Foreign Policy Analysis

Foreign Policy Analysis:
A Comparative Introduction

Marijke Breuning

FOREIGN POLICY ANALYSIS
Copyright © Marijke Breuning, 2007.
All rights reserved. No part of this book may be used or reproduced in any manner what-
soever without written permission except in the case of brief quotations embodied in
critical articles or reviews.

First published in 2007 by
PALGRAVE MACMILLAN™
175 Fifth Avenue, New York, N.Y. 10010 and
Houndmills, Basingstoke, Hampshire, England RG21 6XS.
Companies and representatives throughout the world.

PALGRAVE MACMILLAN is the global academic imprint of the Palgrave
Macmillan division of St. Martin's Press, LLC and of Palgrave Macmillan Ltd.
Macmillan® is a registered trademark in the United States, United Kingdom and other
countries. Palgrave is a registered trademark in the European Union and other countries.

ISBN-13: 978-0-3122-9619-3
ISBN-10: 0-312-29619-3

Library of Congress Cataloging-in-Publication Data

Breuning, Marijke, 1957–
        Foreign policy analysis: a comparative introduction / Marijke Breuning.
        p. cm.
        Includes bibliographical references and index.
        ISBN 0-312-29619-3 (alk. paper)
        1. International relations—Research. 2. International relations—Study
        and teaching. I. Title.
JZ1234.B74 2007
327.1—dc22   2007014791

A catalogue record of the book is available from the British Library.

Design by Scribe Inc.

First edition: November 2007

10 9 8 7 6 5 4 3 2 1

Printed in the United States of America.

Contents

Tables

Preface

This text reflects a specific point of view about the field of foreign policy analysis. It places the individual decision maker at the heart of the foreign policy decision making process. For this reason, the book starts with a discussion of the role of leaders and then proceeds to situate these individual decision makers in the context of advisors and bureaucracies, as well as domestic and international constraints. Each chapter is organized around puzzles and questions to which undergraduate students can readily relate. The book does not assume prior study of international relations. Quite the contrary, this text assumes no prior knowledge of either international relations or foreign policy analysis. Hence, the focus is on explaining concepts and theories rather than on authors and literature.

The book's focus on the individual decision maker makes it easy for students to identify with the problems inherent in foreign policy making and to place themselves in the shoes of decision makers. The case studies that help explain the concepts are drawn from a variety of countries and time periods and include non-crisis as well as small state foreign policy making. Most of the concepts discussed in this book have been developed in the context of the study of U.S. foreign policy. Their applicability to other countries has been tested only infrequently. This book does not test the applicability of these concepts in a systematic way, but suggests the value of a comparative approach to foreign policy analysis.

This text reflects my perspective on foreign policy analysis first and foremost, but it is also the product of the many people who assisted me along the way. Of those, I would specifically like to thank David Pervin, who first persuaded me to take on this project. David was instrumental in the initial conceptualization of the book and provided important feedback on early chapters. John Ishiyama convinced me that it was a worthwhile endeavor and served as an important sounding board for my ideas. His insights and his questions have helped me to write a better book than would have been possible without our many conversations. My students at Truman State University provided positive feedback on the draft chapters I assigned in several classes. They liked what they read and encouraged me to complete the book. Toby Wahl at Palgrave made sure that I did. His insistence shortened the road to the completion of this project. I owe a great debt to these and many other individuals who have, in small and large ways, shaped my thinking about the field of foreign policy analysis. Of course, the responsibility for the final product is mine alone.

Last, but not least, I want thank my spouse, John, and my daughters, Fasika and Bedelwa. You deserve my undivided attention, but accepted much less. Maybe now that the book is done, we can travel without the laptop coming along.

M.B.

Chapter 1

Why Study Foreign Policy Comparatively?

Chapter Preview

- Explains what distinguishes foreign policy analysis as an approach to the study of international politics.
- Explains the difference between foreign policy options, decisions, behaviors, and outcomes.
- Explains the difference between individual, state, and system levels of analysis.
- Explains the value of studying foreign policy comparatively and the basics of the comparative method.

Why Study Foreign Policy?

Leaders have made many puzzling foreign policy decisions across the years. Although some of those decisions turned out to be of little consequence and have been largely forgotten, on many occasions such decisions have plunged countries into major crisis or war. Consider the following decisions, which both reporters at the time and historians who wrote about them later found puzzling.

Saddam Hussein, leader of Iraq, invaded Kuwait in the early 1990s only to find that the United States, under President George H. W. Bush put together a coalition to push him back out. Saddam Hussein knew that the United States was more powerful and much better armed than Iraq. Although Iraq had, in those days, one of the stronger militaries in the region, it was no match for a superpower. Saddam Hussein may have calculated that the United States was too preoccupied with the demise of the

Soviet Union and the collapse of the latter's economy to worry about his invasion of a small neighboring state. A meeting with the American ambassador to Iraq, career diplomat April Glaspie, reinforced his assessment. She made the now-famous statement that "we have no opinion on the Arab-Arab conflicts like your border disagreement with Kuwait."[1] Saddam Hussein may have interpreted this to mean that the United States would not take action if his military attacked Kuwait. Should he have realized that the United States, no matter how much it appeared to be otherwise engaged, could not accept his seizure of the small, but oil-rich Kuwait?

Decades earlier, Neville Chamberlain, prime minister of Britain, made a fateful deal with Adolph Hitler of Germany during the infamous Munich conference of 1938. Britain would not object to Germany's seizure of the Sudetenland, a portion of Czechoslovakia bordering on Germany and with a German-speaking population, as long as Hitler promised he would respect the sovereignty of the remainder of Czechoslovakia.[2] This small country in the heart of Europe was a very recent creation at that time: it had been carved out of the Austro-Hungarian Empire at the end of World War I, just two decades earlier. It was a multiethnic state, home to the Czechs and Slovaks as well as German, Hungarian, and other smaller ethnic minority groups. Chamberlain returned home confident he had made a deal that would preserve the peace in Europe—an important consideration in a time when the memory of World War I and its enormous toll in human lives was still very fresh. He thought that meeting personally with Hitler had allowed him to judge the latter's character and trustworthiness. He could not have been more wrong. Hitler continued his conquests and soon Europe found itself immersed in World War II.

In the early 1960s, Nikita Khrushchev of the Soviet Union made a decision to build launching sites for nuclear missiles in Cuba and soon found himself embroiled in a crisis. American U-2 spy planes photographed the launchpad while it was still under construction. The discovery came on the heels of the Bay of Pigs fiasco, during which American-trained Cuban exiles had attempted, and failed, to topple Fidel Castro, Cuba's communist leader. The Cold War was still in full swing, and President Kennedy was presiding over a military buildup that would give the United States clear superiority in strategic weapons—something Khrushchev could not ignore. Under those circumstances, the possibility of being able to reach U.S. soil by placing missiles in Cuba was quite tempting, especially since the Soviet Union did not yet have the capacity to launch intercontinental missiles. In addition, the United States had missiles close to Soviet soil in Turkey. Khrushchev may have concluded that placing missiles in Cuba was comparable. Should Khrushchev have been able to foresee that no American president during the Cold War could have accepted that the Russians were building missile-launching capacities so close to American shores?

Each of these leaders made a decision that was, certainly in retrospect, puzzling. Saddam Hussein stumbled into a war with a coalition of countries headed by the United States that he could not win and that became a prelude to another war a little over a decade later. In the interim, Iraq suffered the economic consequences of the destruction during and the sanctions that followed the war of the early 1990s.[3] Neville Chamberlain lost his position as Prime Minister of Britain and is frequently cited as the man who gave appeasement its bad name. Nikita Khrushchev stumbled into the Cuban Missile Crisis, which brought his country to the brink of war and contributed to the premature end of his political career.

From the vantage point of a foreign observer or with a historian's hindsight, the decisions made by these leaders are puzzling mostly because they "should have known better." Often, such decisions are deemed "irrational," and the leaders who made them are judged to be crazy or just fools. While being dismissive of such policy choices and the leaders who made them may be tempting, it does not help us understand these puzzling decisions very well. There are on occasion leaders whose rationality may be questioned, but there are far fewer such individuals than those who are commonly labeled irrational. Hence, when seeking to explain foreign policy decisions, it is more fruitful to start with the assumption that the leaders who made these puzzling decisions were rational human beings trying their best to make "good" foreign policy decisions for their countries.[4] Once we make that assumption, however, we must also begin to ponder what motivates these leaders, what they understand about the situations they face, and what factors made their decisions turn out to be "bad" ones.

Before we proceed, let's consider two important concepts introduced in the last paragraph: rationality and good foreign policy decisions. It can be difficult to accept that Saddam Hussein was not crazy, Chamberlain not naive, and Khrushchev not a fool. Commonsense notions of rationality demand that each of these leaders should have known better. Yet if we stop to think about the world from the perspective of each leader, knowing what that leader knew *at the time* of the decision, it becomes a little more difficult to maintain this attitude. We might disagree with the goals Saddam Hussein or Khrushchev pursued, and we might judge Chamberlain too preoccupied with preserving peace, but in each case, we can make the argument that these leaders consistently pursued their goals. And this is the main requirement of **rationality**: the demand that the means—or the policy choices—are logically connected to the ends—or the leader's goals. In other words, rationality demands *only* that a decision maker have some purpose in mind and make choices designed to achieve those predetermined ends.[5]

To argue that a decision maker is rational, therefore, does not mean that you agree with his or her goals—or that you, even if you had the same goals, could not make different choices. You may find the goals objectionable. Or you may share the goals and yet be convinced that different policies would better achieve those objectives. Additionally, and even more important, rationality does not guarantee a desirable outcome, because the outcome is in part dependent on the reactions of other actors.[6]

That brings us to the second concept, that of **good decisions**. All too often, foreign policy decisions are judged to be good or bad in hindsight. Such evaluations are frequently based on the knowledge that the decision led to a desirable or disastrous outcome.[7] The examples of Saddam Hussein, Chamberlain, and Khrushchev are all decisions that, in hindsight, were judged to be disastrous. They "should have known better." But is hindsight a fair standard? The answer is no. Just as good decisions do not guarantee a good outcome, flawed decisions do not inevitably lead to bad results.

If hindsight and a desirable outcome are problematic guides to judging whether a foreign policy decision was good, then how to we arrive at such judgments? An alternative is to judge decisions based on *how* they were made: were they based on a sound analysis of the situation and careful thought regarding the consequences of possible courses of action?[8] Such judgments rely on insight into the decision process and assessments of the priorities and motivations of leaders. The advantage of judging foreign policy decisions in this manner is that decisions can be evaluated *without* resorting to hindsight. There are two disadvantages, however.

First, such process-oriented judgments are likely to overestimate the degree to which leaders make reasonable decisions. When leaders engage in sound analysis on the basis of a very narrow and skewed perception of the world or on the basis of obviously flawed information, a process-oriented evaluation would lead us to judge the decision as a reasonable one. After all, the proper process was followed. Does that sound like satisfactory analysis to you? Or does it sound like a case of "garbage in, garbage out"? Can a good decision process based on faulty information be expected to yield a reasonable, or even good, decision? More likely than not, you will conclude that it cannot. Hence, a process-oriented assessment is better at helping us understand why a policy maker, or group of policy makers, arrived at a specific foreign policy decision rather than at judging whether that decision was good. That is still valuable because it helps us achieve a greater awareness of the problems and pitfalls involved decision making.

The second disadvantage of judging foreign policy decisions by the process used to achieve them is a practical problem: it can be quite difficult to figure out whether a foreign policy decision was based on sound analysis and careful thought. Frequently, relevant information may be classified or the necessary records may not exist. Governments and countries differ in their record keeping. They may also have different policies regarding declassification of the documents that do exist and making them available to researchers. This does not make analysis impossible, but it does mean that we sometimes need to *infer* process variables from the available information, rather than knowing for sure. A skilled analyst can often make very effective use of available information.

In sum, there is no easy way to define good foreign policy decision making. Nevertheless, it is a subject worth pondering. When we judge that leaders should have known better, we are voicing the expectation that, given the responsibilities of their positions, we may expect them to transcend the narrowness of their own time and place to view the world from multiple perspectives.[9] We return to the subject of good decision making in chapter 3.

So far, the focus has been on leaders and decision making, but the study of foreign policy involves more. At the heart of the study of foreign policy is the desire to understand countries' actions and behaviors towards other countries and the international environment generally. **Foreign policy** is defined as the totality of a country's policies toward and interactions with the environment beyond its borders.[10] This definition is quite broad and encompasses a variety of issue domains or **issue areas**, which are defined as a set of interrelated concerns in policy making that are, however, more loosely tied to other sets of interrelated concerns. Traditionally, the study of foreign policy has focused primarily on the quest to maintain and enhance a country's power and security. It centered on questions of averting war when possible, deciding to fight if necessary, and—first and foremost— ensuring the integrity of the country's borders. Increasingly, economic relations between countries have gained attention. Since the end of the Cold War, globalization has become an important process that highlights the interconnectedness of the world's economies. This has had a greater impact on countries with economies that, in earlier eras, were less connected to the international economy. For those countries that traditionally have depended greatly on international trade, economic issues have had a higher priority on the foreign policy agenda much longer. The foreign policy agenda does not stop with security and economic issues: in recent decades, environmental issues have increasingly gained attention; so have issues such as human rights, population growth and migration, food and energy policies, as well as foreign aid, development, and the relations between richer and poorer countries.

In addition to the increased diversity of issues on the foreign policy agenda, there is also an increasing variety in the actors who engage in foreign policy making. Traditionally, investigations of foreign policy looked primarily at states and leaders. This is still largely the case, although there has been increased recognition of, and interest in, the foreign policy roles of decision makers who were not traditionally associated with international diplomacy, such as a secretary of commerce or a minister of justice. Moreover, investigators are increasingly interested in **public diplomacy**, or a government's diplomatic efforts that target citizens, the press, and other constituencies in other countries rather than their governments, and they also occasionally look beyond the government to study **citizen diplomacy**, or the efforts and effects abroad of actions by actors who are not official representatives of the state or its government. Often-cited as examples of U.S. public diplomacy are the efforts of the United States Information Agency (USIA). Other countries also engage in public diplomacy to influence the perceptions citizens in other countries have of their society and government. An example of citizen diplomacy is the Reverend Jesse Jackson's 1984 negotiation with Syria's government for the release of U.S. Navy pilot Lt. Robert Goodman, who had been captured after his plane was shot down over Syrian-controlled territory in Lebanon.[11]

The foreign policies of countries—whether large and powerful, small and weak, or somewhere in between—drive the course of world history. At times, countries and their leaders have pursued wise policies that have yielded peace and prosperity. Yet at other times, they have made choices that have been destructive of both, as the previous examples show. What drives the study of foreign policy is the quest to understand not just why leaders make the choices they do, but also how and why domestic and international constraints and opportunities affect their choices. After all, leaders do not exist in a vacuum; they are surrounded by advisors and a bureaucracy, influenced by domestic constituencies, and dependent on the power their state can project in the international arena. Untangling the relative impact of these various factors on foreign policy is no easy matter.[12] The best explanations of the foreign policy choices of countries are frequently found in the complex interplay of multiple factors.[13]

Untangling the relative impact of various factors on foreign policy decision making may not be an easy matter, but it need not be an impossible task, either. First, we need to be clear about what it is we seek to explain. Next, we will investigate where to look for explanations and discuss a framework that helps to organize the various factors or "causes" of foreign policy. Subsequently, we will turn our attention to the benefits of studying foreign policy comparatively.

What Do We Wish to Explain?

Foreign policy analysts do not always seek to explain the same thing. So far, the descriptors "choice," "decision," and "behavior" have been used interchangeably in connection with foreign policy. But are foreign policy choices, decisions, and behaviors really the same thing?

Consider, once again, Saddam Hussein's incursion into Kuwait. He had several options available to him. Instead of invading Kuwait, he could have pursued a variety of other strategies to achieve his objectives, such as amassing troops on the border to underscore a threat (which he had tried at an earlier time) or some other form of coercive diplomacy. He could have gone to the Arab League or the Organization of Petroleum Exporting Countries (OPEC) to address his grievances. He could have called for a summit meeting with the leaders of Kuwait, possibly with the aid of a neutral third party. He could even have decided to do nothing at all. The bottom line is that he could have acted differently than he did.

If the term options refers to the range of possible choices, **decision** refers to the option that was chosen, i.e., the choice. Not all of the options listed in the previous paragraph would have been equally attractive to Saddam Hussein. To understand how he evaluated different options, which options he would have rejected out of hand, and why he chose as he did, we must learn more about how he viewed the world and Iraq's role in it, as well as domestic factors—in other words, what objectives generally guided his foreign policy. It may also be helpful to learn more about his personality to gain insight into his perceptions of the international political environment and the motivations behind his actions. Since foreign policy decision making is often the task of not one person but of groups of individuals, we may need to understand the predisposition and worldviews of multiple individuals and how these views intersect before we can fully understand a specific foreign policy decision.

Foreign policy **behavior** is the acting out of the decision. In our example, it would be the act of invading Kuwait. Foreign policy behavior can often be described fairly straightforwardly: it consists of the actions taken to influence the behavior of an external actor or to secure a benefit for the country itself. Especially the policy makers of smaller countries often focus more on securing tangible benefits for their own state (such as military assistance or development aid) than on obtaining political influence globally (by, e.g., promoting free trade or democracy). To figure out why states undertake certain foreign policy behaviors, however, it is often necessary to dig into the decision making process; as we shall see, the outcome of actions depends not just on the decision taken by the leaders of one country, but also on how other actors in the international environment react to those actions.

Although we often assume that foreign policy behavior is simply the acting out of a decision, the implementation phase has its own problems and pitfalls: those who are implementing the decision may misunderstand the orders they have been given, they may disagree with their orders and carry them out in a subtly or more overtly different manner than had been intended, or they may simply ignore the order and hope no one in the higher ranks notices. In sum, much can still happen between the making of a decision and its implementation, which means that the observed foreign policy behavior is not always exactly what the decision makers intended.[14]

Outcomes are a further abstraction. The argument that Saddam Hussein should have known better than to think he could get away with invading and annexing Kuwait implies a focus on the relative power of states. Although Iraq was, at the time of the invasion, a well-armed regional power, it was not as powerful as the United States. Its leader should have known that it could not hold on to its newly acquired territory if the United States chose to flex its muscle. Notice, however, that the ultimate outcome is interactive: it required the United States to decide that Kuwait mattered enough to assemble a coalition of allies and to go to war. Despite popular wisdom to the contrary, the United States could have decided otherwise. President George H. W. Bush and his team of foreign policy decision makers also had multiple options: prior to going to war with Iraq, the United States and its allies provided for the defense of the (previously poorly secured) Saudi Arabian border to prevent Saddam Hussein from continuing his conquests. Bush could have decided that preventing Saddam Hussein from extending his reach was a good enough solution. Sanctions might have helped to further contain Saddam Hussein. And the United States could have chosen to do nothing and stay out of disputes between Arab countries—one interpretation of what the American ambassador to Iraq had suggested to Saddam Hussein. Although one could argue that some of these options are less plausible than others, the point is that President George H. W. Bush's decision to push Iraq out of Kuwait was *not* a foregone conclusion. And this is true more generally: decision makers almost always have options. Even very powerful states often do not use all the resources at their disposal, and therefore, knowing what a state is capable of is only one ingredient in predicting the outcome of a conflict. Hence, outcomes require that we understand the foreign policy decisions and behaviors of not just one country but of two or more countries in interaction.

Students of foreign policy, as a specialization within the field of international relations, focus less frequently on outcomes than on options, decisions, or behaviors. A recurrent theme is the quest to help leaders make better decisions.[15] In the previous section we discussed some of the problems involved in defining what constitutes a good decision. The problem, in part, lies in the tendency to work backwards from good outcomes: if it ended well, then this must have been due to a good decision. Such thinking leaves no room for the possibility that the good outcome is due to the way another actor chose to react to what may have been a rather poor decision. Even great decisions may not lead to desirable outcomes, because decision makers do not control how the leaders of other countries will react to their decisions—although strong insight into the personality and motivations of leaders of other countries is likely to improve the odds of a desirable outcome. Nevertheless, an effort to understand how, why, by whom, and on what basis decisions are made, as well as how the contexts within which decisions are made affect decision making processes, is worthwhile: the better we understand why leaders react as they do, the better the odds that we can figure out how to help decision makers transcend their own biases. That won't always guarantee good outcomes, but it gives us the best odds for achieving them.[16]

Where to Look for Explanations

Who or what influences foreign policy? Although leaders are quick to take credit for foreign policy successes and the public is often quick to blame them for failures, leaders rarely make foreign policy alone. Advisory systems and government bureaucracies may be organized differently in different countries, but they always play some role in foreign policy decision making and implementation. Domestic constituencies may vary in influence, depending on the attentiveness of a public to foreign affairs or the structure of government in a specific country. Finally, the world beyond the borders affects the possibilities for foreign policy action. It may present opportunities, but it also presents constraints.

With so many factors affecting foreign policy, how do we unravel the contributions each of these multiple factors makes? First, we will not consider all these factors at once. Although foreign policy behavior is rarely caused by one person or one thing alone, it makes sense to investigate various factors separately before thinking about their interaction. It is simpler to focus on one explanatory factor at a time. After analyzing various factors separately, we can then assess their relative contributions to foreign policy behavior, taking into account also the possible interactions among these different explanatory factors. The strategy is to initially analyze different factors that influence foreign policy making in isolation and to subsequently attempt to integrate these into a comprehensive explanation, assuming that foreign policy is generally purposive or goal-directed behavior.

Second, it is possible to group the different factors into categories that have something in common. Consider, for instance, the contrast between two potential explanations for Iraq's invasion of Kuwait: one, Saddam Hussein's personal lust for power, territory, and oil led him and his country's military to invade Kuwait; two, the preoccupation of the United States with events in Russia and other former Soviet Union states led to a power vacuum in the Middle East, which in turn created the opportunity for Iraq to invade Kuwait. Remember that Iraq was the strongest actor within the region, even if on a global level it was no match for the United States

The second explanation focuses on the relative power of states in the world and sometimes also in specific regional subsystems. It assumes that the United States had an interest in maintaining the relative balance of power among the states of the Middle East but was simultaneously not particularly focused on that region at that time. Hence, Iraq's decision to invade Kuwait was a response to an opportunity provided by the American lack of attention. It also implies that it was fairly unimportant who was in charge of foreign policy decision making in Iraq: any leader perceiving this opportunity would have been tempted to take advantage of the situation to acquire territory and oil and enhance his or her country's power. In this view, leaders and their personalities, perceptions, and motivations are less important. Rather, the emphasis is on understanding the incentives and constraints the international environment places on the behavior of states. Superficially, this would appear straightforward: the United States is a more powerful state than, for instance, the small island nation of Haiti (in the Caribbean) or tiny, landlocked Luxembourg (in Europe). But general assessments of relative power alone do not explain the specific relationships the United States has with these two small states.

The example of Iraq's invasion of Kuwait also shows that the constraints imposed by being a small and weak country are generally enduring factors affecting that state's foreign policy. Kuwait's smallness makes it vulnerable to belligerent neighbors and in need of more powerful allies. Opportunities, on the other hand, are often dependent on specific circumstances that may be temporary; they present a window of opportunity that may in time close. Saddam Hussein, Iraq's leader, acted upon just such an opportunity, convinced that the United States would stay on the sidelines. In fact, that window closed rather rapidly as the United States leadership quickly refocused its attention.

Note that the previous explanation makes certain assumptions about the motivations of leaders, namely that leaders will take advantage of opportunities when they present themselves. In this case, the leader who happened to be in power in Iraq at the time did act upon the opportunity presented by the international environment. But would any leader have acted in this manner? It is quite conceivable that a different leader, who either had a different personality or who was differently constrained by domestic political institutions or public opinion, might have decided that the potential risks of this opportunity—the chance that the United States would act as it in fact did—were not worth the potential gains. Although we can never know for sure whether Iraq would have invaded Kuwait if there had been a different leader in power in that country in the early 1990s, it is at least plausible that another leader might have decided against such a move. Indeed, even in authoritarian countries there often is lively debate among leaders and advisors as they seek to define the best policy for the country.

This implies that individuals and the decisions they make are a major determinant of foreign policy.[17] In order to understand foreign policy decisions and behaviors, then, we must understand leaders—and their personalities, perceptions, and motivations. In addition, domestic political institutions and public opinion may also play a role, depending on the nature of the political system.

The two explanations—the motivations of individual leaders on the one hand and the opportunities and constraints presented by the international environment on the other—can be seen as competing, but also as complementary.[18] The preceding paragraphs indicate that it is ultimately leaders who make decisions, which would argue in favor of a focus on leaders. This is certainly appropriate, but it must also be noted that leaders make decisions within the context of an environment that presents them with problems, opportunities, and constraints. Hence, we must understand both the circumstances and the individual, as well as the interaction between them.[19]

This distinction between the circumstances and the individual is captured by the concept of **levels of analysis**.[20] In this book, we will use three levels of analysis: the individual, the state, and the international system. These three levels of analysis correspond to the different foci of foreign policy analysis: individuals ponder options and make decisions, states engage in foreign policy behaviors, and the interaction between states in the international system yields outcomes. These connections are summarized in table 1.1.

The **individual level of analysis** focuses on leaders and decision makers in an effort to explain foreign policy. It assumes that individuals shape the course of history, because it is their choices and decisions that drive the course of events. The analysis of individuals might focus on either their personalities or on their perceptions—how they make sense of their world and the events occurring within it. The first focus leads to the study of personality traits, beliefs, and values as the factors that explain foreign policy decisions. It emphasizes the enduring qualities of an individual decision maker. Insight into the personality, character, beliefs, and values of the individual enhances our ability to gauge what motivates that decision maker. Does it make a difference whether a leader is extremely power hungry? Does it make a difference whether he or she enjoys the political game? Students of personality and other enduring qualities of leaders (such as their character) suggest that the answer is most often affirmative, as we explore further in chapter 2. The second focus leads to the study of the perceptions and how these influence foreign policy decision making. The individual's perceptions, or the process by which a person makes sense of events and situations in her or his world, are specific to that situation or event. Students of perception, framing, and problem representation do not negate the importance of personality, but they are more interested in how policy makers make sense of—or define—specific decision making situations.[21] Research at the individual level of analysis frequently employs concepts borrowed from psychology, such as **framing**—defined as a tendency for people to judge risk in terms of how a situation is presented to them.[22] We explore perception in greater detail in chapter 3.

Furthermore, individuals often do not make decisions alone but instead work together with others in a group or in a bureaucratic setting.[23] In such instances, their individual personalities and perceptions interact as they jointly determine how best to define the problem before them. Group interactions are often classified at the individual level of analysis because the focus tends to be on understanding the dynamics of interpersonal interaction rather than on the group as an undifferentiated unit. Group decision making, as well as other aspects of the advisory system and bureaucracy, is the subject of chapter 4.

The **state level of analysis** focuses on factors internal to the state as those that compel states to engage in specific foreign policy behaviors. Such analyses include the institutional framework of the state (such as the relationships between the executive and legislative branches of government, the

Table 1.1 Levels of analysis and the study of foreign policy

Level of Analysis	Foreign Policy Focus
Individual	Options/Decisions
State	Behaviors
System	Outcomes

organization of the government bureaucracy, or whether the state is a democracy), domestic constituencies (such as interest groups, ethnic groups, or public opinion more generally), economic conditions, and also the state's national history and culture. At this level of analysis, the emphasis is on how factors internal to the state influence the behavior of that state on the global stage.[24] From a decision making perspective, these factors are often characterized as constraints that determine the parameters of the possible for leaders. Of course, the relationship between leaders and the domestic environment is much more complicated than this simple characterization suggests, as we will see in chapter 5.

Finally, the **system level of analysis** focuses on comparisons (and interactions) between states. This level of analysis asks questions about the relative power of states.[25] The international system is defined as a set of states whose interactions are guided by their relative capabilities, such as their power and wealth, which influence their possibilities for action and for success on the global stage. These relative attributes may change across time as a country's economy yields more wealth or as it attains technological or military capacities. The reverse may also be true: countries can lose as well as gain power. Changes in relative capabilities of states may create opportunities, but they may also serve to increase the constraints on states. An increase in military capacities may embolden a state, while an increasingly interdependent world economy presents constraints.

Note that the system level of analysis makes certain assumptions about the political interests of countries, among which is first and foremost the idea that a state's power is central to its ability to maintain the integrity of its borders. However, the definition of political interest, sometimes called **national interest**, is not necessarily straightforward. Remember that the U.S. response to Iraq's invasion of Kuwait was not a foregone conclusion. In fact, Saddam Hussein may have calculated that the United States would decide it was not in its interest to intervene. Hence, the systems level of analysis can provide insight into the capabilities of states and explain outcomes, but it cannot explain foreign policy decisions or behaviors very well, as we explore further in chapter 6.

On the dividing line between the state and system levels of analysis sits the **two-level game**. This concept describes the fact that foreign policy decision makers try to satisfy domestic constituencies and international imperatives simultaneously, which oftentimes requires a delicate balancing act.[26] This is especially true when the domestic and international environment push decision makers in different directions. Such is often the case in the economic sector: workers may prefer protectionist policies that keep their jobs secure even if the industry in which they work is no longer internationally competitive. On the other hand, countries that have similar industries that are internationally competitive will try to preserve access to as many markets as possible. Hence, decision makers are caught between the international principle of free trade and the interests of their constituents, who may lose their jobs as a result of international competition. Adhering to the internationally accepted principles while not antagonizing domestic constituencies can be tough.

Much has been written about the merits of studying international politics at different levels of analysis. Some scholars have staked out clear preferences for one or another level of analysis,[27] while others understand them to be complementary.[28] The complementarity of the different levels of analysis can be illustrated by linking them to an analysis of the causes of events. We might classify causes into different categories, such as deep, intermediate, and precipitating causes.[29] Consider the following explanation of the outbreak of World War I:

The assassination of Archduke Franz Ferdinand, the heir to the throne of the Austro-Hungarian Empire, by a Serbian nationalist during a visit to Serajevo (now located in Bosnia-Herzegovina) is frequently portrayed as the cause of World War I. This assassination occurred in a context: the rise of nationalism and class conflict preoccupied leaders in many European countries at the time. These factors had been present for decades, but had not led to war. The Austro-Hungarian and Ottoman Empires were particularly vulnerable to unrest and nationalist secession, while Germany had only recently become a unified entity and was rapidly expanding its industrial base—an important source of power. Russia was trying to expand its industrial capacity and modernize its military, but it faced increasing turmoil domestically. Both this turmoil within many of the states of Europe and a changing balance of power among them made conditions favorable for conflict. In addition, the relationships between the larger powers in Europe were changing: since the end of the Napoleonic wars in 1815, the Austro-Hungarian Empire, Russia, Britain, France, and Prussia (the predecessor to Germany) had maintained a balance of power among themselves. Around the turn of the twentieth century, this Concert of Europe began to disintegrate as Germany strengthened itself economically and militarily after its unification in 1871. To counter this rising power, Britain, France, and later Russia allied themselves, while Germany responded by establishing closer ties with the Austro-Hungarian and Ottoman Empires. In other words, the Concert of Europe split into two camps.

Despite these circumstances, war was not inevitable; the leaders of Europe still had options—even if these leaders perceived themselves to be hemmed in by their agreements and plunged ahead into war without much reflection. The assassination, which can be classified as the precipitating cause, was sure to cause a crisis against the backdrop of domestic national-ist agitation and class conflict (intermediate causes) and the changing bal-ance of power among the larger European states (a deep cause), but a crisis does not inevitably lead to war. Different decisions could have been made, and a different outcome might have resulted. Hence, in the final analysis, the decisions made by leaders are the key to understanding international politics.

This does not mean that the domestic and international environments are irrelevant. Leaders must be understood in the context of their time and place. The changing balance of power in the period leading up to World War I certainly created a situation in which a crisis might be more difficult to manage than in a more stable and predictable international environ-ment. Note that what we earlier termed the deep cause of the war corre-sponds to the system level of analysis. Moreover, the domestic nationalism and class conflict prevalent in European countries at the time created a context in which a political assassination could be interpreted as a threat to the integrity of the state. The Ottoman Empire had already begun to disin-tegrate. The Austrian leaders knew that their own multinational empire was vulnerable as well. This certainly colored their perceptions and inter-pretations of what, from historical distance, looks like a relatively minor event. Note that this intermediate cause corresponds to the state level of analysis.

Was war inevitable in 1914? No. The state (intermediate) and system level (deep) causes certainly created a tense environment in which such a decision became more likely, but the environment did not unequivocally determine either the decisions or the outcome. Leaders made decisions.[30] They acted upon their evaluations of the situation they faced and chose from the options they perceived they had. In turn, other leaders reacted with their own assessments and decisions. Collectively, their decisions yielded the outcome: world war. Note that the decisions of leaders in reac-tion to the assassination correspond to the individual level of analysis. Table 1.2 summarizes this comparison.

So, where do we look for explanations? We can choose from the indi-vidual, state, or system level of analysis. Alternatively, we may seek to understand the relative importance of causal factors at each of these levels

Table 1.2 Levels of analysis and causation

Level of Analysis	Type of Causal Factor
Individual	Decisions in response to Precipitating Event
State	Intermediate Cause
System	Deep Cause

of analysis. Whether we choose one or another level of analysis depends largely on what we seek to explain: decisions, behaviors, or outcomes.

What Is to Be Gained by Studying Foreign Policy Comparatively?

The goal of foreign policy analysis is to gain generally applicable knowledge about how foreign policy decisions are made; why leaders make the decisions they make, why states engage in specific kinds of foreign policy behaviors, as well as to assess the opportunities and constraints presented by the international system.[31] How is this best achieved?

Historical events happen only once, and each is unique. However, focusing on what makes each event unique gives us little general knowledge. Knowing all available details of, for instance, the Cuban Missile Crisis, tells us very little about how leaders *generally* respond to foreign policy **crises**. The latter concept can be defined by three elements: there is a high threat to something that is valued and important, leaders perceive that they have only a short amount of time to make a decision, and the occurrence of the threatening situation takes the decision makers by surprise.[32]

Most decision makers and observers of foreign policy intuitively recognize a crisis when one occurs. However, one task of foreign policy analysis is to move beyond intuitive knowledge to explicit knowledge. Making knowledge explicit helps us reexamine our assumptions and question the lessons we have derived from our experiences. This is what foreign policy analysis aims to do: to systematically contrast and compare. Although decision makers derive knowledge from their experiences, they often interpret the lessons narrowly, fail to reexamine their gut reactions, and they compare previous and current crises only superficially. In doing the latter, leaders may make analogies on the basis of superficial commonalities while ignoring significant differences between situations.[33]

Consider for instance, the often-heard saying that leaders are prone to fight the last war. Chamberlain may have appeased Hitler because he hoped to avoid a repetition of the seemingly automatic sequence of events that had led to war in 1914. However, because Chamberlain faced a very different kind of threat, his actions were disastrous—showing that those with knowledge of history may still be condemned to repeat it unless they gain the deeper insights that can be derived from a more comprehensive comparative analysis of such historical events. Chamberlain was comparing the crisis of 1938 with a (then fairly recent) historical event. Since he wished to avoid the outcome of that previous event, he judged that he should avoid the kind of rigid attitudes that had sent Europe into war so quickly in 1914. Hence, he compromised.

There is quite a bit of evidence that leaders use analogies when trying to make sense of a foreign policy situation that demands a decision.[34] However, from a scientific point of view, such comparisons can be quite problematic: a single observation is used to predict another, when closer (or deeper) comparison or the use of additional observations might have helped evaluate whether the expectation of "same action, same outcome" would have been warranted.[35] Additional observations, in particular, can often help to establish to what degree a current problem really is similar to one that occurred in the past. Additional observations help decision makers reexamine the lessons they have intuitively gleaned from past experience. Such a reexamination can move decision makers beyond simple comparisons to a more generalized understanding of crises and, ideally, a better understanding of how to best manage a particular crisis.

This is what foreign policy analysts aim to do: to arrive at generalized knowledge that can enhance our understanding of the similarities and differences between foreign policy events. This can help guide the state's foreign policy decision makers so they do not stumble into a war when they wish to preserve peace, or it can enable them to understand the personalities of other leaders to facilitate productive negotiations and increase the likelihood of desirable outcomes.[36] Imagine for a moment the difference it might have made if Chamberlain had had access to a psychological profile of Hitler, rather than relying on his own intuitions about the German leader. Chamberlain was not the first (or the last) decision maker to think that, after meeting with another leader in person, he could trust that individual. Although politicians are often astute judges of character, their intuitions have their limitations when judging people from different countries and cultures, often after meeting them in highly formal situations for only a short period of time.

In sum, studying foreign policy comparatively and systematically has the potential to yield knowledge that is far more helpful than merely knowing historical facts: a systematic understanding of foreign policy events as alike or different can help decision makers to fashion appropriate responses. Moreover, understanding the peculiarities of the personalities of specific leaders can facilitate more useful and productive diplomacy.[37]

How to Compare

Understanding the need to make comparative and systematic assessments leads to the next question: how does one compare different foreign policy decisions, behaviors, or outcomes? Foreign policy analysis is not satisfied to merely describe decisions, behaviors and outcomes, but is defined by the quest to understand *why* such decisions were made, *what* options were considered (and why not others), *who* or *what* explains behaviors as well as outcomes, and—if the outcomes were unfavorable—what could have improved the likelihood of a better result. This requires us to think in terms of *causes* and *effects*.

Causes are the factors that contribute to various foreign policy options being considered in a decision process, that compel decision makers to choose a specific decision as—in their view—best suited to achieving the desired outcome, that explain specific foreign policy behaviors, and that contribute to the occurrence of an outcome. In foreign policy analysis, causes are called **independent variables**. The effect (or the set of options considered, the decision, the behavior, or the outcome) that we seek to explain is call the **dependent variable**. The effect, or dependent variable, would not have occurred if the independent variables had not been present. In addition, the dependent variable would have taken a different shape if different independent variables had been present or if the independent variables had been of different relative strength. Table 1.3 illustrates the comparison of these different terminologies. In the opening section of this chapter, Saddam Hussein's invasion of Kuwait, Chamberlain's appeasement of Hitler, and Khrushchev's decision to build missile sites in Cuba were all dependent variables (or the things to be explained). Each of these was a decision that was followed by behaviors (or actions) that carried out the decision. Each of these was also preceded by a set of possible options that were considered and out of which a choice was made. Each of these decisions was widely perceived as puzzling—and in need of an explanation—largely because the outcomes were not what the leaders intended. These examples reflect the emphasis of foreign policy analysis on explaining option selection, decisions, and behaviors—or on the individual and state level of analysis.

Although the terminology of independent and dependent variables may be unfamiliar to you, thinking in terms of causes and effects is not. What makes foreign policy analysis different from nonscientific forms of cause-and-effect thinking? Foreign policy analysts try to structure their investigations so that they maximize the gain in generalized knowledge and minimize bias. Consider once again Chamberlain: he compared the crisis he faced in 1938, when Hitler threatened to invade Czechoslovakia, only to the crisis on the eve of World War I and concluded that standing firm would lead to war, because it did in 1914. The limited comparison, combined with Chamberlain's desire to avoid war, biased his thinking in favor of appeasement. What might he have done to achieve a more generally applicable understanding of crisis and how best to deal with the one that confronted him?

Table 1.3 Foreign policy analysis and social scientific terminology

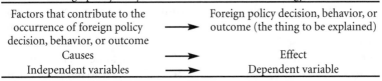

Factors that contribute to the occurrence of foreign policy decision, behavior, or outcome	→	Foreign policy decision, behavior, or outcome (the thing to be explained)
Causes	→	Effect
Independent variables	→	Dependent variable

One, he could have studied many crises and have investigated how often, and under what circumstances, they led to war or were resolved peacefully.[38] Two, he could have made a much more detailed comparison between the known facts of the current and previous crises.[39] In doing so, he could have outlined the similarities between the two situations, but he might have focused especially on how the two events differed. Although the urgency of the situation would have made it difficult to carry out extensive research projects at that moment, foreign policy analysts are in a position to produce such generalized knowledge and make it available to decision makers.

The two types of investigations previously outlined loosely follow the two main research strategies foreign policy analysts use: comparisons of large or small numbers of cases. The former are called **large-N comparisons** and the latter **small-N comparisons** (N is the statistical notation for number of cases). What are the relative advantages of large-N versus small-N studies? Comparisons of large numbers of cases enable researchers to evaluate general cause-and-effect patterns—or relationships—through the use of statistical methodologies. It would be possible to include information on all states in the world for a given period of time, provided one could get the information for all of them. On the basis of such comprehensive data, it would be possible to make general statements about, e.g., whether democracies are less likely to initiate war than nondemocratic countries. However, it would not be possible to make fine distinctions between how democratic (or not) various countries are. In its most simplistic form, we would have two categories: democratic and nondemocratic. We could create a finer-grained scale, but we would inevitably lose some information about the nature of democracy in each country. Whether that loss of information jeopardizes our ability to make valid assessments depends on how well the categorization suits the research question: war-proneness may depend less on finer-grained distinctions about how democratic a country is than on the fact that leaders are held accountable in democracies.

Comparisons of smaller numbers of cases allow for more detailed analyses of similarities and differences among both the independent and dependent variables of the cases.[40] When studying fewer countries, it is possible to make finer distinctions between the nature of democracy in each country, for example. Rather than using categories or numerical indicators to summarize our assessments of specific countries, small-N comparisons use descriptions that can be nuanced and rich in detail. Less information is lost, but the selection of countries to be studied must be done very carefully to ensure that the cases reflect the variation that can be found in the larger set of countries to which we expect our findings to apply.[41] After all, the goal is to acquire generalizable knowledge: whether we study a large or a small number of cases, we hope to learn something that translates beyond the cases studied and not only helps us understand historical foreign policy decisions, behaviors, and outcomes but helps us recognize patterns in new situations as they emerge. In other words, we hope that our findings apply also to foreign policy problems we have not studied, including those that have not yet occurred.

An alternative strategy is to evaluate what might have happened if some aspect of the historical circumstances of a historical situation had been different. Historical events happen only once, and it is tempting to conclude that they were *bound to* happen because they *did* happen. To avoid thinking in such deterministic terms, it can be useful to think about **counterfactuals** in our efforts to evaluate the multiple factors that influenced a specific foreign policy decision, behavior, or outcome. Counterfactuals are essentially decisions, behaviors, or outcomes that differ from the actual facts of history.[42] They help us evaluate whether we have accurately determined the independent variables in historical cases. Consider, for instance, whether Hitler could have been stopped if Chamberlain had taken a firmer stand in 1938. Would Hitler have backed down? Or would Britain have found itself engaged in war sooner than it did? The answer to these questions hinges on interpretations of Hitler's personality. One might conclude that, faced with stronger pressure from the more powerful countries in Europe, he might have decided to contain his ambitions. However, it is also quite possible that diplomacy could never have contained his desire to create a strong German empire. A careful assessment of Hitler's character would be necessary to evaluate the likelihood of either result. Pondering how the course of history might have been different helps us understand what decisions and behaviors were most responsible for the historical outcomes.[43] The usefulness of a counterfactual, or alternative, history depends on a careful reconstruction of actual history and on a meticulous assessment of the impact a changed value of one of the independent variables would very likely have had on altering the actual historical outcome.

Studying foreign policy comparatively, whether studying different foreign policy decisions made by the leaders of one state or comparing the foreign policies of multiple states, has the advantage of allowing the identification of patterns in decisions and decision making processes. Without the ability to compare cases, it would be exceedingly difficult to assess what lessons are to be derived from a specific event—and, as Chamberlain's appeasement of Hitler illustrates, deriving the wrong lesson from an event, or making a faulty analogy, can have disastrous consequences for policy making!

Chapter Summary

- Foreign policy analysis is motivated by the desire to understand the interactions of countries. It assumes that individual decision makers, alone or in groups, make foreign policy decisions. It also assumes that foreign policies are usually determined by the complex interplay of multiple factors.
- Foreign policy analysis can seek to explain different aspects of foreign policy. It may seek to understand what options decision makers had and why they made the decisions they did; it may seek to explain the foreign policy behavior of states; or why certain outcomes occurred.
- Foreign policy decisions, behaviors, and outcomes are studied at different levels of analysis. In this book, we use three levels of analysis: the individual, the state, and the system level of analysis.
- Studying foreign policy comparatively provides greater insight into the conduct and consequences of foreign policy than does studying single cases or drawing simple analogies.
- The objective of foreign policy analysis is to attain generalizable knowledge about foreign policy decision making, behavior, and outcomes. Foreign policy analysts think in terms of independent and dependent variables. They may compare large or small numbers of cases. They sometimes use counterfactuals to evaluate independent (or causal) variables.

Terms

Rationality
Good decisions
Foreign policy
Issue Areas
Public diplomacy
Citizen diplomacy
Foreign policy options

Foreign policy decisions
Foreign policy behavior
Foreign policy outcomes
Levels of analysis
Individual level of analysis
Framing
State level of analysis
System level of analysis
National interest
Two-level game
Crisis
Independent variable
Dependent variable
Large-N comparison
Small-N comparison
Counterfactuals

Study Questions

1. What is foreign policy analysis, and what is the objective of those who study it?
2. What makes it so difficult to determine whether a foreign policy decision was a good decision?
3. What is the difference between foreign policy decisions, behaviors, and outcomes? Why would you wish to distinguish between them?
4. What are the three levels of analysis? How do they relate to foreign policy decisions, behaviors, and outcomes? What is their use in the study of foreign policy?
5. Why is it important to study foreign policy comparatively? How does doing so improve judgment?
6. What are independent and dependent variables? How does thinking in terms of variables help foreign policy analysts in their quest to attain general knowledge?

Suggestions for Further Reading

A classic work in the study of foreign policy is Snyder, Bruck, and Sapin, *Foreign Policy Decision Making: An Approach to the Study of International Politics*. It was recently reissued with two new essays as *Foreign Policy Decision-Making (Revisited)*.

A book that discusses how decision makers often use historical analogies and how they might improve their use of history is Neustadt and May, *Thinking in Time: The Uses of History for Decision Makers.*
Several books have discussed the connection between the academic study of foreign policy and diplomatic practice: George, *Bridging the Gap: Theory and Practice in Foreign Policy*; Nincic and Lepgold, eds., *Being Useful: Policy Relevance and International Relations Theory.*
There are a number of excellent essays on the history of foreign policy analysis as a field of study. The most recent is Hudson, "Foreign Policy Analysis: Actor-Specific Theory and the Ground of International Relations"; Gerner, "The Evolution of the Study of Foreign Policy"; Hudson and Vore, "Foreign Policy Analysis Yesterday, Today, and Tomorrow."
Much has been written about the comparative method. Especially helpful on how to create well-crafted case study research designs are: George, "Case Studies and Theory Development: The Method of Structured, Focused Comparison"; King, Keohane, and Verba, *Designing Social Inquiry: Scientific Inference in Qualitative Research.*

Notes

1. Quoted in Bob Woodward, *The Commanders*, 212.
2. Czechoslovakia ceased to exist when on January 1, 1993, it split into the Czech Republic and Slovakia, two sovereign states, as a result of what was widely touted as a "velvet divorce" because the dissolution took place without a war.
3. In 2003, the U.S. went to war with Iraq, in part to topple Saddam Hussein. There was no question the U.S. had the military capacity to be successful in this effort, although the reconstruction effort has, as of this writing, proven more difficult than anticipated.
4. Philip E. Tetlock, "Good Judgment in International Politics: Three Psychological Perspectives"; Lloyd S. Etheredge, "Wisdom and Good Judgment in Politics."
5. James D. Morrow, *Game Theory for Political Scientists*, 17. This definition of rationality is generally accepted by rational choice theorists. Many foreign policy analysts, including many who study foreign policy from a psychological or cognitive perspective, define rational decision making in a more global manner. Such definitions make more comprehensive demands on both the leader's knowledge and the process by which various options are weighed and evaluated. For a classic enumeration of a rational decision making model, see Graham T. Allison, "Conceptual Models and the Cuban Missile Crisis"; Graham T. Allison and Philip Zelikow, *Essence of Decision: Explaining the Cuban Missile Crisis, 2nd ed.* ; for a well-known critique, see Herbert A. Simon, "Human Nature in Politics: The Dialogue of Psychology

with Political Science." Vesna Danilovic argues that the psychological or cognitive perspective misrepresents rational choice theory ("The Rational-Cognitive Debate and Poliheuristic Theory," in *Integrating Cognitive and Rational Theories of Foreign Policy Decision Making*, ed. Alex Mintz). This book argues that the difference between rational and cognitive approaches lies in the aspects of the decision making process which are investigated and that cross-theoretical communication is facilitated by adopting the rational choice theory definition of rationality. For a comparable approach, see Alex Mintz, "Integrating Cognitive and Rational Theories of Foreign Policy Decision Making: A Poliheuristic Perspective," in *Integrating Cognitive and Rational Theories of Foreign Policy Decision Making*, ed. Alex Mintz. The concept of rationality is investigated further in Chapter 3.

6   Morrow, *Game Theory for Political Scientists*, 20–22.

7. Tetlock, "Good Judgment in International Politics"; Stanley A. Renshon, "Psychological Sources of Good Judgment in Political Leaders: A Framework for Analysis," in *Good Judgment in Foreign Policy: Theory and Application*, ed. Stanley A. Renshon and Deborah Welch Larson; Stanley A. Renshon and Deborah Welch Larson, *Good Judgment in Foreign Policy: Theory and Application*.

8. Renshon, "Psychological Sources of Good Judgment in Political Leaders."

9. Welch, "Culture and Emotion," 208, makes this point.

10. Overviews of the development of the field of foreign policy analysis are provided by Gerner, "The Evolution of the Study of Foreign Policy"; Hudson with Vore, "Foreign Policy Analysis Yesterday, Today, and Tomorrow" and Hudson, "Foreign Policy Analysis: Actor-Specific Theory and the Ground of International Relations." For a recent critical assessment of the field, see also Houghton, "Reinvigorating the Study of Foreign Policy Decision-making: Toward a Constructivist Approach."

11. See, e.g., Karin L. Stanford, *Beyond the Boundaries: Reverend Jesse Jackson in International Affairs*.

12. Indeed, Houghton charges that foreign policy analysis has paid too little attention to the impact of either the domestic or international environment on decision making ("Reinvigorating the Study of Foreign Policy Decision-Making," 40, 34).

13. Richard C. Snyder, H. W. Bruck, and Burton Sapin, *Foreign Policy Decision-making: An Approach to the Study of International Politics*.

14. Allison, "Conceptual Models and the Cuban Missile Crisis."

15. George, *Bridging the Gap*; Nincic and Lepgold, *Being Useful*; Renshon and Larson, *Good Judgment in Foreign Policy*.

16. Renshon, "Psychological Sources of Good judgment," 48; Welch, "Culture and Emotion," 208.

17. Hudson, "Foreign Policy Analysis."

18. See Knill and Lenschow, "Seek and Ye Shall Find"; Nye, *Understanding International Conflicts*.

19. Houghton, "Reinvigorating the Study of Foreign Policy Decision-Making."

20. Singer, "The Level of Analysis Problem"; Rosenau, *The Scientific Study of Foreign Policy*; Waltz, *Man, the State, and War*; see also Nye, *Understanding International Conflicts*; Rourke, *International Politics*; Kegley and Wittkopf, *World Politics*; Hughes, *Continuity and Change*.

21. Representative of the emphasis on leadership and personality is the work of M.G. Hermann (see, for instance, her "Explaining Foreign Policy Behavior" or "Who Leads Matters"). Representative of an emphasis on perception and problem representation are works by Jervis, *Perception and Misperception*, and Sylvan and Voss, *Problem Representation*.

22. Vertzberger, *Risk Taking and Decisionmaking*; Kahneman and Tversky; Levy, "An Introduction to Prospect Theory"; "Loss Aversion, Framing and Bargaining."

23. There is a rich literature on bureaucratic politics. Some well-known examples are Allison, "Conceptual Models and the Cuban Missile Crisis"; Allison and Zelikow, *Essence of Decision*; Bendor and Hammond, "Rethinking Allison's Models"; George, *Presidential Decisionmaking*; 't Hart et al., *Beyond Groupthink*.

24. One example of work at this level of analysis is Hudson, *Culture and Foreign Policy*.

25. Waltz, *Theory of International Politics*; see also Keohane, ed., *Neorealism and its Critics*.

26. Putnam, "Diplomacy and Domestic Politics: The Logic of Two-Level Games"; Evans, et al., *Double-Edged Diplomacy*.

27. Waltz, *Man, the State, and War*; Waltz, *Theory of International Politics*; Singer, "The Level of Analysis Problem."

28. Snyder, Bruck, and Sapin, *Foreign Policy Decision-Making*.

29. Nye, *Understanding International Conflicts*

30. See, for instance, Snyder, Bruck, and Sapin, *Foreign Policy Decision-Making*; Rosenau, "Pre-Theories and Theories of Foreign Policy."

31. Snyder, Bruck, and Sapin, *Foreign Policy Decision-Making*; George, "Case Studies and Theory Development"; George, *Bridging the Gap*.

32. Hermann, *Crises in Foreign Policy, 29–30*. There are other definitions of the concept. However, these mostly boil down to the elements enumerated by Hermann. See, e.g., Lebow, *Between Peace and War, 7–9*.

33. Neustadt and May, *Thinking in Time*; Spellman and Holyoak, "If Saddam is Hitler then Who is George Bush?"; Keane, "What Makes and Analogy Difficult?"

34. Neustad and May, *Thinking in Time*; Hemmer, *Which Lessons Matter?*; Reiter, *Crucible of Beliefs*; Peterson, "The Use of Analogies in Developing Outer Space Law."

35. King, Keohane, and Verba, *Designing Social Inquiry, 212–13*; see also Khong, *Analogies at War*, Hemmer, *Which Lessons Matter?*

36. George, *Bridging the Gap*; Nincic and Lepgold, *Being Useful*.

37. Neustadt and May recognized that such a comparative understanding of history is useful not just for diplomats. They taught their strategy for comparing

historical events to business students, believing that such skills can serve individuals in different professions.

38. Such an investigation was undertaken by Lebow in his *Between Peace and War*.
39. Such investigations were undertaken by, e.g., Hemmer, *Which Lessons Matter?*; Houghton, "The Role of Analogical Reasoning"; Khong, *Analogies at War*; Neustad and May, *Thinking in Time*.
40. Lijphart," The Comparable-Cases Strategy in Comparative Research."
41. George, "Case Studies and Theory Development"; George and McKeown, "Case Studies and Theories of Organizational Decision Making"; King, Keohane, and Verba, *Designing Social Inquiry*, 226–27.
42. Tetlock and Belkin, *Counterfactual Thought Experiments*; Lebow, "What's So Different About a Counterfactual?"
43. Fearon, "Counterfactuals and Hypothesis Testing"

Chapter 2

Do Leaders Shape Foreign Policy?

Chapter Preview

- Explains the value of studying leaders for understanding foreign policy making.
- Explains the difficulties as well as the benefits of studying leaders.
- Explains various strategies for studying leaders, such as the operational code and leadership trait analysis.
- Explains the importance of understanding emotions in foreign policy decision making.

Why Study Leaders?

Some scholars accept without question that leaders shape the course of world politics. Others argue that individuals are to a considerable degree constrained by their historical circumstances and that they are compelled to make certain decisions. The most obvious example of such a scenario is when another country attacks or declares war. In such a case, leaders have very few options: they can fight or surrender. Which course of action is chosen may depend on the relative might of the opponent and the likelihood of successfully resisting the attack, but it may also reflect a desire to defend one's country against all odds. Consider for example the Dutch decision to fight the German invasion during World War II. The Netherlands had stayed out of World War I, had a tradition of neutrality, and expected to stay out of World War II as well. On May 10, 1940, the Germans launched an attack that took the Dutch government by surprise. Nevertheless, its ill-equipped and poorly trained military fought as hard as it could for five days, which was much longer than the German government had expected.[1] Rather than surrendering to the obvious outcome, the Dutch leadership decided that, despite the certainty of defeat, the violation of its sovereignty required active resistance.

As this example illustrates, there are times when circumstances force a leader's hand. Immediate surrender may theoretically have been an option for the Dutch leadership in 1940, but it was not realistic or feasible within the circumstances at that moment. However, few circumstances provide leaders with such severe constraints; more often than not, there are options. This means that leaders generally have at least some possibility of putting their stamp on history. Their impact may be small when circumstances severely constrain their options, and their impact may be bigger when they have a broader scope of options, or when they create their own opportunities.

Consider the story of how Belgium, a small European country, became a colonial power. Ever since it became an independent state in 1830, Belgium had been highly dependent on international trade, which it conducted primarily with the surrounding European countries. It did not have a merchant marine or a tradition of overseas exploration, as the other European colonizers did. It did not, in other words, appear to be a country that was likely to be competitive in the nineteenth-century scramble for Africa.[2] How, then, did Belgium colonize a territory in central Africa that was roughly eighty times its own size?[3]

The answer to this question can be found in an unparalleled story of personal ambition. King Leopold II of Belgium displayed a strong interest in trade and colonialism well before he ascended to the throne in 1865.[4] He traveled widely to visit other European countries' colonial possessions and read extensively on the subject. Importantly, his interest was driven by knowledge of the profits generated by other countries' colonies, although he was also interested in aggrandizing his power—Leopold occasionally exhibited a certain disdain for the small country he ruled, as well as for domestic pressures to institute an elected parliament (which would have constrained his power).[5]

By the time the European powers met in Berlin in 1884–85 to settle conflicting claims on Africa, King Leopold II had laid the groundwork to make himself the biggest beneficiary of that meeting. In his younger years, he had been quite blunt about his desire for profit,[6] but he had long since learned to cloak his ambitions in the rhetoric of humanitarianism. Just short of a decade prior to the conference in Berlin, Leopold had begun his quest by hosting an International Geographic Conference.[7] This meeting brought together a group of notable geographers, explorers, and missionaries, who were delighted to be invited to stay at the royal palace and went home to advertise the king's benevolence—exactly the effect Leopold had intended. The meeting also created the first of a series of organizations that, despite the façade of being humanitarian and scientific associations, were all controlled by the king and aided him in acquiring the land that became the Congo. During this period, King Leopold II employed the famous explorer Henry Morton Stanley to map the Congo river basin and to conclude treaties with local African leaders, which in effect ceded their land to the king's various associations, and thus to him. Meanwhile, the king collected vast amounts of intelligence on the interests of other European countries in Africa, which permitted him to craft his arguments for best effect. In the end, the European powers gathered at Berlin agreed to Leopold's territorial claims in the center of Africa, largely because they were under the impression that the Belgian king would permit free trade in the Congo—he had led them to believe that his colony would be open to traders from across Europe. Although Leopold's agents in the Congo did indeed originate from an assortment of different countries, they served the sovereign and his desire for profit.

Through meticulous study; the careful cultivation of geographers, explorers, and diplomats; the use of payments and payoffs; and a good dose of duplicity, King Leopold II managed to acquire the colony he so much craved. The Congo remained his personal possession until it was transferred to the Belgian state in 1908, after an international movement exposed the extreme coercion and violence that had accompanied the acquisition and exploitation of the territory.[8]

King Leopold II's interest in acquiring a colonial empire is perhaps understandable in the international context of the nineteenth century, when powerful countries tended to have colonial empires and sought to solidify their claims in Africa. After a number of unsuccessful attempts to buy a colony from another country (and discovering that none were for sale), the Belgian king worked tirelessly to partake in the scramble for Africa. Domestically there was not much interest in such faraway ventures, which many feared would be too costly for a small country. In order not to antagonize other powers, nor to invite the scrutiny of the Belgian public, the king was careful to cloak his activities in the decade leading up to the Berlin Conference. Behind the scenes, he steadily worked to claim a large part of central Africa and to get his claims recognized by the leaders of other countries.

So, do leaders matter? One example certainly is not sufficient to answer this conclusively, but it does show that leaders *can* have an impact. After all, it is unmistakable that King Leopold II influenced the course of history:

without enormous ambition and effort, he would never have acquired the Congo, Belgium would not have become a colonial power, and the Congo would have had a different history as well. The king's efforts overcame both an unfavorable international environment and unfavorable domestic opinion. The story is notable because it is unusual: not only did Belgium not have a tradition of worldwide exploration, but it was a relatively new and small country that conducted its foreign affairs—and trade!—primarily with the surrounding states in Europe. This is quite common for **small states**, which often lack the resources for a worldwide network of diplomatic representation.[9] Smallness, in other words, generally serves as a constraint on foreign policy. In this particular case, however, the Belgian king was able to manipulate the country's smallness into an advantage.

The European powers assembled in Berlin in 1884–85 did not perceive the acquisition of the Congo by Leopold II as a threat to their own power or to the European **balance of power**. In fact, recognition of Leopold II's claims represented an attractive solution for the larger powers: this way, they could deny their main rivals the acquisition of yet another colony— and with it the potential increased wealth (which could be translated into more power). France would have objected if the territory went to Britain, and vice versa, because both countries would have perceived this as upsetting the balance of power between them. It was in some ways a replay of the London Conference that had guaranteed Belgium's independence and mandated its political neutrality after the small country broke away from the Dutch Kingdom in 1830. Then, too, the big powers tried to ensure that Belgium's presence in the European political landscape did not upset the balance of power. Now, King Leopold II worked hard to create the impression that all would be welcome to enrich themselves in the Congo. Hence, Belgian administration of the territory would be in the interest of all—or so the European leaders assembled in Berlin thought. Clever diplomacy, based on extensive research, aided Leopold II in achieving his ends on the international stage.

The other constraint, an unfavorable domestic public opinion, was perhaps easier to overcome at a time when the average citizen did not yet have the right to vote and when news was much slower to travel than in our era of instant electronic communications. However, do keep in mind that King Leopold II's rule shares features with today's nondemocratic regimes, which often control their countries' media and thus the information to which their citizens have access. Although the Internet has made government control of the media less effective, there are still quite a few countries where Internet access—and indeed computers—are relatively scarce, especially beyond the capital city. This makes it easier for leaders in those societies to either manipulate or ignore their domestic audience. Consider, for instance, that Egyptian leader Anwar al-Sadat did not consult domestic **public opinion** before embarking on his momentous journey to Jerusalem in the late 1970s. It was a bold move for the leader of an Arab country to make the decision to so visibly enter into negotiations with Israel. Sadat made this decision, which represented a radical shift in his country's foreign policy, against the backdrop of a domestic economic crisis. He hoped that his overture would help bring an infusion of aid to Egypt's economy—which it did. His efforts to sell the changed policy to the domestic public were facilitated by the benefits the new policy brought in terms of aid.

Neither the Belgian King Leopold II nor the Egyptian President Anwar al-Sadat were elected leaders. However, neither could totally ignore public opinion: the Belgian public was not interested in colonial ventures, so the king acquired the Congo as a personal possession. The Egyptian public did not view peace with Israel as its foremost priority, but the benefits that flowed from Sadat's decision facilitated acceptance by many, though not all, citizens of his country. Sadat's leadership ended when he was assassinated by members of the Egyptian military in October 1981, almost exactly four years after his journey to Jerusalem. Do note, however, that his peace treaty with Israel was only one of their grievances.

The lack of **accountability** may make it easier for the leaders of nondemocratic societies to make unpopular decisions, but they cannot do so with impunity. Conversely, the leaders of democratic countries are not always wholly beholden to public opinion. They may be able to shape public opinion to a smaller or larger extent, depending on the public's attentiveness to foreign policy and the centrality of the issue. Public opinion is a constraint irrespective of the domestic political system, although its weight can vary across situations and issue areas. Similar variability applies to other constraints leaders face. Although it is possible to point to some commonalities in the constraints faced by, for instance, the leaders of small or developing countries,[10] there is quite a bit of variability, a topic to which we return in chapters 5 and 6.

Despite such constraints, it is difficult to explain foreign policy decisions and behaviors without reference to leaders. The perception (and perhaps even the creation) of opportunities, as well as the successful conduct of diplomacy depend on the foreign policy skill of individuals. This implies that the impact a leader can have depends not only on the constraints and opportunities presented by the environment but also on that leader's interest and involvement in foreign policy.[11] A leader who has a genuine and deep interest in foreign policy is likely to play a more active role and be involved in a larger number of foreign policy problems than someone who lacks such an interest. Nevertheless, an international crisis is likely to involve decision making at the highest levels even if the leader does not have a special interest in foreign policy. The degree to which constraints diminish (and the degree to which opportunities expand) the number of alternatives is therefore mediated by the interest and attention a specific leader brings to foreign policy making. King Leopold II started out with little opportunity and much constraint, but through his interest and effort he expanded his opportunities to take part in the scramble for Africa.

The skill and experience of leaders is not always sufficient to ensure a desired outcome, because outcomes depend not only on the accurate assessment of opportunities and constraints but also on the interaction of the state's foreign policy behavior with that of other countries. However, decisions that have the best possible chance of yielding desired outcomes depend on perceptive assessments of the opportunities and constraints presented by the international and domestic environments, as well as on insight into the personalities of the relevant decision makers of other countries. It may not be possible to fully predict the actions of those decision makers, but it *is* feasible to develop sufficient insight to understand the predisposition of such leaders. Knowing how another country's leader is likely to react to certain proposals and actions can help tailor messages and behaviors to increase the likelihood that desired responses are elicited and disastrous ones avoided. In sum, understanding leaders is a significant ingredient of successful diplomacy.

Leaders' Personality and Public Persona

Not every leader will have the sort of ambition that motivated King Leopold II. Not every leader will put his or her stamp on history in such a clear manner, but leaders almost invariably have options when they make decisions. This means that the choices they make are not foregone conclusions. What makes it possible for some decision makers to have more impact than others? Why are some leaders satisfied with shaping their environment in small ways while others seek to have a much bigger impact?

The story of how the king of a small country acquired a vast colonial empire illustrates some of the answers. Although individual decision makers must be understood within the domestic and international context within which they find themselves, they are not merely reacting to the pressures provided by that environment. On the contrary, they are best seen as agents with goals who actively seek to influence the world in which they find themselves. Their success in doing so depends to a considerable degree on their personality, which influences decision making in two ways: One, it colors leaders' perceptions of specific events and the world in general. Personality focuses on the enduring qualities of the person and assumes that we can predict the actions and reactions of leaders once we understand the personality or character of that individual.[12] Personality also interacts with perception and cognition, which are discussed separately in chapter 3. Two, leaders' personalities affect how they utilize and organize the staff on which they rely for information and advice. In most countries, the entire government bureaucracy does not change when a new leader ascends to office, but the leader's immediate circle of advisors generally does consist of political appointees. The organizational structure of this group of advisors and the regulation of access to the leader are dependent on the latter's preferences, which are in turn dependent on personality. The advisory system and its impact on decision making are discussed in greater detail in chapter 4. In this chapter, the focus is on personality.

A focus on the personality or character of leaders is often motivated by questions such as these: What sort of personality makes a good leader? What sort of leader will this person make? What sort of personality is the leader of that country? As discussed in chapter 1 in connection with the concept of good decisions, it is not easy to define the qualities that make a *good* leader. It is easier to determine the personality of a leader and predict what sort of leadership we might expect from that individual.

A number of authors who have examined leaders and decision making have concluded that good leadership is often a matter of fit between the person and the circumstances,[13] but this is not a very satisfactory guide, because it is difficult to predict the circumstances a leader may face during her or his tenure in office. In addition, leaders frequently do not just respond to their environment but also seek to influence it. Some personalities may expend more effort than others in attempts to manipulate their environment, but the point is that the relationship between the person and the situation is interactive—which complicates the notion of fit between leader and situation. Is there a good fit when a leader manages a crisis well? Is there a good fit when a leader manipulates his environment to suit his ambitions? Does it matter what sort of strategies a leader employs to achieve desired ends?

Let's examine the case of King Leopold II a bit further. Although he argued even as a crown prince that Belgium needed a colony to enhance its status among the states of Europe, in the end he acquired the Congo as a personal possession. The Belgian state was not involved until much later and did not reap the economic benefits that were derived from the Congo. In fact, the state went so far as to loan money to its king to support his investments in the Congo! It took a great deal of insight into—and clever manipulation of—the personalities of other countries' leaders and the various people he employed for King Leopold II to achieve his ultimate objective. It was a sort of diplomacy the king became quite good at: he knew just how to flatter Stanley to convince the famous explorer to work for him. He exploited this talent many times over with numerous other individuals. He was also quite good at managing his own public relations, gaining quite a bit of publicity both domestically and abroad for his supposed humanitarian and scientific ventures. On the downside was the observation that the king was a "Machiavellian amoralist" who was prepared to use coercion and brute force to squeeze as much money out of a colony as he could.[14] Interestingly, this observation about the king pre-dated not only his actual acquisition of the Congo but also his ascendance to the throne of Belgium. It was based on statements the king had made as a younger and less savvy crown prince, when he displayed his ambition in raw and unpolished form. These insights derived from the king's younger years support the notion that a person's early life may provide important clues to his or her orientation toward life and leadership.[15]

Do notice that the use of a person's early life to predict their performance in office is predicated on the notion that personality is formed early and remains fundamentally unaltered throughout life. While some aspects of personality may be indeed be hardwired or stem from important childhood experiences, it would be problematic to use a person's early life for more than general tendencies, which may manifest themselves in many different ways in later years. This does not mean that insights derived from a person's early life are useless, but it does indicate that we must exercise caution: it is easy to overinterpret the significance of early experiences, especially in hindsight. After all, the attitude Leopold displayed as a young man toward the moneymaking potential of colonies took on heightened significance only *after* an international movement exposed the atrocities that accompanied the rubber trade—the most important source of wealth during the time the king controlled the Congo. Had the atrocities never been exposed, he might have been remembered as a humanitarian rather than an opportunist. In fact, some continued to portray King Leopold II's involvement in the Congo as benevolent. King Baudouin, the grandson of Leopold II's nephew (who succeeded him on the throne), painted his ancestor in this manner at the Congo's independence day ceremony in 1960.

On the other hand, evidence from Leopold's upbringing and the international climate of his lifetime could easily be used to argue that it would have been difficult for him to be satisfied merely with managing the affairs of a small country. His father, Leopold I, had been an ambitious German nobleman who, as the result of a strategic marriage and his own political efforts, was tapped for kingship when Belgium emerged as an independent state. King Leopold I had sought to enhance the status of the new Belgian royal family by arranging a politically expedient, but personally miserable, marriage for his son. Added to the misfortune of an unhappy marriage was the death of Leopold II's only son at a young age.[16] Leopold II may have poured so much energy into his colonial ambitions to escape his private misery.[17] Or perhaps he was merely following in his father's footsteps. After all, his father had also been interested in acquiring a colony for Belgium, though that interest had not been as single-minded as his son's was. Moreover, an interest in acquiring a colony was not all that unusual among leaders in the nineteenth century Europe. What set King Leopold II apart was the enormous drive and persistence he brought to the task, as well as the lengths to which he went to present a humanitarian persona to his European and North American audiences while simultaneously condoning and even advocating brutal practices to squeeze wealth out of the Congo. Given his bluntness as a young man, he made quite a transformation.

In sum, although statements made by Leopold II as a young man seem prophetic in hindsight, other details regarding his upbringing might also lead to the suspicion that as king he would feel the need to demonstrate his royal prowess—and in nineteenth-century Europe the acquisition of a colony was an acceptable way to aggrandize one's stature. Nevertheless, the dramatic shift from the blunt young man to the later humanitarian **public persona** brings up an important dilemma in studying the personalities of leaders. Not all are so blatantly **Machiavellian** as King Leopold II, but most engage in some form of public image making. Niccolo Machiavelli, a fifteenth-century political thinker, counseled that it was more important for a king to *appear* benevolent than to actually *be* good.[18] Machiavelli's advice was based on the notion that most people will judge a leader on the basis of his or her public image and will not perceive the true character hidden behind it. Although Machiavelli's advice has made his name synonymous with duplicity and unscrupulous behavior, most people also accept that a person's public face and private thoughts cannot be equated.

Conversely, information about the private person is not necessarily a good guide regarding the sort of leader a person would be. Consider, for instance, a historical figure that did not smoke or drink, ate a vegetarian diet, and was monogamous.[19] You might consider such a person to be morally upright and expect him or her to be a leader who does not engage in demagoguery or deception. You might consider voting for such a person. However, this same historical figure instituted a policy of systematic and institutionalized discrimination against several ethnic and religious groups, including the systematic killing of six million Jews. Although the institutionalized discrimination was public knowledge, the large-scale murders were not advertised. In fact, many Jews were led to their death believing they were simply going to take a shower. By now, you will have guessed that this historical figure is Adolph Hitler. Superficial biographical information can be quite misleading regarding a person's political leadership qualities and performance.

Treatments that focus on the person's early life are not without problems either. The Soviet leader Joseph Stalin and the Iraqi leader Saddam Hussein were both brutal dictators. Biographies of both frequently report that they had abusive fathers who abandoned their families while their sons were still young. Psychologists have found that children of abusive parents are very likely to become abusive adults themselves. Hence, recounting this childhood experience makes sense of their later performance as leaders of their respective countries. The pieces of information about these men's lives fit together nicely in hindsight. As you may have noticed, psychologists note a greater *likelihood*, but not a certainty, that children of abuse will become abusers. More important for our purposes, it is not clear whether private abusive relationships are in any way predictive of a person's actions as a political leader. And not all leaders who have perpetrated heinous acts have had such backgrounds: Hitler, for instance, did not have an abusive father and had a doting mother. There was not much in his early life that would have predicted his rise to power or the genocide that his regime perpetrated.

This does not mean that an interest in the biographies of leaders is fruitless. It does mean, however, that we must be careful to not overinterpret the significance of snippets of information about a person's life and seek to gain a more comprehensive picture. In addition, we must ask whether the early life experiences of Stalin and Saddam would have seemed equally predictive of their brutality as leaders at the start of their political careers. Hitler's youth provided little indication of his later leadership, and he himself recalled his extended stay in pre–World War I Vienna, where he arrived as an eighteen-year-old, as a formative experience. While there, he experienced poverty and rejection, but he also absorbed many of the ideas that would later shape his political philosophy.[20] Not all leaders express their political philosophy as clearly as Hitler did in his book *Mein Kampf*. Most often, it is a lot more difficult to decipher a leader's character and personality and a lot less clear how the individual views the world and what motivations drive him or her.

Foreign policy analysts are thus faced with a problem: how do we evaluate personality when a leader's early life is at best a rough guide and we cannot assume that a leader speaks his or her mind? Before we attempt to answer this question, let's take a step back and summarize the reasons we want to look beyond the public persona and learn about the personalities of leaders. One, doing so helps us evaluate what sort of leader a person is (or would be). More than merely evaluating whether a person is a good or bad leader, understanding what drives a person can help to evaluate the strengths a person brings to a leadership position—and the weaknesses for which a good advisory system could perhaps compensate. Such information serves the public interest. Two, assessments of the personalities of leaders can facilitate diplomatic negotiations. It can help leaders understand why their counterparts in other countries make the foreign policy decisions they do. It can also help them structure their own foreign policies to have the best possible chance to achieve the desired outcomes. In short, accurate assessments of leaders provide useful knowledge.

The Quest to Understand Leaders

We must begin with the assumption that the public persona and private individual are not synonymous. Given this assumption, how do we go about our quest to understand leaders' personalities? Studies of leaders frequently borrow concepts from psychology, which has devised many instruments for studying individuals and their motivations, their approaches to problem solving and decision making, and their basic view of the world around them. Psychologists have arrived at their notions about personality through carefully constructed experiments that have provided insights into the general tendencies of human behavior. Most often, psychologists will avoid making definitive predictions about a single individual's behavior but will instead cast their assessments in terms of the behavioral patterns that are *likely* to be associated with specific personality types. Foreign policy analysts who study leaders are similar to their colleagues in psychology in that they also discuss their assessments in terms of the *likely* patterns of behavior associated with leaders' personalities. There is, however, an important difference between the two disciplines: psychologists are interested in general knowledge about human behavior, whereas foreign policy analysts are interested in evaluating specific individuals—domestic and foreign leaders. And unlike the counseling psychologist, who tends to focus on individuals for therapeutic reasons, foreign policy analysts are interested in assessing what sort of leader a specific individual is (or would make) and what kind of foreign policy decisions can be expected from a specific leader. A second important difference is that psychologists, whether they are engaged in research or counsel individuals, have direct access to their subjects, whereas foreign policy analysts usually do not: foreign policy decision makers are unlikely to make themselves available for such testing. This means that the study of leaders must rely on indirect methods.

Foreign policy analysts, who are interested in understanding how leaders view the world, what motivates them, and how they make decisions, have no choice but to devise ways to read between the lines of the public persona to find hints of the individual behind the image. This is not an easy task. A number of different strategies have been proposed. Some of these rely on biographical information, as well as interpretations of a leader's public pronouncements and actions. Others rely primarily on official speeches and less formal comments made during interviews or press conferences. In some cases, the strategy is dependent on the availability (or paucity) of information. For example, an effort to understand Soviet leaders during the Cold War would not have been able to rely on as much information as an assessment of a current or former U.S. president. Details about the decision making process, such as transcripts or notes taken by participants in policy meetings, would simply not have been available—nor would spontaneous interview responses. Students of the Soviet Union often had to make do with interpretations of subtle shifts in the use of language in official newspapers.

An early study of the leaders of the Soviet Union juxtaposed Russian literature and texts produced by that leadership to investigate the "unexpressed content" of the latter.[21] The study sought to describe the Soviet **operational code** that, presumably, provided some insight into the likely foreign policy behavior of that country's leadership.[22] It was one of the first studies to consciously apply psychological concepts to the study of leaders. It relied heavily on psychoanalysis. Although the study is now regarded as a classic in foreign policy analysis, there was much skepticism about its findings among area specialists: the study cited the work of two anthropologists who had argued that certain Russian characteristics had their origins in the practice of swaddling babies.[23] The study of the Soviet operational code focused on the personalities of the Politburo members rather than on the possible childhood origins of personality traits, but because it included references to a discredited theory, the potential contributions of the operational code as a methodology were not widely recognized among area specialists.

The operational code as a methodology seeks to describe a leader's fundamental beliefs, which provide norms, standards, and guidelines for decision making.[24] The operational code does not tell us what, specifically, a decision maker will decide. Instead, it provides insight into the decision maker's perceptions and evaluations of the world, and estimates of how he or she will weigh the benefits and risks of various courses of action. In other words, the operational code is designed to allow us to "get inside the mind" of decision makers.

Although later studies that employed the operational code methodology invariably focused on individual decision makers,[25] the pioneering study of the Soviet operational code actually sought to delineate the collective preferences of the Politburo, the Soviet Union's highest decision making body. It justified this focus on the basis of the centrality of this group for Soviet policy. One of the fundamental tenets of the Soviet operational code was, quite consistent with Marxist philosophy, that history was not accidental. The larger trends of history, such as the transition from capitalism to communism, were regarded as predictable, even if the specific path and pace that would bring the world to that future state of affairs was not. This deterministic view of history did not mean that gains for communism would emerge easily: on the contrary, gains could only be the result of struggle.[26]

The point here is not to render a verdict about the correctness of the Soviet view of history. Rather, what is important to note is that the study's author used the publicly available writings of Soviet leaders and the imagery in Russian literature to read between the lines of the official pronouncements in an effort to grasp how Soviet leaders understood the world around them and what motivated them. The objective was not to predict specific foreign policy decisions but to understand what policy options the members of the Politburo would entertain seriously in a given situation—and to exclude those that would be ruled out quickly or not even considered. Although the initial version of the operational code was met with skepticism, the idea was later revised into a framework for systematic analysis and has become an important strategy for evaluating leaders, as we shall see.

Foreign leaders are not the only subjects of efforts to understand the personalities of decision makers. A good amount of effort has been expended on strategies to study the personalities of American presidents, motivated to a large extent by the knowledge that these leaders can affect the course of world politics in important ways. One strategy to assess **presidential character** is centered on two questions:[27] One, how active or passive is the leader? That is, how much energy does the person invest in his or her political office? Two, does the leader rate political life positively and derive satisfaction from it, or does he or she perceive elected office negatively in terms of duty? The answers to these two questions yield four types of leaders, as summarized in table 2.1. The first category is leaders who invest a lot of energy and derive a lot of satisfaction from the job (**active-positive**). Think about presidents like Harry S. Truman, John F. Kennedy or George H. W. Bush. Each of these men made efforts to be well informed. Each was willing to listen to the perspectives of their advisors but also comfortable making tough decisions after evaluating the information presented to him. The second type of leader invests a lot of energy but perceives the job as a chore (**active-negative**). These are leaders who are primarily interested in getting and keeping power. Lyndon Johnson and Richard Nixon are often mentioned as fitting this category. The former had a tendency to micromanage rather than to defer to specialists within the administration. Nixon's preoccupation with power—and his fear of losing it—led him to engage in secretive and dishonest tactics that eventually cost him his presidency.

The third type of president is less energetic but does find the job satisfying (**passive-positive**). Consider Ronald Reagan's jovial demeanor. His emphasis was on speechmaking and playing host, not on reading extensive briefing papers. In fact, he preferred to receive one page "mini-memos" and left much of the negotiation and deal making to his staff. The fourth and last personality category is also a less energetic leader. In contrast with the previous category, this one perceives the presidency as a chore (**passive-negative**). Like the active-negative type, this personality is motivated by a sense of duty. Dwight D. Eisenhower personifies this well-developed sense of service to country.

Although the first type, the active-positive president, appears on the surface to be most desirable, none of the categories are invariably desirable or problematic—each has its own pitfalls. The potential problems of passivity may be most obvious: if a president is not engaged in the subject matter of the political problems of his time and reads only summaries rather than full briefing papers, he (or she) may be open to manipulation by advisors and lose control of the decision making process. The active-positive personality

Table 2.1 Classification of leader personality types

1. Does the leader invest a lot of energy in his or her political office? How active or passive is the leader?	2. Is politics a satisfying and enjoyable career or does the leader seek office out of a sense of duty to serve? Does the leader view politics positively or negatively?	
	Positive	*Negative*
Active	**1. Active-Positive** Harry S. Truman John F. Kennedy George H. W. Bush	**2. Active-Negative** Lyndon B. Johnson Richard Nixon
Passive	**3. Passive-Positive** Ronald Reagan	**4. Passive-Negative** Dwight D. Eisenhower

may appear to be well suited to leadership, but the focus on rational problem solving may lead to a tendency to ignore the rough-and-tumble of political deal making. The classification of leaders into four categories is, of course, a relatively crude approximation of personality. The three presidents listed as examples of the active-positive category—Truman, Kennedy and Bush—may have shared certain traits, but they were also distinctly different individuals. That point is obscured by the relatively simple classification scheme, although studies based on this scheme did address these differences between individuals who were placed in the same category. Such studies relied on the interpretation of biographical material, speeches, and writings of and about the individual. The study of presidential character drew on a more comprehensive set of source materials than the original operational code study. Both approaches, however, relied on the (foreign) policy analyst's personal expertise—including knowledge of the principles of psychoanalysis—as the foundation for interpretation of these materials. This made it difficult for others to replicate these studies and limited the possibility of broad application of these strategies to efforts to understand the personalities of leaders.

More systematic and more easily replicated strategies for reading between the lines of the public persona—strategies that also use publicly available materials—have emerged. One of these methodologies was a reinvention of the operational code, a strategy for determining a leader's fundamental premises and beliefs about politics, discussed earlier in this chapter. The original study was distilled into ten questions; the first five of these address the leader's the philosophical approach to politics and second five address instrumental beliefs about how to attain desired objectives.[28] The complete list of questions can be found in table 2.2. This list of questions provided a systematic approach that permitted comparisons of the operational codes of different leaders who had been evaluated using this strategy. It also permitted, at least in theory, comparison of the results of different researchers studying the same foreign policy decision maker. This last point is important: even if no second or third analyst ever completed an operational code study of the same leader, the systematic investigation guided by these ten questions made it much clearer to anyone reading the results to understand how the analyst had reached his or her conclusions.

Operational code studies have relied on the writings and recorded verbal comments of decision makers. An investigation of the operational code of former U.S. Secretary of State Henry Kissinger, for instance, relied primarily on his academic writings.[29] It found that important themes of Kissinger's philosophical beliefs can already be found in his undergraduate honors thesis and remain quite stable. This former policy maker is known for a role in ending the Vietnam War and for "shuttle diplomacy"

Table 2.2 The operational code: determining the philosophical and instrumental beliefs of leaders

A. Philosphical Questions	1. What is the "essential" nature of political life? Is the political universe essentially one of harmony or conflict? What is the fundamental character of one's political opponents?
	2. What are the prospects for the eventual realization of one's fundamental political values and aspirations? Can one be opmistic, or must one be pessimistic on this score; and in what respects the one or the other?
	3. Is the political future predictable? In what sense and to what extent?
	4. How much "control" or "mastery" can one have over historical development? What is one's role in "moving" and "shaping" history in the desired direction?
	5. What is the role of 'chance' in human affairs and in historical development?
B. Instrumental Questions	1. What is the best approach for selecting goals political or objectives for action?
	2. How are the goals of action pursued most effectively?
	3. How are the risks of political action calculated, controlled, and accepted?
	4. What is the best 'timing' of action to advance one's interests?
	5. What is the utility and role of different means for advancing one's interests?

to investigate possibilities for negotiations among Israel and its Arab neighbors. Kissinger believed that the control that an individual can have over the course of history is limited. Rather, the role of chance and the shadow cast by past events are important. While policy makers are not on the sidelines of history, they cannot expect to have a major influence on historical developments, because they must play the game according to existing rules that can be manipulated but rarely changed. The impact that leaders can have is, in his mind, contingent upon their insight into the forces of history and their strategic responses to these. This operational code explains Kissinger's tactics regarding the end of the American involvement in Vietnam, which was incremental: strategic demonstrations of power were followed by overtures for negotiations. In sum, Kissinger operated not from some grand vision for a future world order but from a point of view that focuses on leaders' tactical and strategic choices in pursuit of the "national interest."

Not all decision makers have such a constant and unchanging set of beliefs. Former U.S. Senator J. William Fulbright evolved in his core beliefs.[30] His changing identification of malignant forces in world politics entailed a changing answer to part of the first philosophical question: What is the fundamental character of one's political opponents? Fulbright started out with the belief that malfeasant leaders of states are a core problem and that, certainly in the United States, the legislature has a key role to play in ensuring that foreign policy is rational and avoids miscalculations. During the Cold War, he shifted to the view that the United States faces an inherently aggressive opponent in the Soviet Union, which must be countered with a single-minded and purposeful response. Power is key in this approach. By the time of the Vietnam War, Fulbright once again changed his identification of the fundamental character of the opponent: he now perceived the arrogance of great powers as a major threat to the international order. He believed this in general, but more importantly, he believed it with respect to the United States in particular—which explains his opposition to the Vietnam War in this time period.

The operational code, as an approach to studying leaders, seeks to utilize their writings and recorded verbal statements. Access to such materials is more straightforward in societies that keep extensive written records. In addition, operational code studies traditionally required that the analyst be able to understand the language in which these materials were written well enough to make nuanced judgments, because such studies employed qualitative analyses. It will come as little surprise that the majority of operational code studies have focused on American and other western leaders.[31] First, these societies have a tradition not only of record keeping but also of providing relatively open access to these materials to foreign policy analysts. Second, not only is it difficult to obtain materials from other countries, but also American foreign policy analysts have a relatively underdeveloped knowledge of foreign languages.

One strategy for overcoming the second problem is the use of translated speeches and other verbal statements. Although it is possible for translated text to miss the subtleties of linguistic expression in a specific language and for errors to occur in translation, the use of such text enables foreign policy analysts to broaden the scope of leaders they can analyze considerably. One effort to understand the personality and style of leaders from a number of different countries utilizes translated text. This is then analyzed systematically for specific linguistic markers that are taken to reveal personality traits. This strategy for **leadership trait analysis** is founded on a set of questions that probe various aspects of a leader's personal characteristics that are relevant to foreign policy decision making.[32] Table 2.3 groups the seven questions into the three dimensions they represent. Leadership trait analysis differs from the operational code. There are fewer questions, and the questions deal more directly with political life. For example, this instrument focuses on whether the leader believes he or she can control events and feels the need to exercise influence rather than whether the person believes that individuals can generally affect the course of history. In addition, where the operational code traditionally relied on the judgment of the analyst on the basis of a qualitative but structured interpretation of the writings and speeches of leaders, leadership trait analysis relies on a systematic **content analysis** of text. The latter scheme looks for specific words and phrases in interview responses and speeches of leaders. For example, the trait of **conceptual complexity** is evaluated on the basis of the frequency with which a decision maker uses qualifiers such as *possibly*, *perhaps*, *sometimes*, and *maybe*, which indicate high complexity, versus qualifiers such as *certain*, *always*, *undoubtedly*, or *indisputable*, which indicate low complexity.[33] How does this trait matter in the conduct of foreign policy?

Table 2.3 Leadership trait analysis

Attitude towards constraints	1. Belief in one's own ability to control events	Perception of control over situations
	2. Need for power and influence	Concern for establishing, maintaining, or restoring one's influence over others
Openness to new information	3. Conceptual complexity	Differentiation in describing or discussing other people, places, policies, ideas, or things
	4. Self-confidence	Sense of self-importance
Motivation	5. Task versus interpersonal	Focus on substance of policy (problem solving) versus interpersonal relations (team work)
	6. Distrust of others	Inclination to suspect and doubt the motives of others.
	7. Ingroup Bias	Degree to which own group is central in view of the world

Lower conceptual complexity correlates with more conflictual state behavior, including less reliance on diplomacy and quicker commitment to action.[34] Interestingly, the two leaders who most closely cooperated to orchestrate the 2003 invasion of Iraq, President George Bush and Prime Minister Tony Blair, both score relatively low on conceptual complexity.[35] In addition, there is evidence that this variable affects the foreign policy making process as well: higher conceptual complexity is linked to greater openness to and use of new information.[36]

The leadership trait analysis focuses on much more than conceptual complexity. It also evaluates whether leaders believe they can control events, as well as their need for power, their self-confidence, their ingroup bias, their level of distrust of others, and the degree of task emphasis. Tony Blair's low cognitive complexity explains why he "did not recognize the caveats and uncertainties" expressed in the intelligence he received on Iraq prior to the decision to invade.[37] He combined this trait with a strong belief in his ability to control events as well as a high need for power. This predisposed him to taking tight personal control over policy making with a small, closely knit circle of advisors.[38] On the other side of the Atlantic, there is evidence that strong scores on distrust of others, coupled with a relatively low conceptual complexity, "help to explain President Bush's insistence that Saddam, his WMD stockpiles, and his links to terror constituted a severe threat to America's security in the post–September 11 world, when others were more skeptical."[39] High scores on distrust predispose leaders to perceive threats as credible and often increase their willingness to confront such threats aggressively. This distrust was characteristic not only of Bush's personality, but also of others within his administration, although there were distinct differences between the scores on this variable for different individuals.[40] Unfortunately, the decision makers with the lowest scores for distrust of others were also least central to the decision making process. In essence, there may have been insufficient questioning among administration officials of their predisposition to distrust Iraq's leader.

The presidential character, operational code, and leadership trait analysis are not the only strategies that have been employed. However, these different strategies do demonstrate the variety of approaches that have been employed to evaluate the personalities of leaders. Initially, many studies employed concepts from psychoanalysis and required that foreign policy analysts read and interpret large amounts of information. The original operational code study and the study of presidential character represent this generation of leadership analysis. The revised operational code infuses qualitative analysis with a systematic approach through the use of ten questions, and in the past decade scholars working with operational code analysis have developed a strategy for machine coding the speeches of leaders.[41]

The advantage of doing this is not only that a computer can code large amounts of text in a fairly short time, but also that the material is evaluated in a very consistent manner.

The leadership trait analysis method of evaluating leaders builds on the expertise of a more recent generation of experimental psychological researchers and relies on quantitative content analysis techniques. Although this strategy initially used human coders to analyze text, it now also employs a machine coding strategy. Both the leadership trait analysis and the current generation of the operational code use transparent methods that make it easier for readers to understand how analysts arrived at their conclusions. Before computer-assisted content analysis, the coding of text—an integral part of content analysis—was very labor intensive and required human coders trained in the specific methodology. This made such analysis time consuming and cumbersome. The move to computerized content analysis techniques has made this sort of analysis easier and quicker and the results more consistent. As a result, more researchers are now exploring the possibilities of both operational code and leadership trait analysis to evaluate the personalities of leaders and their advisors. This creates possibilities for increased usefulness: quick turnaround on the assessment of current leaders can provide foreign policy decision makers with insights into their counterparts in other countries that can help them understand how best to approach and negotiate with those leaders.

The Impact of Emotions

Thus far, leaders have been portrayed as goal-directed, and purposeful. This is not incorrect, but it is incomplete: it implies that foreign policy decision makers have a cool and rational distance from the problems they face. That is not always the case. Affect, or emotion, influences foreign policy decision making in a myriad of ways, some of which are not yet well understood.

The impact of emotions on decision making is not wholly separate from the impact of personality. Consider that one of the characteristics measured by the leadership trait analysis method is the leader's propensity to distrust others. The operational code includes among the philosophical questions a measure of the subject's optimism or pessimism regarding the prospect of realizing his or her values and aspirations. Both trust-distrust and optimism-pessimism have their foundations in personality: people often are predisposed toward trusting or distrusting others, or they tend toward optimism or pessimism. Of course, such a predisposition can be modified by hard-won life experience. In addition, moods are not constants but vary across time for each individual. The impact of these moods or emotions on decision making is the subject matter of this section.

What are emotions? Emotions consist of both psychological and physical components. Individuals describe the psychological (or mental) aspects to others as feelings, and these feelings may be accompanied by physical changes.[42] Emotions are often described as spontaneous reactions. Because of this, emotions are sometimes perceived as detracting from reasoned judgment,[43] although others liken them to stress: while a little stress enhances performance, too much impairs it.[44] In either case, there is a recognition that emotion affects judgment: individuals in a positive mood tend to rely on general knowledge and make judgments on the basis of stereotypes, prior judgments, and other mental shortcuts, whereas decision makers in a sad mood tend to be much more attentive to detail and engage in careful step-by-step analysis of the situations they face.[45] Consider, for instance, the impact of King Leopold II's personal unhappiness on his devotion to his colonial ambitions. Would he have pursued the Congo as single-mindedly if he had been happily married? Would he have done so had his only son survived to adulthood? We cannot be certain of the answers; such speculation amounts to counterfactual history. What we do know, however, is that the king was not a happy man, and it is not unreasonable to suspect that this affected his decision making.

Emotion influences not only the decision making process but also judgments about the object of attention. Although people in different cultures experience the same range of emotions, different societies have different norms regarding the expression of emotion. Hence, it may be difficult for decision makers to accurately interpret the emotions of their counterparts in other countries—especially if social norms and cultures are very different.[46] Trade negotiations between the United States and Japan long suffered from misunderstandings between the two countries' representatives. The Americans would walk away from negotiations thinking they had a deal, while the Japanese interpreted their responses to be merely polite pleasantries—not commitments. The former value directness in communication, but the latter value politeness and subtlety. The social norms with regard to overt display of emotion are very different in the two societies, making it difficult for diplomats of either country to interpret the other's motives and intentions accurately.

This points at a problem that is central to foreign policy making: interpreting the foreign policy behaviors of other countries and their leaders is rarely straightforward. Emotions affect these judgments. Preexisting positive or negative feelings about other countries and their leaders influence judgments about their foreign policies. Chapter 3 discusses how leaders make sense of the world around them. As you read, remember that leaders' emotions have an impact on foreign policy decision making that is not trivial, but that has not yet received much systematic attention.

Chapter Summary

- Leaders do not impact the foreign policy behavior of their state equally under all circumstances. At times, circumstances leave them with few options. At other times, leaders either have, or create for themselves, great leeway in their ability to shape the foreign policy of their country.
- An important difficulty in studying leaders' personalities is that their public persona may portray a very different image from the person they are in private. Their early years and formative experience represent at best a rough guide to their motivations as leaders.
- There are several different strategies available to assess leader personality. The chapter describes the operational code, presidential character, and leadership trait analysis. The first generation of operational code analyses and presidential character studies were less systematic and more dependent on the analyst's insight and expertise. Leadership trait analysis employed systematic content analysis. Both leadership trait analysis and the operational code now employ computer-assisted coding strategies, which provide consistent analyses and complete the task fast.
- Human emotions influence decisions but are an under-studied subject. Not much is yet known about the impact of emotions on foreign policy decision making.

Terms

Small states
Balance of power
Public opinion
Accountability
Personality
Public persona
Machiavellian
Operational code
Presidential character
Active-positive
Active-negative

Passive-positive
Passive-negative
Leadership trait analysis
Content analysis
Conceptual complexity
Emotions

Study Questions

1. How does a leader's personality influence foreign policy decision making?
2. Are leaders free to pursue their foreign policy ambitions? What are some of the factors that influence leaders' abilities to do so?
3. What are some of the differences between the public persona and private person? Why do they matter for the study of foreign policy?
4. What are some of the strategies foreign policy analysts have used to figure out what motivates the man or woman behind the public persona?
5. In what ways do emotions influence foreign policy decision making?

Suggestions for Further Reading

An essay that makes the case that leaders matter and that they are a worthy subject of investigation is Hermann, Preston, Korany, and Shaw, "Who Leads Matters: The Effect of Powerful Individuals."

The classic study of presidential character is Barber, *The Presidential Character: Predicting Performance in the White House.*

A classic essay regarding the operational code is: George, "The 'Operational Code': A Neglected Approach to the Study of Political Leaders and Decision-making." Another important study in this tradition is: Walker, "The Interface Between Beliefs and Behavior: Henry Kissinger's Operational Code and the Vietnam War." More recent works in this area, using computer-assisted coding, are Marfleet and Miller, "Failure after 1441: Bush and Chirac in the UN Security Council" and Malici and Malici, "The Operational Codes of Fidel Castro and Kim Il Sung: The Last Cold Warriors?"

An explanation of Leadership Trait Analysis, its components, and their measurement can be found in Hermann, "Assessing Leadership Style: A Trait Analysis." Also look for the many studies of leaders by Hermann. Other recent works utilizing computer-assisted leadership trait analysis are

Dyson, "Personality and Foreign Policy: Tony Blair's Iraq Decision," and Shannon and Keller, "Leadership Style and International Norm Violation." The role of emotions in foreign policy making is under-studied. One work in this area is Crawford, "The Passion of World Politics: Propositions on Emotion and Emotional Relationships."

Notes

1. Wels, *Aloofness and Neutrality*.
2. Pakenham, *The Scramble for Africa*.
3. Dunn, *Imagining the Congo*, 37; see also Hochschild, King Leopold's Ghost, 87.
4. Coolsaet, *België en zijn Buitenlandse Politiek*.
5. Hochschild, *King Leopold's Ghost*, 36–39; Dunn, Imagining the Congo, 28–29.
6. Coolsaet, *België en zijn Buitenlandse Politiek*, 145.
7. Hochschild, *King Leopold's Ghost*, Dunn, *Imagining the Congo*.
8. According to some estimates, the population of the Congo was reduced by about ten million during the period King Leopold II controlled the territory. See Hochschild, *King Leopold's Ghost*, 233.
9. East, "Size and Foreign Policy Behavior"; "National Attributes and Foreign Policy."
10. Hey, *Small States in World Politics*; Braveboy-Wagner, *The Foreign Policies of the Global South*; Korany, *How Foreign Policy Decisions are Made in the Third World*.
11. Hermann et al., "Who Leads Matters."
12. Schafer, "Issues in Assessing Psychological Characteristics at a Distance," 517; see also Greenstein, *Personality and Politics*.
13. Larson, "Politics, Uncertainty, and Values," 314; Barber, *Presidential Character*; Farnham, "Perceiving the End of Threat"; Welch, "Culture and Emotion as Obstacles to Good Judgment."
14. This phrase is translated from Coolsaet, *België en zijn Buitenlandse Politiek*, 145. See also Hochschild, *King Leopold's Ghost*.
15. Barber, *Presidential Character*. See also George and George, *Woodrow Wilson and Colonel House*; George and George, *Presidential Personality and Performance*.
16. Hochschild, *King Leopold's Ghost*, 39. The king had three daughters as well, but only male heirs mattered in terms of the royal succession.
17. This is implied by Hochschild, *King Leopold's Ghost*.
18. Machiavelli, "The Prince," 135.
19. Shirer, *The Rise and Fall of the Third Reich*.
20. *Mein Kampf*, cited in Shirer, *The Rise and Fall of the Third Reich*.
21. Leites, *A Study of Bolshevism*, 21–22; see also Leites, *The Operational Code of the Politburo*.
22. Leites, *A Study of Bolshevism*, 16–17.

23. Leites cited the work of Gorer and Rickman, *The People of Great Russia*. The association between the two studies and the negative connotations for Leites' work are expressed in, e.g., Tucker, *Political Culture and Leadership in Soviet Russia*.

24. George, "The Operational Code," 191; see also George, "The Causal Nexus."

25. George, "The Operational Code," "The Causal Nexus"; Tweraser, *Changing Patterns of Political Beliefs*; Walker, "The Interface Between Beliefs and Behavior," "The Motivational Foundations of Political Belief Systems," "The Evolution of Operational Code Analysis." More recent studies employing a machine-coded version of the operational code are, e.g., Malici and Malici, "The Operational Codes of Fidel Castro and Kim Il Sung"; Marfleet, "The Operational Code of John F. Kennedy"; Marfleet and Miller, "Failure After 1441"; Schafer and Crichlow, "Bill Clinton's Operational Code"; Schafer, Robison, and Aldrich, "Operational Codes"; Schafer and Walker, "Democratic Leaders and the Democratic Peace"; Walker and Schafer, "The Political Universe."

26. Leites, *A Study of Bolshevism*.

27. What follows is based on Barber, *Presidential Character*.

28. George, "The 'Operational Code'", "The Causal Nexus between Cognitive Beliefs and Decision-Making Behavior"; Holsti, "The Operational Code as an Approach to the Analysis of Belief Systems"; for more recent iterations, see Schafer, "Issues in Assessing Psychological Characteristics at a Distance"; Walker, "Assessing Psychological Characteristics at a Distance."

29. Walker, "The Interface of Beliefs and Behavior."

30. Tweraser, Changing Patterns of Political Beliefs.

31. The largest number of studies concern American decision makers; Marfleet, "The Operational Code of John F. Kennedy During the Cuban Missile Crisis"; Schafer and Crichlow, "Bill Clinton's Operational Code"; Tweraser, *Changing Patterns of Political Beliefs*, focuses on J. William Fulbright; Walker, "The Interface Between Beliefs and Behavior," focuses on Kissinger and "Psychodynamic Processes and Faming Effects" on Woodrow Wilson; Walker and Schafer, "The Political Universe of Lyndon B. Johnson and His Advisors." A few recent studies have focused on the Russian leader Vladimir Putin (Dyson, "Drawing Policy Implications from the Operational Code") and on Israeli decision makers (Crichlow, "Idealism or Pragmatism?" which focuses on Yitzhak Rabin and Shimon Peres). An extensive listing of published and unpublished operational code studies can be found in Holsti, "The Operational Code as an Approach to the Analysis of Belief Systems." His listing also demonstrates a distinct focus on American and western decision makers.

32. Hermann, "Assessing Leadership Style," "Assessing the Foreign Policy Role Orientations of Sub-Saharan African Leaders," "Explaining Foreign Policy Behavior," Leader Personality and Foreign Policy Behavior."

33. Schafer, "Issues in Assessing Psychological Characteristics at a Distance."

34. Hermann, "Explaining Foreign Policy Behavior," "Personality and Foreign Policy Decision Making"; Hermann and Hermann, "Who Makes Foreign Policy Decisions and How?"
35. Dyson, "Personality and Foreign Policy"; Shannon and Keller, "Leadership Style and International Norm Violation."
36. Kaarbo and Hermann, "Leadership Styles of Prime Ministers"; Preston, "Following the Leader"; Schafer, "Explaining Groupthink."
37. Dyson, "Personality and Foreign Policy," 299.
38. Ibid., 300.
39. Shannon and Keller, "Leadership Style and International Norm Violation," 97.
40. Ibid., 96–97.
41. Walker, Schafer, and Young, "Systematic Procedures for Operational Code Analysis."
42. Crawford, "The Passion of World Politics," 124.
43. Elster, "Sadder but Wiser?"
44. Crawford, "The Passion of World Politics," 137.
45. Bless, "The Interplay of Affect and Cognition"; Schwarz and Bless, "Happy and Mindless, but Sad and Smart?"; Crawford, "The Passion of World Politics."
46. Crawford, "The Passion of World Politics," 131–33.

Chapter 3

How Leaders Make Sense of the World

Chapter Preview

- Explains the ways in which "rationality" has been defined and used.
- Explains different models of the decision making process.
- Explains several ways of capturing the impact of perception on decision making.
- Explains why history can be a poor guide to decision making.
- Explains the difficulties in evaluating "good" decision making.

Do Perceptions Matter?

September 11, 2001, is etched in the minds of Americans. The terrorist attacks on the World Trade Center in New York City and the Pentagon in Washington, DC, are almost universally perceived as an unprecedented attack on the United States. Are the simultaneous bombings of multiple locations of the London Underground of July 7, 2005, etched in the minds of the British in the same way? While less devastating in their consequences, these bombings were also an attack on an unprecedented scale. But consider the differences in the context: whereas the British have long endured smaller attacks as a result of Irish Republican Army (IRA) terrorism, Americans generally perceived themselves as immune from attacks on their home soil. In addition, earlier bombings of the World Trade Center and Oklahoma City's Murrah Federal Building did not alter American perceptions of immunity from terrorism nearly as much as did the attacks of September 11, 2001. Perhaps only events of the scale of those of that day had the power to change the long-held perception that the country was safely ensconced between two oceans. In earlier times, that perception was certainly valid, but as military technology has changed, so has the value of vast oceans as borders—long before that fateful day when Americans suddenly realized their vulnerability.

How we perceive our world is not only dependent on context but also quite resistant to change.[1] Perceptions that may have been accurate at one time endure. They become the perspective from which we view the world—the image we have of the world—even if the circumstances have changed. That image guides our interpretation of new information about our environment and the actors in it.

This is true not only of average citizens but also of decision makers. Their perceptions are guided in part by their personality, beliefs, experiences, and expertise, but also by how the information is presented, in what context, and by whom. It is tempting to assume that decision makers are different from average citizens. Sometimes they are. There are examples of leaders who did try very hard to view the world from different perspectives and who "asked themselves hard questions about the accuracy and wisdom of their own beliefs and judgments,"[2] but there are also many examples of leaders who were not able to transcend the perspectives from which they customarily viewed their world—perspectives that were informed by their roots in their own society and its culture and history. Those are the leaders who have made decisions that others regard as puzzling or even irrational.

For instance, why would the leaders of Argentina decide to invade a group of small islands off their coast in 1982 and risk a war with Britain?[3] Argentina was at the time led by a three-person junta (or military dictatorship), consisting of the President and Commander in chief of the Army, General Leopoldo F. Galtieri, the Commander in chief of the Navy, Admiral Jorge I. Anaya, and the Commander in chief of the Air Force, Brigadier Basilio Lami Dozo.[4]

There was a longstanding dispute between Argentina and Britain about sovereignty over the islands, called the Malvinas by the Argentineans and the Falklands by the British, which were of "negligible strategic and economic value."[5] Hence, it would seem odd for the Argentine junta to risk a war with Britain, which had occupied the islands since 1833, even though the Argentine claim to jurisdiction over the islands predated the British occupation of them. The disputed sovereignty of the islands had been a factor in the relations between Argentina and Britain for a long time and had been the subject of (partially successful) negotiations between the two countries. The issue acquired a heightened urgency for the Argentine government as the 150-year anniversary of the occupation of the islands by Britain approached. The "recovery" of the Malvinas acquired "an artificial but powerful significance in the Argentine imagination" as 1983, the year of the anniversary, approached.[6] In early 1982, the Argentine government called for renewed talks with Britain that were to lead to the recognition of the former's sovereignty over the islands. Soon, however, negotiations were overtaken by events.

The story starts with the actions of an Argentine scrap-metal dealer, Constantino Davidoff, who had a contract with a Scottish company to salvage an abandoned whaling station on South Georgia Island, which was part of the disputed archipelago. As was the case on an earlier trip, he failed to observe the requisite formalities when traveling to the islands. In addition, the Argentine naval transport on which he traveled observed strict radio silence. The British suspected that Davidoff's trips deliberately challenged their country's sovereignty over the islands and objected to his presence and to the involvement of the Argentine military in his transportation.

The foreign ministries of the two countries negotiated the quiet departure of the naval transport so as not to jeopardize the upcoming negotiations over the transfer of the islands' sovereignty. However, when the naval transport left, Davidoff and his party were not on board. The British press subsequently reported the presence of Davidoff and his group as an "invasion" of the islands. British Prime Minister Margaret Thatcher responded by dispatching the HMS *Endurance*, the only vessel of the British Royal Navy in the South Atlantic, to evict the Argentineans. The Argentine government countered by sending an ice patrol vessel to land marines on the island to protect Davidoff and his group. Despite the belligerence of these actions, both countries' governments still sought a diplomatic resolution.

Then, the British governor of the Falklands, Rex Hunt, asked his government to insist that Davidoff and his group present their passports. Margaret Thatcher's government followed that recommendation. The Argentine junta interpreted compliance with this demand as "tantamount to acknowledging British sovereignty" over the Malvinas and, hence, they saw the governor's demand as an act of British aggression against Argentina.[7] In response, the Argentine junta decided to invade the islands. They did so on April 2, 1982.

The Argentine leaders did not expect the British to respond militarily.[8] They were convinced that theirs was a just cause. They expected that world leaders would agree with them, since many already saw the Malvinas as Argentine territory.[9] In addition, the Falklands are very far from Britain, creating an enormous logistical problem for any military effort. It was inconceivable to the Argentine leaders that Thatcher would be willing to make the effort with so little at stake, as the islands held little strategic or economic value. The Argentine Foreign Minister, Nicanor Costa Mendez, reasoned that Britain would act as it had earlier in Suez and Rhodesia, where it had favored negotiation over the use of force.[10] The Argentine junta accepted Mendez' interpretation that these historical precedents were analogous to the situation they faced. It perceived its own motives in terms of "right, justice, and national honor" and saw its actions as serving to correct a historical injustice.[11] Reasoning that international opinion was on their side and the effort not worth the small stakes, the Argentine leadership fully expected Britain to relinquish the islands.

Prime Minister Thatcher, however, interpreted the situation very differently. To her, the relevant historical precedent was Munich, where British Prime Minister Neville Chamberlain had made a deal with Hitler and given appeasement a bad name. It compelled her to stand tough in the face of Argentina's invasion of that small, insignificant, and faraway piece of British territory.[12] Her decisions were informed by the right to self-determination of the settler population, who wished to remain under British rule.[13]

Despite the logistical problems of conducting a war at the other end of the globe, Britain easily reclaimed the Falklands, and the leaders of Argentina were soundly defeated, both on the world stage and domestically—the junta lost power and served jail terms.[14] Could the leaders of Argentina have avoided the catastrophe that befell them?

The case of the Falklands (or Malvinas) war has been described as the "quintessence of poor judgment."[15] The Argentine leaders certainly could have benefited from a stronger ability to understand how the British government might interpret the situation. They might have considered whether Costa Mendez' analogies with Suez and Rhodesia were appropriate and, especially, whether it would be reasonable to expect Thatcher to act as Eden (Suez) and Wilson (Rhodesia) had. They might have considered that their historical claim to the Malvinas had to be reconciled with the British emphasis on the right to self-determination of the islanders. The decisions made by the Argentine junta seem puzzling until we begin to take seriously their interpretations of the situation.

By developing the ability to see the world the way the leaders of different countries see it, we can better understand the logic behind their foreign policy decisions. What may have seemed puzzling or even irrational from our own perspective may be perfectly reasonable once we understand the perspective of the leader at the time she or he made the decision. That does not mean we have to think it was a good decision, nor that the decision makers should not have tried harder to see the world from different perspectives—particularly those of the other leaders with whom they were dealing. We may still conclude that they could have made a wiser decision. Our first step, however, is not to evaluate the decision as good or bad, rational or irrational, but rather to understand how and why a decision maker arrived at it.

Rationality or Reason?

In chapter 1, we defined rationality simply as purposeful action. Foreign policy decisions are rational if they are logical in light of the decision maker's goals. That definition provides us with a good start, but there is much more to be said about rationality. First, assessments of foreign policy decisions frequently neglect to make a distinction between individual decision makers and the government as a collectivity of many persons. In such assessments, foreign policy decisions are treated as if they were made by a single, homogeneous entity. Second, rationality has been used both normatively and empirically. Both these issues are discussed in this section, and we define each concept as we discuss it.

It is especially tempting to assume that the foreign policy decisions of another country are made by a homogeneous entity, but analysts have made such an assumption not only when evaluating other countries' foreign policies. As observers, we are not privy to the debates that occur among high-level decision makers. We sometimes get a glimpse of them when decision makers write their memoirs after leaving government service or when we get access to declassified documents. Knowledgeable and insightful observers interpret signals when decision makers are still in office. These observers do not have access to classified information, but their knowledge of government and decision making permits them to utilize publicly available information to derive critical insights. Their assessments can be remarkably accurate even if they are largely based on inference. Making accurate inferences is not an easy task, because most of the time, the debates among decision makers at the pinnacle of government are not carried out in public. In addition, it is not always clear what information decision makers receive from within the bureaucracy and how they weigh it. This makes it tempting to assume that the united front presented to the outside world is reflective of what happens behind closed doors.

This assumption that decision makers act as a homogeneous entity is also called the unitary actor assumption. It means treating the government *as if* it were a single individual, rather than (at minimum) a group of decision makers or (more generally) a composite of many agencies and offices, each staffed with many people at various ranks within a hierarchy. Looking from the outside in and not knowing what really goes on inside a government administration, we are greatly tempted to treat foreign policy as if it is the result of the government acting as a unified entity. Doing so makes it unnecessary to know the inner workings of an administration by imposing the assumption that the collectivity acts in unison and with purpose. It is not surprising, then, that analysts of foreign policy have often posited that they can treat a government as a purposeful and rational unitary actor.[16] Interpretations of the Falklands/Malvinas crisis, for instance, often judge that the Argentine junta initiated the crisis to divert domestic attention away from the country's economic problems and to gain public support.[17] If so, the Argentine government would have acted according to the **diversionary theory of war,** which suggests that leaders may take their country to war to focus the public's attention on foreign policy rather than on the domestic problems and at the same time generate support for their regime.[18] At first glance, the theory appears to fit the circumstances quite nicely. There *were* economic problems, and the government was losing public support. However, this explanation leaves us with a puzzle. Leaders may indeed wish to refocus the public's attention when faced with domestic problems, especially ones they cannot address successfully in the short term, but heightening international tensions or starting a war can be risky. If we consider the situation from the perspective of the system level of analysis, it makes no sense for a less powerful actor (Argentina) to confront a more powerful actor (Britain) as a diversion. At the very least, it would be shortsighted, because the chances of emerging successfully from such a crisis would be small. In addition, we have already seen that the evidence suggests that the Argentine leaders did not themselves identify a desire to create a diversion from domestic problems as a reason for engaging in this conflict with Britain.

In the study of foreign policy decision making, the unitary actor assumption is made at the system and state levels of analysis (see chapter 1). At those levels of analysis, researchers focus primarily on the outcomes of the foreign policy behaviors of states, and also seek to describe and evaluate the foreign policy behaviors of states. At the individual level of analysis, the unitary actor assumption is questioned: do governments or states really act *as if* they are single, purposeful actors?

The explanation of Argentina's invasion of the Malvinas/Falklands that relies on the unitary actor assumption—and that holds that the invasion was a rational response to domestic problems faced by a regime—leaves us with the puzzle that this diversion also created the not-so-rational decision to take on a much more powerful international actor. Here, the assumption of a rational unitary actor gets tangled with itself: what may be rational given the domestic circumstances is not rational given the dynamics of the international system. Is there, perhaps, a better explanation than the rational actor assumption can provide? This would require an investigation into the motives of the Argentine junta.

As previously discussed, the evidence suggests that the junta had a strong desire to correct a perceived historical injustice. This explanation requires research into the Argentine perspective but preserves the idea that the government acted as a unified entity. Did it? Several participants in the decision making process during the crisis later said that President Galtieri suddenly changed course after the invasion.[19] The initial plan was to place the islands under a temporary international administration after the governor had been removed and a small British garrison had been disarmed.[20] This would demonstrate Argentinean resolve but also provide an incentive to resolve the dispute through diplomacy. After the invasion Galtieri suddenly announced to a cheering crowd that was celebrating the invasion that Argentina would never leave the Malvinas.[21] His announcement surprised the other members of the junta. It is certainly possible that Galtieri got caught up in the excitement of the moment. Had he stuck by the original plan and placed the islands under an international administration, war might still have been averted. That might have been wiser foreign policy, but it would also have poured cold water on the triumphant atmosphere and disappointed his domestic audience. This story illustrates the possible tensions between domestic and international imperatives (something to which we will return in chapter 5), but it also shows that governments are made up of individuals who do not always act in concert—something that calls the unitary actor assumption into question even more fundamentally.

Although the unitary actor assumption can lead to plausible explanations, it does not always fit the facts well. Sometimes the plausible explanation is good enough, but at other times we are left with important puzzles, as in the case of Argentinean decision making during the Malvinas crisis. What is easily dismissed as bad judgment with the benefit of hindsight may appear more reasonable once we figure out how the relevant decision makers viewed their world, what motivated them, what options they perceived, and how they evaluated those options.

The study of foreign policy decision making seeks to understand decisions that are puzzling to those making the unitary actor assumption. It takes as the starting point that foreign policy is made by individuals, acting alone or in concert with others and taking advantage of opportunities or acting within constraints. Should we expect these individual decision makers to act rationally? What do we mean when we voice that expectation? That brings us to a discussion of theories of rationality.

A **normative theory of rationality** provides a model for rational behavior and judges actual behavior in light of that model.[22] The model specifies the process by which decisions should be made: confronted with a situation that requires a decision, leaders define that situation, establish their goals, investigate their options, weigh the advantages and disadvantages of their options, and decide on the option that achieves the goal best and at the lowest cost, as summarized in the left-hand column of table 3.1. In addition to specifying the process, normative theories often imply that everyone judging the same situation will have the same information or understand the situation in the same way. Any time we argue that decision makers should have known better, we imply that there is a standard, or norm, for rational decision making against which we can judge an actual decision—and we simultaneously render the verdict that the decision makers have failed to live up to that standard.

Table 3.1 Comparing normative and empirical rationality

	Normative Rationality	Empirical Rationality
Start with:	A situation that requires a decision	A situation that requires a decision
Process:	1. What are the relevant foreign policy goals?	1. Who were the relevant decisionmakers?
	2. What are my options?	2. What did they know and when?
	3. What are the advantages (expected benefits) and disadvantages (expected costs) of each option?	3. How did they interpret the information?
	4. Make a decision. Choose the option that performs best in the cost/benefit analysis.	4. What options did they perceive as realistic?
		5. How did they evaluate those options?
Finish with:	A decision	A decision
Theory or model:	Prescribed decision process serves as standard for judgment.	The decision making process is itself the subject of investigation.
Assumption:	Closely following the prescribed process leads to the best possible decision.	The quality of the process is related to the quality of the decision. (We want to be able to repeat good decision making and learn to avoid bad decision making.)

Empirical theories of rationality, on the other hand, are less interested in judging a decision than in understanding how leaders arrived at it. That does not mean that researchers employing empirical theories of rationality do not care about good decision making. On the contrary, they care a great deal about finding ways to lessen the likelihood that decision makers accidentally stumble into war or otherwise make a decision that has strongly negative consequences for their country. Researchers who favor empirical theories of rationality think that, rather than evaluating a decision against a standard of good decision making (as the normative theory of rationality does), it is important to understand how and why policy makers arrived at their decision as a first step to suggesting ways in which decision making can be improved. Empirical analysts try to determine what decision makers knew, when they knew it, and what they did with the information. The right-hand column of table 3.1 outlines a typical set of questions. Researchers who employ empirical theories of rationality do not always study the entire decision making process; rather, they frequently focus on one or a few of the questions listed. Instead of judging decision makers on the basis of options they *should* have considered, such analysts ask what options were *actually* considered, how those options were evaluated, and how decision makers arrived at their decision.

At the core of empirical theories of rationality is the assumption that better decision making leads to better decisions and, ultimately, better outcomes. Of course, even the best and most thorough decision making process does not guarantee a good outcome. It does, however, make the desired outcome vastly more likely.

The model of rational decision making provided by the normative theorists is not irrelevant for empirical theorists. You probably noticed that empirical theorists are also interested in option selection and evaluation. In fact, most empirical theorists would agree that normative theories of rationality provide a useful framework, but criticize such theories for ignoring the difficulties of acquiring information, the impact of personality and prior experience, as well as the interactions among decision makers (which is addressed more fully in chapter 4). Empirical theories of rationality address questions such as these: How does a decision maker's personality predispose her or him to understand information in a specific manner? If information is incomplete, as it often is in foreign policy decision making, how do decision makers gain the confidence that they do indeed have a good understanding of the situation? Do decision makers weigh options, as the normative model of rationality suggests? If so, how do they decide what options to consider or discard, and how to evaluate the options they have in front of them?

Weighing Options and Defining Interests

The evidence suggests that decision makers do not always employ the kind of decision making process that requires them to weigh options. In some cases, they take the first solution that seems reasonable. That's a quick way to deal with a problem, and it frees up time to devote to other issues. This way of responding to a problem is called **satisficing**. Decision makers satisfice when, rather than seeking an optimal solution, they merely look for one that is "good enough." Instead of going through an exhaustive search for options and evaluating these by weighing the pros and cons of each, decision makers search for and evaluate options sequentially, discarding those that do not meet their criteria until they find one that seems adequate. They do not subject these options to a comparative assessment but judge each option in light of what their experience tells them will be a satisfactory solution to the problem. Such an experience-based rule of thumb is called a **heuristic**. Decisions made in this way are not optimal, but they work—they are deemed good enough and allow decision makers to move on to the next problem.[23]

From the point of view of normative rationality, satisficing is a terrible way to make a decision. But is it? Consider that making a decision according to the procedure specified by normative rationality takes time, energy, and resources. None of these are limitless. Consider also that there are a lot of issues that require a decision and that not all of them are equally important. It makes sense for decision makers to devote their time and energy first and foremost to the highly important issues—the ones that are likely to affect the future of the country in significant ways—and to satisfice regarding other issues.[24]

That presumes that decision makers readily understand the relative importance of various issues before them. This will sometimes be obvious, for instance, when the country is experiencing a foreign policy crisis or an attack. Consider the consensus regarding the importance of the terrorist attacks of September 11, 2001, or the attack on Pearl Harbor at the start of the official American involvement in World War II. At other times, whether or not an issue is regarded as highly important (and deserving of top-level attention) is itself a political decision—one that is contingent upon the worldview and perhaps also the policy agenda of the decision makers.[25]

There was a well-publicized disagreement between the American President George W. Bush and the French President Jacques Chirac (and other member countries of the United Nations Security Council) regarding the need to go to war with Iraq in 2003. The two presidents agreed on their assessment of the nature of Saddam Hussein's rule and on the importance of containing his ambitions, but they diverged on how best to confront his government.[26] Disagreement between American and European leaders is not a new phenomenon. During the Cold War, European leaders increasingly disagreed with the United States about the nature and severity of the threat posed by the Soviet Union. This disagreement influenced discussions on "burden sharing" (or: how much each state would contribute to the joint defense effort) within the North Atlantic Treaty Organization (NATO), although they were not guided by such differences in perception exclusively.

In addition to the question of whether in issue is regarded as important, decision makers also tend to focus more readily on issues that require immediate attention. Consider the global AIDS crisis, which is devastating societies and could politically destabilize entire countries, but which has only recently begun to be treated with the urgency accorded to foreign policy crises. Leaders have long expressed their concern and agree that the problem is an important one, but they have not made the AIDS crisis central to their foreign policy. Why not? How is the global AIDS crisis different from, e.g., the Cuban Missile Crisis? The latter was a short period of thirteen days in October 1962, when the American president of the time, John F. Kennedy, confronted the highly threatening prospect that the Soviet Union might soon be able to launch (nuclear) missiles at the United States. Prior to that time, the Soviet Union, although it had acquired nuclear weapons, had not yet acquired the ability to launch them in such a way that they could reach U.S. soil. U.S. reconnaissance flights discovered the missile sites that were being built in Cuba. If these had been completed and become operational, Soviet missiles immediately would have gained the capability to strike the United States—making the latter a lot less secure at the height of the Cold War. This situation fits the classic definition of a crisis: high threat, short decision time, and surprise.[27]

In contrast, AIDS is a "creeping crisis": it has not emerged into our consciousness suddenly, the full scope of the problem has been difficult to estimate, and there do not appear to be any immediate consequences to doing nothing. In short, the AIDS crisis does not fit the conventional definition of a crisis very well. This makes it easier to ignore the global, long term impact of the AIDS crisis, and to see it as a problem that affects "others" and is centered "elsewhere." With so many unknowns, the AIDS crisis is best defined as an **ill-structured problem**. Such problems are characterized by a lack of contours: the problem is not well defined and, as a result, it is also not clear how it is best confronted, what constraints stand in the way of solving the problem, and what means are best employed to do so.[28] Especially when other problems that are better defined or more urgent also vie for attention, the easiest solution is to take a wait-and-see approach.

Urgency helps focus the attention. Foreign policy problems are not regarded as important only because they are urgent, however. Importance derives also from the degree to which decision makers perceive a problem to affect vital **national interests**. Traditionally, the concept of the national interest denoted security issues, usually defined in terms of the ability to maintain the integrity of the state's borders through military defense. According to classical **Realist theory**, decision makers "think and act in terms of interest defined as power."[29] Realist theory has been very influential in the study of world politics. It is characterized by a concern with maintaining and possibly enhancing a state's power and, thereby, the integrity and autonomy of the state. Realists assume that (military) security issues are paramount and that economic issues matter to the degree that they affect the state's power. Social and cultural issues are largely deemed not relevant. Therefore, Realists do not readily perceive global health problems like AIDS as a threat to national security.

The concepts of power and national interest are deceptively simple: we intuitively understand them. Yet both concepts are vague and open to interpretation. Part of the problem with power is that it can take many different forms and can be exercised in many different ways. A large, well-trained, and state-of-the-art military can make a state powerful, but so can control over a strategic resource, as was demonstrated by the Organization of Petroleum Exporting Countries (OPEC) under the leadership of Saudi Arabian oil minister Sheikh Zaki Yamani in the early 1970s. At that time, the OPEC countries were unified in an embargo. They not only wanted to be paid better for the sale of this finite resource, they also wanted concessions regarding the policies of the oil importing states toward the long-standing conflict between Israel and its Arab neighbors. Although embargoes are not universally successful, this one resulted temporarily in a severely limited availability of gasoline and, after the end of the embargo, higher oil prices. At least some countries modified their Middle East policies as well.

Power cannot be exercised only through military or economic means. It can also take other, more subtle forms, as captured by the concept of **soft power**. Soft power is defined as "the ability to shape the preferences of others" through persuasion and the attraction of one's ideas.[30] Power is a concept that most of us understand intuitively, but it has been quite difficult to capture adequately for purposes of empirical investigation, a topic to which we will return in chapter 6.

The national interest—what it is and what foreign policy actions best serve it—turns out to be equally difficult to pin down. As a result, there is no one-size-fits-all guide regarding what makes a specific foreign policy problem important, as is illustrated by a comparison of the United States and Japan. American decision makers generally understand national security to be a military concept, but Japanese leaders perceive national security in economic terms.[31] The United States is resource rich and militarily powerful, while Japan is resource poor, and the size of its military is limited by its post–World War II constitution. Unlike the United States, which can supply about half of its own energy, Japan's economy is not only highly dependent on imported materials for its industry but also critically dependent on imports for its energy needs.[32] As a result, energy security has long been quite prominent in the Japanese conceptions of national security and has shaped decision makers' conceptions of the country's national interest.[33]

American and Japanese decision makers face different sets of constraints that are shaped by their states' respective international positions and strategic resources. These constraints both shape decision makers' world views and their ability to pursue specific foreign policy strategies. They also affect which problems they perceive as important.

Poliheuristic Theory

Once a problem is perceived as sufficiently urgent and important to warrant the expediture of substantial time and resources, decision makers are more likely to try to evaluate multiple options and discuss the merits of each. But can we assume that decision makers will follow the template specified by normative theories of rationality? Empirical investigations indicate that the answer is, most often, not quite. However, the decision making process is not random and does tend to follow certain identifiable patterns.

One effort to investigate to what degree decision makers make an effort to implement the ideas specified by the normative theory of rationality is the poliheuristic theory. The poliheuristic theory incorporates elements from normative and empirical theories of rationality. It suggests that foreign policy decision making takes place in two stages and that each stage is characterized by a different approach. During stage one, decision makers use a **noncompensatory principle** to determine their options. They evaluate a range of policy responses and discard any that are unacceptable on one (or more) critical dimensions. This means that a policy response that is quite attractive in some respects will be eliminated if it has at least one disadvantage that negatively affects either the (perceived) national interest or the decision makers' political interests.[34] In other words, one or more advantages of an option cannot compensate for that option's critical disadvantage. The disadvantage is in essence given veto power over the policy option, and it is eliminated from further consideration.

After a set of options is generated using the noncompensatory principle, the poliheuristic theory posits that decision makers will subject the remaining options to careful analysis during the second stage of the decision making process. This second stage frequently involves a careful weighing of the costs and benefits of the remaining alternatives in a manner similar to that specified by normative rationality, albeit with the difference that not *all* possible alternatives are being evaluated but only those that have already passed a minimum threshold of acceptability.

The poliheuristic theory thus delimits rational behavior: it holds that decision makers are rational, in the sense of seeking the optimal policy, but that their rational cost-benefit analysis is conducted over a set of alternatives that have already been deemed acceptable. The poliheuristic theory thus seeks to integrate aspects of psychological models with those of normative rationality. In doing so, the stage two decision making process of the poliheuristic theory represents something akin to **bounded rationality**. The latter concept is used to separate normative and empirical rationality: it defines decision makers as rational within the scope of their knowledge. This means that in order to determine whether a decision maker arrived at a rational decision, we need to know what that decision maker knew at the time they made the decision.[35] The poliheuristic theory agrees with bounded rationality in the sense that the options that were deemed acceptable on the basis of the non-compensatory decision rule used in stage one are subjected to the sort of cost-benefit analysis normative rationality would specify during stage two. However, bounded rationality delimits options on the basis of a decision maker's knowledge, whereas the poliheuristic theory adds the requirement that policy options must meet a minimum requirement of political acceptability in order to be considered during stage two of the decision making process.[36]

By adding the acceptability requirement, the poliheuristic theory adds a distinctly political dimension to the question of which policy alternatives are to be considered and assumes that "politicians will rarely choose an alternative that will hurt them politically."[37] Bounded rationality, on the other hand, makes the broader assumption that the inclusion of policy options is determined solely by the information the decision maker has at his or her disposal. It assumes decision makers will seriously consider the advantages and disadvantages of all options they know to exist, not just the ones that have met some minimum standard of political acceptability.

Both bounded rationality and the poliheuristic theory point to the importance of investigating what decision makers know and how they interpret information. Both fit under the larger umbrella of empirical approaches to rationality. However, both emphasize the option evaluation process rather than the selection of options—an issue to which we will turn in the next section.

Framing and Problem Representation

How do decision makers determine what their options are? According to the poliheuristic theory previously discussed, decision making can be divided into two discrete stages. During the first stage, decision makers determine their realistic options using a noncompensatory decision rule. Bounded rationality implies that the enumeration of options is limited by what decision makers know. The poliheuristic theory adds that options must also pass a political acceptability threshold, which means that there must not be some critical disadvantage that makes an option unacceptable to the decision makers. Neither explicitly addresses the mechanism that ties the decision makers' knowledge base or the noncompensatory evaluation to the enumeration of the options that will be seriously considered in the decision making process.

This is not unique to bounded rationality or to the first stage of the poliheuristic theory. The emphasis in the study of foreign policy decision making has most often been on how leaders choose between options, rather than on how those options emerge.[38] That leaves us with another puzzle: why do leaders fail to recognize certain options? To return to the case study of the Malvinas/Falklands: was invading the island the only option the Argentine leadership had after the British governor insisted that Davidoff and his group present their passports? Did they consider the potential consequences of this action? At this point in the crisis, the situation had become quite tense. However, the invasion escalated the situation even further, a fact that the junta failed to recognize, largely because they simply could not imagine that British Prime Minister Thatcher would make the decision to go to war to recover control over the islands. Having accepted Foreign Minister Costa Mendez's argument that the situation was analogous to the crises Britain had faced in Suez and Rhodesia, they convinced themselves that their opponent would respond as it had done in those historical events. In other words, the Argentine junta framed the situation in a specific manner that had consequences for their actions.

It is quite reasonable to suggest, as bounded rationality does, that leaders conceive of options within the context of their knowledge. But that knowledge is not neutral: leaders have a specific window on the world, which is shaped by their personality (as discussed in chapter 2), background, education, knowledge, and experiences, as well as formative historical events. The resulting predispositions affect the tasks of making sense of (the events in) the world, determining what policy options are available, and choosing a specific foreign policy decision. To put it another way, decision makers approach the world from a specific vantage point.

Their perceptions are likely to be affected by the way in which information is presented. This is the subject of **prospect theory**, which takes into account that the preferences of decision makers change in predictable ways depending on how a problem is presented or framed. For instance, in problems that can be phrased in terms of gains and losses, most people prefer a small chance of a gain to the certainty of a loss. If the problem is presented differently, however, most people prefer a rather small (but certain) gain over a small chance to win big. So, while most people are willing to take a risk at the prospect of a loss, they also prefer a certain but small gain, rather than taking a chance to win big.[39] In short, whether or not people are willing to take a chance depends on how they perceive their prospects (or odds).

At the core of prospect theory is the **decision frame**, defined as "the decision maker's conceptions of the acts, outcomes, and contingencies associated with a particular choice."[40] The concept of the decision frame thus focuses on the calculations of the likelihood that particular actions will yield the desired outcome. Prior events (or the sequence of events in which the problem is situated), as well as the decision maker's vantage point, affect the decision frame.[41] However, decision makers are "not normally aware of the potential effects of different decision frames on their preferences."[42] In fact, they often convince themselves that their *framing* of the situation represents it *objectively*, i.e., that their framing is the best—or the only—way to understand it. The Argentine junta did this and was not able to conceive of the possibility that the British leaders would frame the situation in a very different way.

The concept of the decision frame does not differentiate between perceptions of the situation on the one hand and the perceived policy choices on the other. The two are certainly linked. Prospect theory places the emphasis on how *choice* is affected by decision frames, whereas **problem representation** privileges investigation into how and why decision makers *represent* situations in specific ways. Problem representations are mental models or schemas that are produced within the context of a decision maker's more general understanding of how the world works. The concept of problem representation is akin to that of worldview. The difference is that worldview is general and denotes a person's understanding of the world globally, whereas problem representation is specific to a problem or situation.[43] A problem representation is "the product of an individual's knowledge level, experiences, and beliefs," each of which influence how (and what) new information is acquired and how it is given meaning in causal interpretations.[44] A decision maker's representation of a problem shapes her or his reasoning about it. In other words, whether options pass the initial, noncompensatory, stage of the poliheuristic theory's screening depends in large part on how the problem has been represented.

Problem representations determine what options are specified and especially what options are seen as plausible ones. Problem representations thus help us understand why certain options are perceived as feasible and others are rejected out of hand. In short, problem representation can be seen as a process that is completed before the poliheuristic theory's stage one (noncompensatory) decision making takes place.

A decision maker's representation of a problem shapes what options are perceived as viable. As we have defined the concept, problem representations are far from random. Instead, they are shaped by a decision maker's knowledge, experience, and beliefs. Knowledge about these elements can help us understand why decision makers represent problems as they do. Consider the differences between Japanese conceptions of national security and those of American policy makers, or the different historical experiences of war and terrorist attacks of the United States and Britain, both of which were sketched earlier in this chapter. Given these differences, would you expect the decision makers of these three countries to represent the problem of global terrorism in the same way? Would you expect them to advocate the same strategies for confronting this problem? Consider that the formative experiences of the leaders of these three countries took place in very different contexts. They were taught different national histories and different perspectives on world history. Yet each of these three countries is considered a powerful actor in world politics.

How different might be the perspectives of leaders from less powerful countries? Consider the analogies that the Argentineans found useful in constructing their representation of the Malvinas crisis: both Suez and Rhodesia concerned British relations with a (former) colony. In contrast, the British prime minister does not appear to have taken the power differential between the two countries into account in her problem representation. She perceived the Falklands crisis as similar to Hitler's challenge to its European neighbors and represented the situation as analogous to Munich. The Argentinean debacle in the Malvinas stems largely from its leaders' inability to imagine the possibility that the British prime minister might define the situation differently than they did.[45] The British representation not only differed from the Argentinean, it also appears to be a gross overestimation of the Argentine leadership's ambitions to portray the situation as analogous to that faced by Chamberlain at Munich. However, that overestimation was far less damaging to Britain than the failure of the Argentine leaders to realize that the British prime minister had framed the situation very differently.

Historical analogies play an important role in problem representation and framing. In the next section, we'll address the use of historical analogies in greater detail. Before we move on to that topic, however, it is important to point out that exposure to a specific national history and other aspects of a culture are not the only factors that influence a decision maker's propensity to represent problems in a particular way. There are also interpersonal differences. Individuals bring different experiences and knowledge to their roles as decision makers.[46] They do not always agree on the best way to frame or represent a problem. When decision makers work together in groups, they need to reconcile such different problem representations to fashion one on which they can collectively agree. The dynamics in groups of decision makers are explored more fully in chapter 4.

Decision makers do not interpret the actions of the leaders of other countries in a vacuum. Previous interactions, ongoing disputes, and historical animosities influence how events are interpreted. Neither the French nor the German government supported the decision of the United States to go to war in Iraq in 2003, but the brunt of American disgruntlement was with France. Of course, unlike Germany, France is a member of the United Nations Security Council, the body where the disagreement over Iraq became very visible. But the Security Council is not the only body where French leaders had openly disagreed with the United States. One memorable instance occurred in 1966, when President Charles de Gaulle, who was very much concerned with France's prestige in the world, challenged the leadership positions of the United States and Britain within NATO in an effort to have France recognized as an equal partner. The effort ended with France's withdrawal from the integrated NATO command. Germany, on the other hand, has long been quite restrained in its foreign policy. The leaders of both states have disagreed with their American ally, but when French leaders disagree it is more readily perceived as a challenge to U.S. power because of France's aspirations. Similarly, in the Falklands/Malvinas crisis, the leaders of both countries interpreted the actions of the other with the suspicion that results from longstanding disagreements. Each perceived the other to have sinister motives.[47]

Making Sense of the Present by Comparing It to the Past

Much of the time, foreign policy decision making situations represent ill-structured problems. Information is available on some aspects of the problem, but there are also numerous unknowns. Making a decision is rendered

more difficult when there is not enough information to construct a complete picture of a situation. Quite frequently, foreign policy problems are a
bit like Swiss cheese. This is especially true during crises but is not limited
to such situations. Incomplete information and its counterpart, secrecy, are
inherent in foreign policy making. At the same time that decision makers
struggle to make sense of a situation on the basis of limited and incomplete
information, they refuse to reveal the complete extent of their knowledge
or the full details of their own strategy to their opponents. Whether this is
done to maintain the edge of a surprise in war or to have leverage in negotiations, it means that incomplete information is inherent in foreign policy
decision making. Although it is not often acknowledged, decision makers
representing all states involved in a problem confront this "Swiss cheese
problem."

One way to achieve an understanding of an ill-structured problem is to
compare it to a historical situation that is deemed similar and about which
more is known. The comparison helps to fill in the blanks in the current
situation. It helps decision makers construct a representation of the current problem and point to potential solutions. This process of comparison
is called **analogical reasoning**.[48] It starts with an attempt to construct a
representation of the problem from the available but incomplete information.[49] Decision makers then search their memories for a potentially useful,
related problem. This analogy is a problem that has been solved in the past
and that decision makers are confident they understand well.[50] The current
problem and the potential analogies are compared to determine what
aspects of the two situations are alike and which are different. Central to
such comparisons is the effort to determine whether a particular analogy
shares meaningful commonalities with the problem at hand.[51] If it does,
the next step is to consider whether the solution used in the analogical situation might be an appropriate response to the current situation as well.[52]

In some cases, the analogy points to what *not* to do. The Munich analogy is a good example: once Margaret Thatcher had framed the situation in
terms of this analogy, it was her cue to stand strong against the Argentinean
incursion into the Falklands.

The Munich analogy is often cited by decision makers to suggest that it
is not a good idea to give in to aggressive actions by the leaders of other
countries. It has acquired the connotation that if you give in even a little to
an aggressive leader (as Chamberlain did with Hitler), that leader will be
emboldened and present a bigger foreign policy problem in the future.[53]
Hence, it is reasonable to stand strong and confront a relatively smaller
problem now, rather than a bigger problem later. On the other hand, the
"lesson" taught by this analogy assumes that aggressive leaders react in predictable ways to certain incentives: *Give in* and you embolden a leader.

Confront and you force that same leader to back down. Would Hitler have backed down if Chamberlain (and other European leaders) had stood up to him from the beginning? Is it reasonable to suggest other aggressive leaders would back down (short of a defeat in war)? What other policy options might be available (and potentially more effective)? There are many questions to ponder as we consider the appropriateness of the Munich analogy and the lesson it represents for most contemporary leaders.

Let's return to Margaret Thatcher and her use of the Munich analogy during the Falklands/Malvinas crisis. The Argentine junta invaded and occupied a group of islands that were part of their country prior to the British occupation of them in 1833. Since that time, the islands had acquired a British settler population. The future of this settler population was one of the topics discussed in the ongoing British negotiations with Argentina over the disputed sovereignty of the islands. The series of events described earlier in this chapter cut short these negotiations. Although there were a number of junctures at which a different decision could have steered events away from war, Galtieri's surprise announcement after the invasion, stating that Argentina would never leave the Malvinas, made a military response from Britain almost inevitable.

Does the Munich analogy fit? Hitler justified his annexation of Austria and the Sudetenland area of Czechoslovakia on the basis of the ethnic and linguistic commonality of the people who lived in these areas. There was no issue of disputed sovereignty. Instead, there was the **irredentist** claim that people sharing a similar German ethnic and linguistic background ought to live together in one national state. In the period between the two World Wars, the quest for **national self-determination** (meaning the desire of a group of people sharing a common national and/or ethnic identity to govern itself in its own state) was still seen as a legitimate pursuit. Although Hitler's irredentist claims and his quest to enlarge German territory generated disquiet, they were not immediately perceived in the same negative light that such claims encounter in our times. It was not until Hitler's conquests reached beyond areas populated by people who identified as ethnically German that the leaders of Europe became truly alarmed. Chamberlain's agreement with Hitler at Munich violated the sovereignty of Czechoslovakia (Austria had been annexed earlier) in favor of honoring an irredentist claim, on the assumption that this diplomatic agreement would be honored. If it had been, war would have been avoided. As it turned out, it was not, and Hitler proceeded with further conquests.

How much similarity is there between the two situations? Other than the fact that in both cases one country invaded another, the differences between the two situations far outnumber the similarities. For example, expansionist desires were much less a motive for the Argentine junta than for Hitler. Rather, the Argentine leaders sought to end what they perceived as the occupation of *territory* they claimed as belonging with their country. The analogy they perceived with Suez and Rhodesia is interesting in this regard: both those situations involved Britain as a colonial power. This suggests that the Argentine junta perceived the situation *not* in terms of aggressive expansionism, but in terms of ending colonial domination over islands they perceived as Argentine territory. Furthermore, the Falklands/Malvinas were of little strategic value. Their importance was primarily symbolic. The Sudetenland, on the other hand, was a valuable strategic prize for Germany.

As stated, the lesson the Munich analogy communicates is that aggressive leaders must be confronted. Beyond that simple—and possibly simplistic—lesson, the comparison with the Falklands/Malvinas crisis demonstrates that decision makers tend to use analogies in a rather superficial manner: they overstate the similarities and downplay important differences between the historical and current case.[54] The problem is usually not that decision makers have a poor grasp of history, but rather that the comparisons they make are poorly executed. They fail to carefully compare the current and historical situations.[55] This means that decision makers make a global judgment that a current situation is similar to a particular historical case, rather than comparing the two point by point for differences as well as similarities.

More careful analysis of such differences and similarities between current and historical foreign policy problems has the potential to be quite useful. There have indeed been efforts to teach decision makers to engage in more careful comparisons.[56] Unfortunately, it will remain difficult for most decision makers to engage in such careful comparative analysis of a current and past situation, because the poor use of analogy is inherent in the psychology of analogical reasoning.[57] Decision makers (as well as people in general) tend to place undue emphasis on surface similarities and ignore deeper, structural differences. They remember lessons learned but not the details; i.e., they remember what Munich stands for but not the details of Chamberlain's negotiations with Hitler, nor the context within which these took place.

In fact, decision makers appear to choose an analogy less for the analogous situation than for the general lesson for which the case stands. In other words, decision makers use historical analogies as if they were **schemas**.[58] A schema is a psychological concept defined as a mental representation of a person's general knowledge about a concept or situation.[59] Using analogies as if they were schemas eliminates the need for careful, point-by-point comparison between the current situation and its historical analog. It also precludes deeper and more careful analysis of the current situation. Once they have classified a situation as "an instance of [insert schema]," decision makers have framed the situation, and their interpretations of the actions of opponents and the viability of particular solutions are viewed through lenses colored by that frame.

The choice of analogy depends on who is making foreign policy. A decision maker's formative experiences have long been thought to weigh disproportionately.[60] Hence, it is not surprising that the post–World War II generation of (Western) leaders so frequently referenced Munich—the event that came to symbolize the failure to arrest Hitler's quest to control Europe before he had conquered a large slice of that continent. Margaret Thatcher, for example, turned thirteen in the year of the Munich agreements and was nineteen by war's end. World War II happened during her high school years—it was her lived experience, not something gleaned from a history book, although both historical treatments and popular media have kept the war and its lessons alive and well for many years (a fact that is not irrelevant to the continued frequent use of the Munich analogy). In addition to formative experiences, more recent events are often remembered more easily—largely because of their recentness they are still more vivid in the decision makers' memory.[61] Finally, the personality of the decision maker matters as well; that is, whether a decision maker has high or low conceptual complexity has an impact on their search for—and use of—analogies. Conceptually complex individuals are more likely to use analogies in a more sophisticated manner than decision makers who are less conceptually complex. The latter focus more frequently on the surface similarities and the "lesson" of a specific historical analogy, whereas the former are more likely to perceive structural similarities between situations that may on the surface not appear analogous.[62] For instance, during the Cuban Missile Crisis President Kennedy used the analogy of the outbreak of World War I to express his concern that miscalculation might easily lead the United States to war with the Soviet Union. Although the two situations did not on the surface appear to have much in common, Kennedy perceived the possibility that a mistake in judgment might have dire consequences.[63]

In sum, the choice of a specific analogy as an appropriate metaphor for a current situation is not necessarily determined by the appropriateness of the comparison. First, analogies are frequently selected because they are historical events decision makers happen to remember, either because they were formative experiences or recent events. In the case of the Cuban Missile Crisis, President Kennedy had recently read a book about the outbreak of World War I, which he used as an analogy and which made him highly aware of the high cost of miscalculation.[64] Second, the higher the conceptual complexity of the decision maker, the greater the likelihood that she or he will move beyond surface similarities (or the basic "lesson" derived from a historical event) and perceive deeper, structural similarities between the current and historical event. What difference does it make whether decision makers use analogies well or poorly? In the example of the Falklands/Malvinas crisis, it mattered more for Argentina than for Britain. The conceptualization of the situation as analogous to Suez or Rhodesia led the Argentine junta to drastically underestimate the possibility of a British military response. The Munich analogy led Prime Minister Thatcher to forego diplomacy. Regaining control of the Falklands might have been obtained through other means. Consider that the two countries had a long history of (partially successful) negotiations about the disputed islands. Thatcher might have achieved her goal with a less belligerent strategy. However, foreign policy decision makers are rarely criticized for a policy that achieves the objective.

Thus far, we have taken the use of analogies seriously. We have accepted that decision makers do indeed use their knowledge of history to think about current problems. It is, of course, possible that analogies are used instead to communicate with an audience, whether that is a private conversation within a group of decision makers or a public speech. It is difficult to know to what degree analogies are indeed used as "thinking tools" versus verbal justification. However, the psychological literature suggests that people do indeed think in terms of analogies. In fact, more generalized schemas are the product of analogical reasoning. Moreover, communication with others is an essential component of decision making, because foreign policy decisions are rarely made by one individual in isolation. Most often, groups of decision makers ponder a problem, even if ultimately one person is responsible for the decision.

Fiascoes, "Good" Decisions, and Learning

The Falklands/Malvinas crisis turned into a fiasco for the Argentine decision makers largely because they underestimated the likelihood of a military British reaction to, first, the Argentine move to occupy the islands and, second, Galtieri's announcement that Argentina would never leave the Malvinas. Once the Argentineans had framed the situation in terms of Suez and Rhodesia, it became more difficult for them to perceive the possibility of military action by their opponent. Had they examined their analogies more closely, and perhaps taken into account that Britain under Thatcher might act differently than it had in those historical situations, the crisis might have had another ending. That, of course, presumes that good decision making *can* make a difference. Not everyone accepts that this is possible. **Skeptics of good judgment** in foreign policy decision making argue that the world is very complex and that, as a result, decisions often have many unintended consequences.[65] If things turn out well, these skeptics argue, this is due much more to luck than wisdom, because outcomes simply are not very predictable: world politics is much too complex and it is extremely difficult to accurately forecast the outcomes of decisions that are meant to have an impact on complex systems.

Not everyone agrees. Students of foreign policy decision making proceed from the notion that it *is* possible to acquire knowledge that can improve decision making processes and, thereby, the odds that decisions lead to desired outcomes. That does not mean that a well-executed decision making process will *always* lead to the desired outcome.[66] Even under the best of circumstances, it is possible that an opponent acts in ways that could not have been foreseen. After all, foreign policy decision makers are human beings rather than robots. They are creative beings who innovate and sometimes defy the patterns in their own previous behavior.

On the other hand, decisions that are made on the basis of faulty information and flawed processes do not consistently lead to disaster. Sometimes decision makers simply get lucky. However, a foreign policy fiasco is certainly more likely under the latter conditions. Conversely, the odds of achieving the desired outcome are much better when the decision has been made on the basis of solid information and a well-considered process.

How, then, can we assure the best possible decision process? Good judgment involves the ability to discern patterns in world politics and foreign policy behavior, but there are distinct differences of opinion about the sort of patterns that would be most helpful to decision makers. One perspective is offered by the **simplifiers**, who argue that good judgment is rooted in the ability to discern the simple patterns that define even the most complex of events.[67] Simplifiers would probably not see a problem with Prime Minister Thatcher's use of the Munich analogy during the Falklands/Malvinas crisis as sketched in the previous section of this chapter. Indeed, they would argue that Thatcher accurately characterized the situation as one that called for Britain to take a strong stand.

More generally, simplifiers think it best for leaders to stay focused on the geopolitical forces that influence the relative power of states in the global arena. Book titles like former National Security Advisor and political scientist Zbigniew Brzezinski's *The Grand Chessboard* or historian Paul Kennedy's *Rise and Fall of the Great Powers* reflect this type of thinking.[68] As these titles suggest, simplifiers tend to focus on the system level of analysis and regard much (but not all!) of what happens at the individual and state level as distraction from the essential outlines of global politics. That said, simplifiers may disagree over what exactly are the fundamental outlines of world politics, but they share the conviction that much of what is reported on a daily basis is simply "noise" that distracts from the "big picture."[69]

The other perspective is that of the **complexifiers**, who see good judgment as connected to the ability to think critically.[70] Although decision makers (and people in general) are often "too quick to rush to judgment and too slow to revise their beliefs in response to new evidence," those who are "explicitly encouraged to think of reasons why they might be wrong" are more likely to reevaluate their initial judgments and arrive at more realistic assessments.[71] By focusing on the reasons why their initial judgment might be erroneous or incomplete, decision makers can counteract three common human tendencies: one, overconfidence in one's judgment; two, resistance to revising one's opinion even when the evidence makes it abundantly clear that the opinion is not tenable; and three, emphasizing the commonalities—and downplaying the differences—between a historical precedent and the current situation. We define these tendencies collectively as **cognitive biases.** Just as decision makers generally assume that their framing of a situation represents that situation objectively, they are usually not aware of their own cognitive biases—unless they are trained to identify and purposively counteract them by looking for evidence and for reasons they might be incorrect. There have indeed been efforts to provide such training.[72] In addition, there is some evidence that cognitively complex decision makers are more likely to overcome their own cognitive biases. In doing so, they are likely to achieve not only an understanding of multiple viewpoints, but also to attempt to integrate them—which may lead them to discover innovative policy responses.[73]

Hence, the complexifiers provide some guidance that can serve to improve decision processes and thereby the odds of desirable outcomes. The simplifiers are less able to guide decision makers with regard to the decision process, but they do provide insights into global system dynamics that decision makers defy at their peril. Both the simplifiers and complexifiers offer something that is useful to leaders, although what they offer is quite different.

Above, we made the point that even the most well-executed decision process cannot guarantee a good outcome, but we did not specify exactly how we define "good" in this context. Good decision making is frequently judged in the context of the decision's ultimate result, the foreign policy outcome. This is problematic, because the outcome may look better or worse, depending on the time horizon: President George H. W. Bush's decision to end the war against Iraq in the early 1990s was initially hailed as a good decision. The military objective, freeing Kuwait from its Iraqi occupation, had been achieved. Mission accomplished, war ended. The United States government was congratulated for not widening or changing the war's objective. But it did not take long for arguments to surface that victory had been declared too soon, because Iraq's dictator, Saddam Hussein, was still in power and would continue to threaten stability in the region (overthrowing him was not an explicit goal of the U.S. military effort at that time). A little historical distance influenced judgments. Such a change in perspective after time has elapsed is not uncommon. Usually, more information is available to those who can judge with hindsight. More is known about the consequences of decisions. Observers know whether the intended consequences did or did not materialize, and have also discovered potential unintended consequences. In addition, the observer's personal biases also affect judgments about foreign policy decisions. One scholar went so far as to state that when one concludes that someone else used good judgment, it is often "just another way of saying that one agrees with them."[74]

The determination that good judgment was exercised certainly deserves to rest on a better foundation than the observer's agreement or disagreement with that decision. Is it fair (or appropriate) to judge a decision on the basis of information that was not known, and could not have been known, to those who made the decision? Certainly, we cannot expect decision makers to be clairvoyant. On the other hand, we can expect decision makers to work hard to obtain a thorough grasp of the foreign policy problems they confront. Whether or not the outcome is successful, a good decision rests on a thorough examination of the available information and a willingness to question both one's own initial judgments and one's beliefs about the opponent. A good decision moreover requires that decision makers make a serious attempt to try to see the world from the perspective of their opponent.[75] This may be easier to achieve for leaders who are conceptually complex. In any case, it requires empathy and a broad knowledge of not only one's own society but of the world beyond the borders.

Unfortunately, the cognitive biases previously mentioned also make it difficult for decision makers to truly be open to new information, especially when it is inconsistent with what they already believe about a specific situation or actor. Most decision makers do not revise their judgments, even when new information makes it abundantly clear that the initial judgment was misguided. This means that it is difficult for decision makers to learn from either history or their own previous decisions. In fact, only rarely do decision makers learn and reframe their understanding of a problem or their judgment about a situation or opposing leader. When they do learn, it is usually as a result of a **formative event**, defined as a crisis or other major event that strongly influences a decision maker's thinking about the nature of world politics and foreign policy.[76] Events experienced personally are likely to have a greater impact than those which a decision maker has experienced secondhand through reading or other vicarious experience.[77] In short, decision makers tend to learn only under certain, narrowly specified conditions.

What lessons do they learn in such cases? This depends on the nature of the formative event: a success suggests a foreign policy action that may be repeated, while a failure suggests a foreign policy action to be avoided.[78] Most important for our purposes is that past experience does not necessarily lead to wiser choices. Rather, foreign policy problems are likely to be "framed as repetitions of past experiences."[79] This has led one observer to note that those "who remember the past *too well*, or dwell on it too much, are the ones condemned to repeat it, because they rarely recognize the novelty of the challenges they face."[80]

Whether learning takes place, what lessons are learned, and whether decision makers reach beyond their own (and their country's) experiences will depend not only on cognitive biases and psychological predispositions, such as conceptual complexity, but also on the context within which decisions are made.[81] The leader's circle of advisors and the foreign policy making bureaucracy can either reinforce such human tendencies or try to mediate them.

Chapter Summary

- Rationality has been conceptualized in different ways. Normative rationality specifies a decision making process that follows specific steps. Empirical rationality seeks to ascertain how decision makers actually make decisions and in what ways their decision process deviates from normative models of rationality.
- Not all decisions are made using elaborate decision making processes. In some instances decision makers satisfice or use a heuristic.
- Decision makers often employ a two-stage decision process, as specified by the poliheuristic theory. During stage one, options are eliminated on the basis of a noncompensatory rule. During the second stage, a more comprehensive evaluation is completed.
- Prospect theory, which investigated how decision makers frame situations, and problem representation are efforts to study the impact of perception on decision making.
- History can be a poor guide to decision making, because decision

makers often employ historical analogies in a superficial manner.
- It is difficult to conceptualize "good" decision making. Skeptics doubt it can be done, simplifiers look for simple patterns, and complexifiers emphasize the value of critical thinking.

Terms

Unitary actor
Diversionary theory of war
Normative theory of rationality
Empirical theory of rationality
Satisficing
Heuristic
Ill-structured problem
National interest
Realist theory
Soft power
Poliheuristic theory
Noncompensatory principle
Bounded rationality
Prospect theory
Decision frame
Problem representation
Analogical reasoning
Irredentism
National self-determination
Schema
Skeptics of good judgment
Simplifiers
Complexifiers
Cognitive biases
Formative event

Study Questions

1. Are decision makers rational? What does it mean to be rational?
2. What are perceptions and how do they influence decision makers?
3. Is history a useful guide for decision makers? How so? Why not?

4. How does problem representation or framing influence decision making?
5. Is the use of heuristics in decision making necessarily bad?
6. Is it possible to distinguish good decision making? Or is good judgment merely a matter of opinion—and agreement with the decision?

Suggestions for Further Reading

A classic work on the role of perception in decision making is Jervis, *Perception and Misperception in International Politics*.

An early critique of rational models of decision making is Allison, *Essence of Decision: Explaining the Cuban Missile Crisis*. An updated version is available as Allison and Zelikow, *Essence of Decision: Explaining the Cuban Missile Crisis, 2nd ed.*

For the poliheuristic theory, see Mintz, ed., *Integrating Cognitive and Rational Theories of Foreign Policy Decision Making*, and James and Zhang, "Chinese Choices: A Poliheuristic Analysis of Foreign Policy Crises, 1950–1996."

Work on problem representation is well represented in Sylvan and Voss, *Problem Representation in Foreign Policy Decision Making*.

A frequently cited work using analogies is Khong, *Analogies at War: Korea, Munich, Dien Bien Phu, and the Vietnam Decisions of 1965*.

A source for work on good judgment is Renshon and Larson, *Good Judgment in Foreign Policy: Theory and Application*.

Notes

1. Fiske and Taylor, *Social Cognition*, chapter 2.
2. Welch, "Culture and Emotion," 208.
3. The discussion of this case draws heavily upon the work of Welch's "Culture and Emotion" and "Remember the Falklands?"
4. Welch, "Remember the Falklands?" 484.
5. Welch, "Culture and Emotion," 193.
6. Welch, "Remember the Falklands?" 488.
7. Ibid., 490–91.
8. See ibid., 493–94.
9. Welch, "Culture and Emotion," 199.
10. Ibid., 207.
11. Ibid., 202.

12. Ibid., 207.

13. Ibid., 194.

14. Ibid., 193.

15. Ibid.

16. One of the early critiques of the unitary actor assumption was Allison, "Conceptual Models." See also Jervis, *Perception and Misperception*; Rosati, "The Power of Human Cognition."

17. Levy and Vakili, "Diversionary Action by Authoritarian Regimes," 118–46.

18. See, e.g., Williams, Internal Woes, External Foes?; Levy and Vakili, "Diversionary Action by Authoritarian Regimes," 118–46; Levy, "The Diversionary Theory of War," 259–88.

19. Welch, "Culture and Emotion," 198.

20. Ibid., 197.

21. Ibid., 198.

22. See, e.g., Allison, "Conceptual Models"; Simon, "Human Nature in Politics." The terminology is adapted from Hill, *The Changing Politics of Foreign Policy*.

23. Simon, *The Sciences of the Artificial*.

24. Whether satisficing is limited to less important matters is, of course, an empirical question.

25. This is akin to Goldgeier's observation that the "existence of threats depends on the perceptions of individuals and societies" ("Psychology and Security," 164–65).

26. Marfleet and Miller, "Failure after 1441."

27. Hermann, *Crises in Foreign Policy*.

28. Voss, "On the Representation of Problems," 11.

29. Morgenthau and Thompson, *Politics Among Nations*, 5.

30. Nye, *Soft Power*, 5.

31. Sylvan, Goel, and Chandrasekaran, "Analyzing Political Decision Making," 78.

32. Ibid.; see also Energy Information Administration, "Oil Market Basics," http://www.eia.doe.gov/pub/oil_gas/petroleum/analysis_publications/oil_market_basics/trade_text.htm#Import%20Dependency.

33. Sylvan, Goel, and Chandrasekaran, "Analyzing Political Decision Making."

34. Mintz, "Integrating Cognitive and Rational Theories"; Mintz, "The Decision to Attack Iraq"; DeRouen, "The Decision Not to Use Force"; James and Zhang, "Chinese Choices."

35. Simon, "Human Nature in Politics."

36. Mintz, "Foreign Policy Decision Making"; Mintz et al., "The Effect of Dynamic Versus Static Choice Sets"; Mintz and Geva, "The Polyheuristic Theory."

37. Mintz, "Integrating Cognitive and Rational Theories," 3.

38. Sylvan, "Introduction," 3.

39. Tversky and Kahneman, "The Framing of Decisions."

40. Ibid., 453.

41. James and Zhang, "Chinese Choices," 45.
42. Tversky and Kahneman, "The Framing of Decisions," 457.
43. Sylvan and Voss, *Problem Representation*.
44. Sylvan and Haddad, "Reasoning and Problem Representation," 189.
45. See Welch, "Remember the Falklands?" "Culture and Emotion."
46. See, e.g., Jervis, *Perception and Misperception*.
47. Holsti, "The 'Operational Code' Approach," identified such a tendency in John Foster Dulles, which became known as the "inherent bad faith" model.
48. Hemmer, *Which Lessons Matter?*; Houghton, "The Role of Analogical Reasoning"; Khong, *Analogies at War*; Neustadt and May, *Thinking in Time*. For assessments that compare analogical reasoning with other reasoning styles, see Breuning, "The Role of Analogies"; Sylvan et al., "Case-Based, Model-Based, and Explanation-Based Styles of Reasoning in Foreign Policy."
49. Novick, "Analogical Transfer"; 1988; Keane et al., "Constraints on Analogical Mapping."
50. Novick, "Analogical Transfer"; Spellman and Holyoak, "If Saddam Hussein is Hitler"; Keane et al., "Constraints on Analogical Mapping."
51. Gentner, "The Mechanics of Analogical Learning."
52. Novick, "Analogical Transfer"; Spellman and Holyoak, "If Saddam Hussein is Hitler"; Keane et al., "Constraints on Analogical Mapping."
53. Reiter, *Crucible of Beliefs*, 23.
54. Khong, *Analogies at War*; Neustadt and May, *Thinking in Time*.
55. Neustadt and May, *Thinking in Time*.
56. Teaching decision makers to employ analogies more effectively is the subject of Neustadt and May, *Thinking in Time*.
57. Khong, *Analogies at War*
58. Khong, *Analogies at War*, 221.
59. Fiske and Taylor, 1984, 13.
60. Jervis, *Perception and Misperception*.
61. Khong, *Analogies at War*, 212–15.
62. Dyson and Preston, "Individual Characteristics."
63. Ibid., 278–79.
64. Allison, *Essence of Decision*, 218.
65. Tetlock, "Good Judgment in International Politics," 523.
66. Renshon, "Psychological Sources of Good Judgment in Political Leaders," 46.
67. Tetlock, "Good Judgment in International Politics," 527.
68. Brzezinski, *The Grand Chessboard*; Kennedy, *The Rise and Fall of the Great Powers*.
69. Tetlock, "Good Judgment in International Politics," 518.
70. Ibid., 518.
71. Ibid., 525–26; see also Welch, "Culture and Emotion," 208.
72. See Neustadt and May, *Thinking in Time*.
73. Tetlock, "Good Judgment in International Politics," 526; see also Kowert, *Groupthink or Deadlock*, 18.
74. Tetlock, "Good Jsudgment in International Politics," 518.

75. Welch, "Culture and Emotion," 208.
76. Reiter, *Crucible of Beliefs*, 38; see also Jervis, *Perception and Misperception*.
77. Reiter, *Crucible of Beliefs*, 39.
78. Ibid., 39, 204.
79. Reiter, *Crucible of Beliefs*, 203.
80. Hirsh, *At War With Ourselves*, 13, italics in original.
81. Snyder, Bruck and Sapin, *Foreign Policy Decision-Making (Revisited)*, 95.

Chapter 4

Leaders Are Not Alone: The Role of Advisors and Bureaucracies

Chapter Preview

- Explains the ways in which leaders are embedded in the institutions of government.
- Explains the intersection of leader personality and the organization of the advisory system.
- Explains the role of government agencies and small groups of advisors in decision making.
- Explains the consequences of various interaction patterns among advisors.
- Explains differences in the advisory structure of presidential and parliamentary systems, as well as specifics of coalition governments.

Leaders Do Not Decide Alone

President Truman had a sign on his desk in the Oval Office that read, "the buck stops here."[1] He referred to its meaning in his farewell address in January 1953, saying that the "greatest part of the President's job is to make decisions—big ones and small ones, dozens of them almost every day. . . . The President—whoever he is—has to decide. He can't pass the buck to anybody. No one else can do the deciding for him. That's his job."[2]

What Truman referenced was that he had the ultimate responsibility for U.S. foreign policy. In his view, others in government could "pass the buck" to someone else up the chain of command, but once on the desk of the president, a decision had to be made. His statement nicely expresses two interconnected elements of political decision making: one, he implies that a single person bears the ultimate responsibility for making foreign policy decisions and two, that policy making is conducted through hierarchical organizations. Is this always the case? Let's examine each point in turn.

Although it is tempting to accept Truman's contention that a single person bears the ultimate responsibility for foreign policy decisions, consider once again the story of the Argentine junta and the Falklands/Malvinas crisis discussed in chapter 3. The junta made a *joint* decision. Later, President Galtieri's surprise announcement after the Argentine invasion of the islands altered the group's decision in a very public manner that was not easy to retract. A public announcement of this nature was probably the only way that Galtieri could override a decision made by the group. The expectation was that they would make decisions together, meaning that the junta expected to govern as a collective of equals. This junta's expectation was not unique. Decision making groups may be of vastly different sizes, be less or more formally structured, and bear different names—junta, cabinet, coalition, parliament, etc.—but all make decisions in concert. That does not mean that Truman's assessment was wrong. He did make the important decisions that shaped the latter days of World War II and the immediate post war period. More generally, American presidents do have the ultimate responsibility for foreign policy decisions. This is not true in all countries and decision making situations, as the Argentinean example shows. Whether one person or a collective of multiple individuals or even multiple organizations is responsible for foreign policy decision making depends on the structure of the institutions of a specific society's government.[3]

Note that whether or not one individual bears the ultimate responsibility for foreign policy decision making does *not* depend on whether that country is a democracy. In fact, in the examples cited here, the democratic country (the United States) has one person who is the ultimate decision maker, whereas Argentina was at the time of the Falklands/Malvinas crisis a nondemocratic country with a group as the ultimate decision maker. Additionally, within one country foreign policy decisions can be made by different **decision units** at different times or concerning different types of issues. An ultimate decision unit is defined as the person or the group who are in a position not only to make a foreign policy decision but also to prevent any other entity within the government from explicitly reversing that decision.[4] Especially important with regard to the first element of this decision is that the person or group can use the resources of the government, such as its military, to enforce their decision. For instance, during the Falklands crisis, Prime Minister Thatcher's decision to send the military to retake the islands was not easily reversed by any other person or agency within the British government. In sum, determining who has the ultimate power to decide is not simply a function of the type of government but depends on identifying whether a single individual or a group has the ultimate authority to make a foreign policy decision. Making such a determination depends on substantive knowledge about the government in question. The bottom line is that the ultimate decision maker is not always a single individual, as Truman noted with regard to his own situation as President of the United States

Truman's farewell address also implied that foreign policy is made through hierarchical organizations. Another part of the previous quotation reads, "The papers may circulate around the Government for a while but they finally reach this desk. And then, there's no place else for them to go."[5]

Truman portrayed his office as situated at the top of the hierarchy and as the last stop in the decision making process. This reflected the way *he* organized his White House and communications with various departments. However, not all U.S. presidents, and certainly not all leaders, strive for this type of streamlined communications. Some leaders purposely build multiple channels of information into their advisory systems.

Take, for instance, Emperor Haile Selassie, who ruled Ethiopia from 1930 until 1974. He had joined the imperial court in the capital city of Addis Ababa as a teenager. There, he found himself surrounded by the constant intrigues that were part of political life. In Ethiopia at the time, there were no formal institutions of government, and rule revolved around personal authority and loyalty to the Emperor.[6] Although Haile Selassie sought to modernize his country, especially after World War II, the political system continued to revolve around personal loyalty to the Emperor. All his ministers reported to him on a regular basis, to ensure that Haile Selassie was fully informed.[7] These ministers had every incentive to report everything the Emperor might possibly wish to know because he maintained multiple channels of information. If a minister neglected to tell him something, the Emperor would surely find out about it from someone else. By telling the Emperor himself, each minister maximized control over how the affairs within his department were portrayed. Besides, ministers would be reprimanded *and* regarded as less trustworthy if they failed to inform the Emperor—something that would not be helpful to their political careers, which depended on remaining in the Emperor's favor. It is not surprising, then, to know that Haile Selassie is characterized as a masterful politician who manipulated others with such great skill that "he sometimes appears to be a master of marionettes, moving in a mysterious way to determine the actions of the lesser individuals who surround his throne."[8]

Interestingly, the description of Emperor Haile Selassie's court shares much in common with the organization of the White House under President Truman's immediate predecessor, Franklin D. Roosevelt. Under

Roosevelt, the executive branch deliberately included overlapping jurisdictions, which led to conflict between departments, but also ensured that the President received information on policy problems from multiple perspectives. In addition, Roosevelt would also occasionally contact individuals working within each of the departments to obtain "independent advice and information."[9] Roosevelt thrived on the political conflict he thus created around him and "manipulated the structure of relationships among subordinates in order to control and profit from their competition."[10] Although no one has described Roosevelt as a "master of marionettes," the institutional organization (or lack thereof) of Emperor Haile Selassie's court and Roosevelt's White House are remarkably similar. So was both men's comfort with political intrigue, or the political game. In contrast, Truman's White House was far more hierarchical.

A leader's personality is likely to affect how she or he organizes the executive.[11] Some leaders gain insight from hearing their advisors debate issues in their presence, while others like to ponder the policy options their advisors provide to them in solitude. Some leaders are intent that their preferences shape policy, whereas others want policy choices to reflect a consensus among various viewpoints. It also matters whether a leader wishes to be actively involved in foreign policy making, actively seeking out information and shaping the policy options, or, conversely, prefers to rely on the expertise of trusted advisors who help define issues and gather information. Leaders are more likely to actively seek out information when they feel knowledgeable about (and comfortable with) foreign affairs and when they trust the bureaucracy.

In sum, there are many aspects of a leader's personality that influence how that leader treats information—and how much information she or he requires. This has implications for the organization of an effective advisory system.

In the remainder of this chapter, the discussion focuses on various aspects of the advisory system that surrounds the leader. Just like the largest part of an iceberg rests below the surface of the ocean, much of that advisory system is not readily visible. The tip of the iceberg consists of the leader and her or his immediate advisors. The rest of the iceberg is the so-called permanent bureaucracy on which leaders rely for the information that shapes their policies and the implementation of their decisions. Although we know the bureaucracy is there, we are not always sure of what those working within the bureaucracy do or how their work influences foreign policy decisions.

The Tip of the Iceberg—Organizing the Executive

The people with whom a leader surrounds her- or himself matter. It is through the leader's conversations with the immediate circle of advisors and associates that policy decisions take shape.[12] Although Truman portrayed himself as the final arbiter in the decision making process, he would have admitted that his advisors shaped his policies in significant ways.

There is no such thing as a perfect advisory system: each system has its own pitfalls. Leaders function best if the advisory system suits their personality,[13] and they always need to guard against the potential problems of the specific advisory system they choose.[14] Let's take a look at some of the ways in which leaders have structured advisory systems.

One categorization scheme, derived from the organization of the White House under several U.S. presidents, identifies three different approaches to organizing the advisory system: formalistic, competitive, and collegial.[15] The following paragraphs discuss each in turn. As you read them, consider how a leader's personality might predispose her or him to organize the executive along these, or perhaps yet other, lines.

The **formalistic approach** to organizing the executive emphasizes a hierarchical structure with a clear chain of command. This does not mean that the executive office of every leader who has employed this type of organization could be depicted with the same organizational chart. Rather, it means that leaders who employ this type of organizational structure endeavor to create an orderly decision process. Advisors each provide the leader with information on those aspects of a problem that is within their area of expertise and under the jurisdiction of their departments. These advisors, in turn, obtain information and advice from the individuals who work in their department or agency. Some leaders will want each department head to provide them with advice, while the leader synthesizes the information, as did Truman. More recently, U.S. presidents have employed their White House staff to synthesize information and advice for them. Other variations are possible within the scope of the formalistic model. They all share in common that the flow of information and the spheres of competence of various advisors are clearly delineated. The emphasis is on analysis and on making the "best" decision possible.[16] Although such a hierarchical structure appears orderly and efficient, it may not be possible for a leader who sits at the top of such an advisory system to know whether information has been left out or distorted as it made its way up the organizational ladder, because leaders who employ this type of organizational structure seldom, if ever, circumvent the official chain of command.[17]

This drawback of the formalistic approach to organizing the executive is the strength of the **competitive approach**. As the example of Ethiopian

Emperor Haile Selassie shows, the leader who organizes the executive along these lines actively uses multiple channels of information. There is little cooperation between advisors in this type of advisory system. Instead, all are keenly aware that the leader can access information from a variety of sources, including the subordinates of the department heads, which creates an atmosphere of competition and conflict. Advisors all vie for the leader's ear and rush to be the first to convey new information, either so they can present the information in a way that portrays their department favorably or so they can play a crucial role in the framing, or representation, of the policy problem. As a result, advisors are likely to present partial, incomplete, or biased information. Leaders arrive at a complete, or at least balanced, view of issues as a result of reconciling these various viewpoints.[18] The internal competition can be hard on the leader's advisors and may result in high staff turnover. It also demands a lot of the leader's time and attention. When used well, it does place that leader at the hub of an extensive informational network. In doing so, this approach can generate creative solutions, because there is a confluence of many different ideas and viewpoints at the center of government. Furthermore, this system is also very good at generating solutions that are feasible: ideas are modified and tempered as a result of the interplay with other ideas, as well as the need to defend ideas in debate with others. Hence, the competitive system, if managed well, can generate solutions that are at once creative, politically acceptable, and bureaucratically doable.

There are leaders who see the advantages of the ability to ponder multiple perspectives and divergent information but who are not comfortable with the high level of internal conflict that the competitive approach is likely to generate. Yet they also wish to avoid the potential loss or distortion of information that is inherent in the formalistic approach. A third alternative takes advantage of the benefits that flow from obtaining a multiplicity of views but endeavors to cultivate a spirit of teamwork rather than competition. This alternative is called the **collegial approach**. As in the competitive advisory system, the leader sits at the center of an extensive informational network. Advisors do not provide their information to the leader individually but debate policy options with one another as a group. The objective of such discussions is to achieve a frank exchange of ideas—but without the conflict that accompanies the competitive system—and arrive at innovative policy proposals. The leader communicates directly with advisors but at times also reaches out to the subordinates of department heads and obtains information outside of the formal chain of command.

In the collegial approach, the emphasis is on teamwork rather than competition.[19] Of course, differences of opinion can always spin out of control, and advisors may become competitors. On the other hand, there is also the risk that the team starts to think too much alike and that the open exchange of ideas turns into too much mutual agreement. The difficulty in making the collegial approach work is that it requires a delicate balance of diversity of opinion, mediating differences, and fostering a team spirit. Not all leaders have the skills to manage the interpersonal relations between their advisors to successfully maintain a collegial system across time.

Each of the three approaches to the advisory system has its own advantages and disadvantages. Table 4.1 summarizes these with the help of four questions that are implied in the description of the pros and cons of each approach to organizing the executive: 1. How likely is it that the advisory system will distort information? The formalistic system has the highest risk of doing so. 2. Is the leader exposed to a lot or to very little conflict, either substantive or interpersonal? The formalistic system seeks to shield the leader from both types of conflict, whereas the competitive system exposes the leader to both. The collegial system stakes out a middle ground by guiding members of a team to debate the issues. 3. How responsive is the advisory system? Does it emphasize optimal or feasible solutions? Here, again, the formalistic and competitive systems are opposites—emphasizing optimality and feasibility, respectively—with the collegial approach staking out the middle ground. 4. What conditions are required for thorough consideration of alternatives? How well each works is likely to depend on whether the leader can effectively manage the chosen arrangement. Each system has the capacity to do well and also runs the risk of performing abysmally.

Above, we introduced Emperor Haile Selassie of Ethiopia, whose advisory system approximated the competitive approach. This masterful politician has been described as an "African Louis XIV," a reference to the centralization of power that took place during his rule.[20] He was born in 1892 as the son of a cousin of his predecessor, Emperor Menilek. Succession to the throne was not predetermined by birth order and family ties (the way it is in "modern" monarchies), but sons of cousins were certainly not the most likely successors to the throne. Haile Selassie's ascension to the throne was itself a testament to his political skill.

How, then, was it possible for Haile Selassie's government in the early 1970s to deny the existence of a widespread famine within the borders of the country? The government claimed that international media reports of the famine were "misinformed and exaggerated"[21] and continued to deny its existence until May 1973.[22] Is it possible that provincial administrators "obscured the magnitude of the tragedy"?[23] Is it possible that officials in the capital initially "did not even inform the emperor"?[24] Could it be possible that the Emperor did not know of the immense tragedy that was unfolding within his own country? This would seem strange given the

Table 4.1 Comparison of executive management styles

	Formalistic	Competitive	Collegial
1. Likelihood that information will be distorted	High No built-in checks on distortion of information	Low Multiple perspectives presented and openly debated	Low Multiple perspectives presented and debated
2. Degree to which leader is exposed to substantive and interpersonal conflict	Low for both	High for both	High for substantive conflict Low for interpersonal conflict
3. Overall responsiveness of decision process	Low Focus on best solution May react slow or inappropriate in crisis	High Focus on feasible solution Highly dependent on leader's skill and involvement	High Aims to identify solutions that are both optimal and feasible Highly dependent on leader's skill and involvement
4. Thoroughness of consideration of alternatives	When it works well: High Thorough, orderly, objectively	When it works well: High Cacophony of voices; leader exposed to partial and biased information	When it works well: High Debate and teamwork ensure multiple viewpoints are considered
	When it does not work well: Low Emphasis on objectivity may distort political pressures and public opinion	When it does not work well: Low Staff competition, self-interested action rather than service	When it does not work well: Low Closed system of mutal support, or groupthink

Adapted from Johnson 1974 and George 1980.

Emperor's multiple channels of information that kept him "in touch with the least event," although he did occasionally use "the claim of ignorance" to be able to deny responsibility for specific policies.[25]

On the other hand, the entire system operated through personal ties and connections, and there was no framework for systematically analyzing information. What advisor would, in such a political system, risk being the bearer of bad news? It would obviously displease the Emperor to hear of such problems within his country.

Of course, it is difficult to establish conclusively what the Emperor did or did not know at a specific point in time. Although he had always aimed to be the fully informed central hub of government, by the early 1970s the Emperor was in his early eighties, and some described him as "too old and senile" to lead effectively.[26] He worked fewer hours and was less actively involved in the policy making process than during his younger years.[27] Although he may have managed a competitive advisory system well at one point in time, it appears that Haile Selassie was less skillful at manipulating his advisors as he aged. In fact, it appears that he may have become the captive of his immediate advisors, who took an active role in the day-to-day administration and who carefully controlled access to him.[28] What became visible at that point was the weakness of a fluid system based on the ability of the leader to manage (and mediate) conflict. Just as Roosevelt's administration "spawned inefficiency" when he could not personally manage the conflict between individuals with overlapping responsibilities,[29] when Haile Selassie's attention to detail diminished in his later years, his advisory system suffered. With little formal (bureaucratic) structure, nor an emphasis on analysis, his advisory system increasingly distorted information. Because it was built on interpersonal connection, there were no mechanisms to prevent, or correct for, such distortion. Under these circumstances, it is entirely plausible that no one informed the Emperor of the famine: doing so would have weakened the position of the advisors closest to him—precisely the ones who also controlled access to him.

The organization of the advisory system has consequences for decision making. In the Ethiopian case, the deterioration of the competitive approach meant that an aging Emperor was increasingly out of touch with events inside his own country. The "master of marionettes" had become the father of a cohort of Pinocchios. It created an opportunity for opposition groups, who ultimately took power and deposed Haile Selassie (and thereby ended the reign of the Ethiopian monarchy).

The story of the last Ethiopian emperor demonstrates the difficulty of managing a competitive advisory system. At its best, it demands much of the leader's time and attention. It also requires a personality that is comfortable with political conflict, as both Haile Selassie (in his younger days) and Roosevelt were. Leaders who are less comfortable in such surroundings will choose either to emphasize teamwork, if they seek a hands-on role in decision making, as did John F. Kennedy, or a more formal system with gatekeepers, if they are more comfortable pondering advice and options in solitude, as was Truman.

The discussion of the advisory system has thus far largely focused on instances where there is a single leader with substantial control over the design of the advisory system. Depending on the political system of a specific society, the leader may have more or less leeway in structuring the advisory system and choosing her or his advisors. The more a leader has the ability to place his or her stamp on the organization of the executive, the more his or her personality will factor into the organizational structure. In a **presidential system** of government, for instance, the executive branch of government is separate from the legislative branch.[30] The president is elected independently and does not owe her or his position to the support of the legislature, although a troubled relationship with the legislature can render policy making difficult. In a presidential system, the president usually has substantial leeway in organizing the executive to suit her or his decision making style, just as she or he has great autonomy in the selection of her or his advisors.

In a **parliamentary system**, on the other hand, the prime minister owes her or his position directly to the support of the legislature. If the legislature withdraws its support, for instance through a vote of no confidence, the prime minister is forced to resign. In a parliamentary system, the composition of the executive is less clearly determined by a single individual, depending in part on the **electoral system** of the country. In cases where a single party tends to win a parliamentary majority, a prime minister may exercise somewhat greater influence over the composition of government and the advisory system. In cases where governments are composed of several political parties, such as in **coalition cabinet** government, the advisory system as a whole is less likely to be structured to suit a single personality. Rather, each member of the executive structures only a small circle of advisors in the department over which she or he presides. A **cabinet government** is a group of ministers who jointly constitute the executive of a country. They usually have **collective responsibility**, which means that each minister is expected to publicly support all cabinet decisions. Personal disagreements with collective decisions may not be voiced publicly. When the cabinet is made up of a **coalition** of political parties, meaning that two or more political parties jointly form the government, the collective responsibility for political decision making is borne by ministers who are affiliated with different political parties and have different political views and priorities. The interactions of coalition governments are discussed in greater detail later in this chapter.

The significance of the structure of the advisory system derives not only from the fact that it is often a function of the leader's personality, but also—and perhaps more importantly—from its implications for the decision making process. In the next sections, we first examine the functioning of the government bureaucracy as a whole and then turn to an examination of the smaller decision making groups that form the immediate advisory circle around a leader.

The Rest of the Iceberg—the Government Bureaucracy

A thread that runs through the discussion of the organizational structure of the advisory system is that inaccurate, incomplete, and biased information makes its way through such policy making bodies. In some cases, information is not accurate simply because someone made a mistake or did not research thoroughly enough to discover (through consultation of alternative sources) that their information was not reliable. As the discussion of information distortion makes clear, not all failures in policy making can be blamed on such problems. That does not mean that distortions are deliberate efforts to misinform. No matter how well the advisory system works, it remains a political system. Advisors have their own perspectives on the world, as well as their own interests and ambitions.[31] Even advisors who are appointed by the leader will not always perceive their interests to be perfectly aligned with that leader. Conversely, members of the permanent bureaucracy are not necessarily antagonistic to the leaders' political agenda. In the end, policy choices are the result of a "dynamic influence process" in which advisors do much more than "merely collecting, processing, and interpreting information."[32]

Each of the three approaches to organizing the advisory system addresses these issues in its own way. Interestingly, the formalistic model endeavors to follow the decision making process prescribed by the normative model of rationality discussed in chapter 3 most closely. Both the normative model of rationality and the formalistic approach to the advisory system emphasize finding the "best" solution on the basis of thorough analysis of the problem and the available policy options. Both downplay the role of politics in decision making. Neither is intended to *describe* the actual practice of policy making. Instead, the normative model of rationality outlines how policy *ought* to be made, whereas the formalistic approach *organizes* the relationships between the various individuals who are employed as members of the leader's advisory system. To achieve a better understanding of the inner workings of the advisory system, we will need to delve into efforts to describe the actual advisory process.

It is tempting to assume that foreign policy decisions are the result of a rational process in which the various agencies, departments, and offices that collectively constitute the government jointly serve an agreed-upon national interest. If this were the case, the **rational policy model** might provide a fairly accurate description of how foreign policy is made.[33] It assumes that foreign policy is made *as if* a single, rational decision maker analyzes a strategic problem and, once the problem is defined, selects a policy response from among the available options. The process by which the policy response is selected starts by outlining the options, investigates the likely consequences of each, and settles on the option that promises the biggest benefit at the lowest possible risk and/or cost. Fundamental to the analysis, as well as the judgment of cost and benefit, is the desire to serve the state's interests.

This rational policy model does not take into account the possibility that information could become distorted in a complex advisory system made up of many individuals, offices, and agencies. Neither does it take into account that identifying the national interest is not necessarily straightforward. The problems surrounding the concept of the national interest were discussed in some detail in chapter 3. Here, we delve into two alternative descriptions of the decision making process, the **organizational process model** and the **bureaucratic politics model**, which were originally created as critiques of the rational policy model.[34] Both models take into account that there are usually multiple perspectives on any given policy problem, but they stress different reasons for the existence of those multiple perspectives. Table 4.2 summarizes and compares these three models of decision making.

The organizational process model envisions the government as a collection of organizations, centrally coordinated at the top, each with their own specialties and expertise, but also its own priorities and perceptions. Each organization, moreover, has its own customary ways or **standard operating procedures,** which is often abbreviated as SOPs. Although it is efficient for organizations to act according to such standard procedures most of the time, rigid adherence also robs them of flexibility when they confront a novel or unusual situation. According to this model, organizations respond to such situations by adapting rather than reinventing their standard operating procedures. Adaptation consists of small and incremental changes to standard procedures. Such changes are easier to implement, even if they are not an adequate response to the problem they are intended to address. And that is the key to this model: it describes government as a large conglomerate of organizations that, singly and collectively, pursues policy responses that permit them to stick as closely as possible to well-worn routines that they know to be feasible rather than to fashion policy responses that best respond to the problem. According to this model, then, inadequate policy responses do not result from a failure to objectively evaluate the risks and benefits associated with various options, but from the inertia of established organizations.

Table 4.2 Models of decision making

	1. Rational Policy Model	2. Organizational Process Model	3. Bureaucratic Politics Model
Policy is determined by:	national interest	organizational inertia and feasibility	complex bargaining among individuals and agencies
Key actor(s):	Government, acting as *if* it is a single, rational decision maker	Organizations, acting on the basis of standard operating procedures (SOP's)	Individuals, guided by role and self-interest
Decision Process:	1. Identify national interest	1. Organizational expertise and interests determine preferences	1. Horizontal: interests determined by role and employing agency
	2. Identify options	2. Adapt SOP's	2. Vertical: interests determined by place in hierarchy
	3. Cost/Benefit analysis of options	3. Feasibility determines policy choice	3. Bargaining and other political maneuvering determine policy choice
	4. Choose policy alternative that best serves national interest		

Adapted from Allison 1969, 1971, Allison and Zelikow 1999.

Interestingly, the competitive style of organizing the executive also predicts an emphasis on feasible policy decisions, but it stresses the interactions among individuals rather than the inertia of organizations as the reasons for that emphasis. To understand the difference between organizational inertia and the interactions among individuals within the advisory system we need to first delve into the details of the bureaucratic politics model.

The bureaucratic politics model focuses on the role of individuals within governmental organizations. Individual advisors within the government occupy specific roles within it: 1. They lead, or work within, a specific agency or department. Each agency and department has its own mandate.

The specific expertise and policy interests of that agency are bound to color the perceptions and opinions of the individuals working within that agency. 2. Advisors are also placed at a specific location within the hierarchical structure of that agency or department. The individual who serves as the head of the agency is dependent upon her or his subordinates to provide information, analysis, and policy options.

Agencies are typically hierarchical structures and run the same risks for distortion of information that we discussed as part of the formalistic style of organizing the executive. The direction provided by the agency head influences that agency's functioning. How much so will depend on both the quality of the leadership and the degree to which follow-through is monitored. In addition, those working within the agency are not robots that simply follow orders, but individuals with their own interests and career aspirations. Some may seek to help their superiors by highlighting information that supports their point of view and downplaying the information that contradicts it. Others may seek to advance their own career by establishing (and getting their superiors to notice) their expertise in a specific policy area. The relationships between superiors and subordinates sketched here provide only a small sampling of the many ways in which these relationships affect the flow of information, and thereby the policy options that are proposed and the choices that are ultimately made.

The bureaucratic politics model stresses that advisors' perceptions and priorities are shaped by both the organizations that employ them and their personal ambitions and interests. As a result, policy choices become the end result of complex bargaining at multiple levels: hierarchically between superiors and subordinates with their own individual agendas and horizontally between heads of agencies that represent different interests within the government. Both the competitive and collegial style of organizing the executive recognize that this occurs and seek to harness the power of multiple perspectives, but both require considerable skill and involvement by the leader. The formalistic style does not take either the complex advisory relationships or the distortion of information that can result from them into account. On the contrary, it emphasizes the efficiency of formal bureaucratic structures and shields the leader from much of the conflict that is likely to occur within the advisory system. Although it is important to recognize that the advisory bureaucracy rarely functions as efficiently and dispassionately as the rational policy model assumes, it is also important to recognize that correctives can come from the leader's advisors as well as from the leader her- or himself. The advisory system surrounding the leader can either mediate or aggravate the distortions in the flow of information from organizations and individuals within the bureaucracy. It is the dynamics of this smaller advisory circle to which we now turn.

Back to the Tip of the Iceberg—Decision Making in Small Groups

Leaders and their advisors depend on government agencies, and the individuals working in those organizations, for information and advice. In the end, however, foreign policy decisions are made closer to the tip of the iceberg: by leaders and their small circle of advisors, or by groups of policy makers. It is in these small **groups** where policy makers meet face-to-face that decisions are fashioned on the basis of the information and analysis provided by the various agencies and departments.[35] Such groups may consist of only a few people or encompass an entire cabinet in a country with parliamentary government. Some scholars even include groups as large as the entire parliament.[36] Larger groups will require more rules and direction to function well than small ones, which can remain more informal in their interactions.[37] The important distinction is that the members of the group speak directly with each other as a collectivity.

Here, we are primarily interested in groups that are no larger (and perhaps smaller) than a **cabinet government**. A cabinet government is a group of ministers who jointly constitute the executive of a country. Officially, cabinets usually have collective responsibility, but the prime minister can become a dominant figure within the cabinet rather than simply one of the collective. This is especially true in electoral systems that yield governments dominated by one political party, rather than a coalition of several parties. British Prime Minister Margaret Thatcher, for instance, was such a dominant prime minister.

Although some scholars include parliaments in their definition of small groups, we will not: the members of parliaments do meet face-to-face as a group, but their deliberations are governed by highly formalized rules and protocols. The kind of group dynamics that are the subject of this section do happen in (subgroups of) parliaments, but they are not usually part of the formal sessions of a parliament. Some of interactions described here could occur in larger groups, others require the more intimate setting of a small group.

Small groups serve a variety of functions in foreign policy decision making. Most popular are two images of the small group: one portrays the advisory group as a **think tank**, where top advisors use the available, but incomplete, information to jointly construct a representation of a foreign policy problem, determine its importance among other foreign policy problems, and debate how best to respond to it.[38] The basic assumption is that decision making in a team is "demonstrably superior to [single] individuals when it comes to processing information about novel, complex, and unstructured problems."[39] In other words, groups or teams are especially good at making sense of the sort of ill-structured problems that characterize most foreign policy decision making situations because the creative interplay between their individual efforts to make sense of the available information yields greater insight than a single person could achieve within a short time frame. That is, provided that the group functions as intended.

The other popular image of the political decision making group is that of the **command center**, where the group jointly determines the foreign policy actions.[40] In this role, the group builds on the think tank role to develop options, evaluates them, selects the most viable ones, and ultimately makes a decision. In cases where a group is jointly responsible, as with the Argentine junta encountered in chapter 3, this may accurately represent the power structure within the government—*if* we can assume equality among the members of the group. Most of the time, even in groups of supposed coequals, there are subtle and informal hierarchies that shape the relationships among the individual members of the group. Consider, for instance, that the Argentine junta accepted the analogies to Suez and Rhodesia proposed by their Foreign Minister, Nicanor Costa Mendez, and estimated the British response on the basis of that assessment.[41] This estimate was crucial to their decision making. Because Mendez was seen as more knowledgeable, he exercised greater influence over the decision than his colleagues. In other situations, such as the example of the U.S. Presidency so aptly described by Truman, groups of advisors may make recommendations, but the responsibility ultimately rests with one individual leader, who may or may not have taken part in the group's deliberations. If the leader accepts the recommendation, the group appears to be the command center without having the ultimate authority. Hence, the accuracy of the image of the group as a command center, and whether we should interpret it as one that makes decisions or one that simply advises, depends on the powers invested in that collectivity.

In the case of both the think tank and the command center role, the group is involved in the actual work of decision making; that is, it works at identifying the contours of the problem, discusses policy options, and so on. Formal and informal small groups perform additional functions as well: One, group decision making can help a government present itself as a unified team that works together in the national interest.[42] The fact that decisions are made or recommended by a unified team helps justify and legitimize these decisions as reflecting the government's, or even the society's, core values. This same emphasis on values can be turned inward: reference to the government's or society's core values can help shape the norms of the group and its members.[43] If such an emphasis is very strong, it can squelch dissent within the group and make the group function less effectively. Two, a small, informal group can also serve as a sanctuary.[44] Such a group becomes an emotional support system for a leader, which can help her or him deal with the pressures and stresses of leadership. It can also devolve into a circle of sycophants, making a leader overconfident in the appropriateness of her or his judgments rather than providing a gentle "reality check" when appropriate. Three, groups that are formally part of the government structure can serve as "smoke screens" behind which informal groups do the actual work of decision making.[45] Such informal groups can be places where differences of opinion can be aired out more readily than in more formal settings. Consider, for instance, foreign policy making in societies that are governed by coalitions of parties with very different ideas about the policies that will best serve the state's interests. Policy makers may prefer to sound out their colleagues in other parties informally and work out major differences before publicly debating the issues with one another. The use of informal networks to work out agreements is common in other situations as well. Once differences of opinion become public, it will be harder for any of the decision makers to change their opinion. Doing so could damage their political reputation or the party's reputation. It could make either look like they are just "blowing with the winds" or compromising for the sake of expediency or their own advancement.

This discussion of the different roles played by small groups in foreign policy decision making is not exhaustive, nor is it meant to be. Rather, it serves to highlight that small groups perform important functions in addition to their role in the decision making process itself and that those additional roles are not wholly separate from that decision making process but influence it.

The actual decision making role of a group of policy makers is twofold, as previously introduced. One, groups play the role of think tank when they gather, organize, and process information to gain an understanding of the problem, i.e., construct a representation of it. Two, groups act as a command center that develops and evaluates options. The command center is responsible for arriving at a decision. The same group of individuals may fulfill both the think tank and command center roles. The distinction roughly mirrors the two stages of the poliheuristic theory (discussed in chapter 3). At each stage, group dynamics influence the process in a somewhat different manner: a more even distribution of power among the group members makes it likely that a wider range of options will be considered and debated as the group fulfills its think tank role, but may also make it more difficult for the group to reach a decision as it moves to its command center role.[46]

Colleagues and Competitors

Advisors are both colleagues and competitors. As we saw earlier, the competitive executive management style aggravates and utilizes the elements of competition among the policy makers who surround the leader. The collegial style, on the other hand, seeks to foster collegial interaction while acknowledging the multiplicity of viewpoints. The formalistic style pushes competition and conflict away from the tip of the policy making iceberg. The thread than runs through each of these three descriptions of government decision making is that individual and organizational factors influence problem representations and decisions. More importantly, you have probably noticed that the policy making process is rife with opportunities to advance the cause of the (perceived) national interest, one's organization, one's superior(s), or oneself. A policy maker can act collegially and loyally to achieve her or his ends or can choose to subvert the career of a superior or a colleague. The small advisory groups at the apex of government are no different from the government as a whole: the members of such groups can interact in a variety of ways to serve a mixture of interests. Their interactions can be summarized into four main interaction patterns: bargaining, concurrence, deadlock, and persuasion. We discuss each in turn.

The bureaucratic politics model specifically mentions bargaining, which implies that the decision making process involves give-and-take and that the preferences of any one policy maker never fully shape the decision but often partially do so. This suggests some form of compromise as the likely result of the bargaining process. A compromise would suggest an **integrative solution**, defined as a result that represents the preferences of all members of the group, albeit modified to some degree.[47] This may be easier to achieve in smaller groups than in larger ones. A small group of advisors close to the leader may be able to arrive at an integrative solution easier than, for instance, a coalition cabinet made up of representatives of several different political parties. The former are much more likely to share assumptions about the core values of the government.[48] In larger groups, bargaining can easily lead to a **subset solution**, in which one faction's ideas end up dominating the preferences of other members or factions within the group. This situation can emerge in small groups as well, especially if the members of the group are of unequal status. In larger groups, the subset solution could favor smaller as well as larger factions, depending on the politics surrounding the specific issue at hand.[49] In either case, the members or factions that emerge on the losing end of the bargaining process must at the very least acquiesce in the group's decision.

When such acquiescence emerges quickly and without much debate, the decision process is more accurately characterized as one of **concurrence**. In this case, other options are barely discussed, or not at all. Instead, the decision makers quickly settle on an option they jointly perceive as a reasonable solution. This can happen for three reasons: One, there may be a **dominant solution**. This means that only one option is credible. In terms of the poliheuristic theory (see chapter 3), it may mean that only one option met the noncompensatory criteria in the first stage of decision making. In other words, other options are sought and considered, and are quickly disposed of because they either are not politically feasible or simply not adequate policy responses to the problem.[50] Two, and likely only when a decision is not of vital national importance, it is possible that the policy makers **satisficed**, or accepted the first option that met their threshold of acceptability (see chapter 3). Depending on the situation and on other simultaneous problems that demand the time and attention of policy makers, this may be a reasonable way to deal with a situation.[51] Three, concurrence can be evidence of **groupthink**, or the premature closure of the search for options.[52]

The problem with groupthink is not just that there is little or no consideration of alternatives (something that is also true when there is a dominant solution). The primary problem is that the decision makers fail to critically examine their problem representations and the option(s) before them or to ask themselves whether there might be other options that they have not yet considered. This may happen as a result of strong cohesion among the members of a small group: they perceive the world in such similar ways that none of them is able to offer an alternative point of view or think of alternative ways of confronting the situation.[53] Think, once again, of the failure of any of the members of the Argentine junta (discussed in chapter 3) to suggest that British Prime Minister Margaret Thatcher might perhaps respond differently than her predecessors had during the Suez and Rhodesia crises. None of the decision makers in Argentina at the time seems to have considered the possibility. And if they did, they kept quiet because they all perceived Foreign Minister Mendez as more expert than themselves. In essence, groupthink is the problem of a distorted and one-sided problem representation based on incomplete or faulty information that no member of the group questions because none of them can conceive of any other way of understanding the problem or no one dares suggest that the person they all see as more expert might be wrong. Hence, no one plays "devil's advocate." Interestingly, U.S. President John F. Kennedy purposely left the deliberations of his small circle of advisors during the Cuban Missile Crisis to avoid precisely this problem. He was aware that his presence might influence the nature and content of the discussions among his advisors. Remember that Kennedy organized his executive along the lines of the collegial style, which routinely takes multiple perspectives into account but which can also devolve into a closed system of mutual support. When the system works well, as it did during the Cuban Missile Crisis, the decision making process can avoid the pitfall of groupthink. When the system does not work well, it is likely to fall into precisely this trap. The formalistic style has no built-in mechanism to counteract the distortion of information. When it works well, the emphasis on analysis helps it avoid the problem of groupthink, but when it does not work well, this style of organizing the executive may also suffer from groupthink without ever realizing that its distorted view of the issue is not an accurate representation of the problem.

On the opposite end of reaching agreement too readily is the failure to achieve any agreement at all. This is called **deadlock**. In countries such as the United States, where the President selects the members of the executive, the occurrence of irresolvable differences among small groups of top advisors should be rare.[54] The leader selects these individuals to suit her or his worldview, policy preferences, and decision making style. Contrast this with the situation of a coalition cabinet in a parliamentary system of government: who becomes part of the group in such cases is not determined solely by the prime minister but is dependent on negotiation and dynamics internal to the political parties that participate in the coalition. When coalition cabinets are truly deadlocked, this may result in the resignation of a minister or even the fall of the government. The frequency with which this happens varies, depending on the issues as well as the political traditions within a specific country. Even in countries where the members of government serve at the pleasure of a prime minister or president, and are presumably selected because they suit this individual's priorities, is it possible for advisors to have very strong differences with regard to specific policy problems. For instance, during the Carter administration a stalemate developed between National Security Advisor Zbigniew Brzezinski and Secretary of State Cyrus Vance with regard to the direction of foreign policy. The two men had very different worldviews.[55] If such problems are allowed to fester, and especially if they become public, they can have negative consequences for a government's ability to respond to foreign policy problems and lead to perceptions of ineptness.[56]

Deadlock may result when several members of a decision making group each have strongly held opinions about the course of action that should be taken in response to a specific foreign policy problem. Such strongly held opinions can also lead to efforts at **persuasion**.[57] In fact, one might imagine that mutually unsuccessful efforts at persuasion could result in a standoff between the members of the group as each advisor digs in his or her heels and refuses to compromise. Efforts at persuasion do not inevitably lead to a deadlock. If they are successful, others in the group come around to seeing the situation from the point of view of the persuader. More likely may be the subset solution mentioned previously, which is a solution that is preferred by a subset of the advisory group rather than the entire group. The difference between persuasion and a subset solution is that the latter does not require that the persuader have fully convinced his or her colleagues, only that he or she have achieved sufficient agreement among them that they are willing to go along with the proposal. The difference between persuasion and compromise is that the former is not an integrative solution that reflects (aspects of) the starting preferences of all members of the group. Instead, the preferences of one member or a subgroup become dominant. Hence, a subset solution can connote either a partial compromise or partial persuasion.

Comparing the preferences of the advisors at the outset of their deliberations with the decision could help evaluate whether a specific subset solution is best characterized as compromise or persuasion. Information about the initial positions of decision makers is not always easy to obtain. Decision makers often cloak their statements about decisions in terms of bargaining, even if that's not exactly what happened. Hence, if foreign policy analysts accept decision makers' own characterization of the decision making process, it is likely that they will overestimate the degree to which bargaining plays a role in decision making.[58]

Political Games, a.k.a. Strategies of Influence

The four decision processes described in the previous section define that process primarily by the manner in which the outcome is achieved. Much more can be said about small group interactions, as each of the policy makers involved is likely to be engaged in efforts to manipulate the decision process to increase the chances that the decision she or he favors will dominate or significantly influence the decision. Political manipulation is defined as the effort(s) made by one or more individuals to influence a situation in which a group is making a decision in a way that increases the chances that the outcome will reflect their preferences.[59] There are a variety of strategies a decision maker can employ to improve her or his chances to significantly influence the decision. Such strategies can be divided into three groups: (1) efforts to influence the composition of the decision making group so as to reduce the impact of opposing viewpoints; (2) efforts to influence the beginning stages of the decision process, such as the framing of an issue or perceptions of its relative importance among the various issues the government confronts simultaneously; (3) efforts to manipulate the dynamics of interpersonal interaction within the group.

If all of this sounds Machiavellian, remember that there is often much at stake in foreign policy decision making and also that the problems are generally ill-structured—in chapter 3 we likened the inevitable gaps in information to Swiss cheese. This means that knowledgeable and well-informed policy makers can differ greatly in their assessments of the same situation. Each of them operates on the basis of partial information and their own political instincts—which are in turn heavily informed by the policy maker's personal operational code (see chapter 2). The impact of these differences of interpretation on the decision making process will depend also on the personal characteristics and ambitions of the individuals involved.

What tactics might decision makers use to improve their chances to influence the decision? Let's examine each of the three types of strategies previously mentioned in a little more detail:[60]

1. *Group composition.* Policy makers sometimes try to influence the composition of the decision making group. This can be achieved either by excluding a colleague whose opinions contradict one's own or by trying to include additional members into the group who will support one's position. Exclusion can be achieved formally only by policy makers who have the clout to play a role in determining membership in a particular decision making group, but it is also possible to schedule meetings at a time when the individual with the opposing opinion happens to be out of town or to hold informal meetings with select group members apart from the officially scheduled ones. Including additional members into the group can sometimes be justified on the basis of their expertise and can be useful in providing additional support for one's position. It is also possible to strengthen the credibility of a viewpoint by claiming to speak for one's superior. Doing so not only includes that person's opinion into the debate, it serves to lend greater weight to one's own point of view.

2. *Framing.* Efforts to influence how an issue is framed are especially effective at the early stages of a decision making process. Framing and problem representation are discussed in chapter 3, although the relevance for group decision making was not highlighted. Individual decision makers are likely to frame problems each in their own distinctive way. Once they join one another in a group to deliberate how to respond to this problem, they will each operate on the basis of this individual problem representation, unless the group first deliberates the contours of the problem before moving on to outlining and discussing options. By influencing the group's *collective* problem representation, an individual policy maker can manipulate which options will then have a greater likelihood of being chosen.

3. *Interpersonal relationships.* In addition to manipulating who participates and how the problem is framed, policy makers are likely to use a variety of tactics to influence how they and others in the group are perceived.

In addition to bolstering one's position by claiming to speak for a superior, a policy maker might seek to discredit the expertise of their opponent. Another tactic is to get others to agree in stages. This is called the "salami tactic." It requires a lot of planning and patience to structure a debate in such a way as to get colleagues to agree with you on minor points to build to the inevitable conclusion you set out and that they cannot escape once they have agreed with you on the smaller points.[61] Still another tactic is to leak information. This is a risky strategy, because leaks can easily backfire and have negative implications for the reputation of the source of the leak. It can damage the advisory system because its members can no longer trust that their deliberations will remain confidential. Yet it can also be an attractive strategy for someone who cannot get his or her voice heard within the group or to circumvent a rival.[62]

The use of such tactics shapes the decision process in the small group. Other strategies may be used by policy makers as they seek to influence the decision process. Whether that process is best characterized by bargaining, concurrence, deadlock, or persuasion will depend on the tactics group members use to influence one another and how those tactics combine to produce the outcome. For instance, if opposing viewpoints have been successfully excluded, the group might reach easy agreement (concurrence), whereas if each seeks to convince others of their viewpoint they may be unable to reach a decision (deadlock).

Small advisory groups, with their strategies and political games, are especially common in political systems with a strong executive, characterized by one individual who has the final responsibility for the decisions, such as is common in presidential systems. The entire advisory system ultimately coalesces at the tip of the iceberg where the president or prime minister can't pass the buck to anybody, as U.S. President Harry Truman said.

A different situation is found in parliamentary governments where coalition cabinets are common. Decision making has a more collective quality. This does not mean that the dynamics of advisory systems, bureaucracies, and political manipulation are irrelevant. It does mean that decisions are ultimately made by a group of policy makers who represent different political parties and policy agendas. It is to the dynamics of such groups that we turn in the next section.

Coalitions: Governing Together

In political systems in which the ultimate responsibility rests with a single chief executive, such as a president, advisory groups are not ultimately responsible for the final decision. Rather, it is the chief executive who bears that responsibility. In parliamentary cabinet government, the heads of the various departments share collective responsibility for policy decisions, at least in a formal or legal sense. The prime minister is in that case considered to be the primus inter pares (Latin for "first among equals"), meaning that the prime minister holds the special position of head of the collective but is not superior in rank to her or his colleagues. In practice, though, the prime minister often carries greater weight in decision making than the other members of the group. This is especially true in parliamentary systems where a single party dominates the government, such as is usually the case in Britain. There, prime ministers like Margaret Thatcher and, more recently, Tony Blair acted as the central figures of their governments, leading to the "presidentialization" of cabinet government.

When the cabinet is created out of a coalition of political parties rather than one dominant party, the situation is different. In such cases, cabinets remain closer to the principle of collective responsibility in their decision making. As discussed earlier, coalition cabinets bring together the representatives of two or more political parties for the purposes of governing a country. The power of these parties is rarely, if ever, equal: Each party's presence in the coalition is proportional to its relative presence in parliament and also reflects its electoral gains in the most recent election. The exact distribution of power among the coalition partners, or the parties that have agreed to form a government together, is the subject of negotiations between those parties. Before signing a **coalition agreement**, the document that governs the cooperation between the coalition partners as they govern together, representatives of these parties negotiate not only the number of ministers each party will provide but also which ministries each will hold, as well as the general outlines of the policy agenda that will guide their government.

Coalition cabinets rest on the foundation of carefully worked-out agreements between the parties that constitute them, but those agreements can never fully specify policy decisions in advance. Hence, coalition cabinets engage in group decision making processes. They bargain and persuade, occasionally they concur, and at other times they deadlock. Such deadlock can have consequences far beyond the policy issue itself. Failure to reach agreement on one important policy problem can spell the end of the coalition government when the representatives of the party that cannot get its way threaten to abandon the coalition. If they make good on their threat, the government falls. This is a high price to pay for disagreement, because it necessitates at a minimum another round of negotiations for a new coalition agreement—with no guarantee that all ministers will be reappointed to a ministerial post—but it can possibly also lead to a new round of elections.[63]

The fact that there can be such a dramatic consequence to the inability to reach agreement affects the dynamics within the coalition. It can give the smaller, or junior, party influence beyond its relative strength in the coalition. In essence, the junior party is in a position to "blackmail" the larger, or senior, party into agreement, assuming that the senior coalition partner would prefer to continue its government role. A more positive interpretation is to view the junior coalition partner as providing a corrective by not permitting the senior coalition partner to always get its way or push through its own policy agenda.

It is important to note that junior parties do not have significant influence on every single decision. Not much is known about the circumstances that permit junior coalition partners to place their stamp on policy, but it appears that the threat to abandon the coalition is an important strategy for exercising disproportionate power.[64] Furthermore, when the senior coalition party is internally divided about the preferred policy option but the junior coalition is united and sides with the faction of the senior party that most resembles their own position, the junior party can have a distinct influence on the decision. Finally, the distribution of ministries matters also. If the junior party has a share of the important, or core, ministries (like foreign affairs, defense, or economics) roughly equivalent to the share of core ministries held by the senior coalition partner, then the junior coalition partner can exercise greater influence than when it is largely relegated to politically peripheral ministries—such as a ministry of culture.[65] The politics of joint governance through coalition cabinets show that such governments are particularly vulnerable: disagreements over foreign policy can, and occasionally do, lead to the dissolution of government.

Whether policy makers function within the institutional constraints of coalition governments or guide a leader who has been able to structure the advisory system that surrounds her or him, in each case the institutional arrangements have an influence on the decision making process. No institutional arrangement is perfect; each has its own advantages and pitfalls. How well each institutional arrangement works will depend on the leader's ability to use the system to its full potential. And this, in turn, depends on how well the leader's personality is suited to the institutional arrangements. It also depends on wisely chosen advisors, who understand the institutional framework in which they operate and the person (or persons) for whom they are working. But even under the best of circumstances, foreign policy outcomes depend on more than good decision making. Domestic and international constraints also play a role in determining whether policy decisions lead to the desired outcome.

Chapter Summary

- Leaders are embedded in the institutions of government. There are three executive management styles: formalistic, competitive, and collegial. Each requires a certain leader personality to work well and avoid that style's disadvantages.
- Government decision making can be conceptualized in terms of the rational policy, organizational process, and bureaucratic politics models.
- Small groups of advisors can function in different ways. Groups can variously be depicted as think tanks and command centers.
- Advisors in small groups may engage in various different patterns of interaction, such as bargaining, persuasion, concurrence, or deadlock. These processes can alternatively lead to an integrative, subset, or dominant solution.
- In coalition governments, which are unique to a subset of parliamentary systems, junior (or smaller) coalition partners can under certain circumstances have extraordinary influence over decision making.

Terms

Decision units
Formalistic approach
Competitive approach
Collegial approach
Presidential system
Parliamentary system
Electoral system
Coalition cabinet
Cabinet government
Collective responsibility
Coalition
Rational policy model
Organizational process model
Bureaucratic politics model
Standard operating procedures
Groups
Think tank
Command center
Bargaining
Integrative solution

Subset solution
Concurrence
Dominant solution
Satisfice(d)
Groupthink
Deadlock
Persuasion
Coalition partners
Coalition agreement

Study Questions

1. What ways for organizing the executive have been identified? Which of these approaches is best? Why?
2. Does final responsibility for foreign policy decision making always rest in the hands of one person? If so, whose? If not, who or what has final authority?
3. If the role of the government bureaucracy politically neutral? Why or why not?
4. What are the roles of small groups of top level advisors in the foreign policy decision making process?
5. Is foreign policy decision making invariably characterized by bargaining? What other group dynamics might occur?
6. How does the authority structure in coalition cabinets differ from those in presidential systems (or even single party parliamentary government)? What are the implications for decision making?

Suggestions for Further Reading

Decision units are conceptualized and explained in Hermann and Hermann, "Who Makes Foreign Policy Decisions and How: An Empirical Inquiry," and Hermann, Hermann, and Hagan, "How Decision Units Shape Foreign Policy Behavior."

Classic works on the organization of the (American) executive are Johnson, Managing the White House: An Intimate Study of the Presidency, and George, *Presidential Decisionmaking in Foreign Policy: The Effective Use of Information and Advice*. A more recent work in this area is Mitchell, "Centralizing Advisory Systems: Presidential Influence and the U.S. Foreign Policy Decision-making Process."

The dynamics of advisory groups are the subject of Kowert, *Groupthink or Deadlock: When Do Leaders Learn from Their Advisors?*, and Garrison, *Games Advisors Play: Foreign Policy in the Nixon and Carter Administrations.*

Decision making in coalition government is the subject of Kaarbo, "Power and Influence in Foreign Policy Decision Making: The Role of Junior Coalition Partners in German and Israeli Foreign Policy."

Notes

1. See Truman Presidential Museum & Library, "'The Buck Stops Here' Desk Sign."
2. Truman, "The President's Farewell Address to the American People."
3. Hermann, Hermann, and Hagan, "How Decision Units Shape Foreign Policy Behavior"; see also Kaarbo, "Power and Influence in Foreign Policy Decision Making."
4. Herman, Herman, and Hagan, "How Decision Units Shape Foreign Policy Behavior," 311.
5. Truman, "The President's Farewell Address to the American People."
6. Clapham, *Haile-Selassie's Government*, 48.
7. Ibid., 53–54.
8. Ibid., 48.
9. George, *Presidential Decisionmaking in Foreign Policy*, 150.
10. Ibid., 149–50.
11. Hermann and Preston, "Presidents, Advisers, and Foreign Policy," 75–96; see also Hermann, "Presidential Leadership Style."
12. Hart, "From Analysis to Reform," 311.
13. Kowert, *Groupthink or Deadlock*, 21.
14. Johnson, *Managing the White House*, 233.
15. George, *Presidential Decisionmaking in Foreign Policy*; Johnson, *Managing the White House*; see also Mitchell, "Centralizing Advisory Systems."
16. Hermann and Preston, "Presidents, Advisers, and Foreign Policy," 78; Johnson, *Managing the White House*, 4.
17. George, *Presidential Decisionmaking in Foreign Policy*, 165; Johnson, *Managing the White House*, 6.
18. Johnson, *Managing the White House*, 5–6.
19. George, *Presidential Decisionmaking in Foreign Policy*, 157–8; Johnson, *Managing the White House*, 6–8.
20. Perham, Foreword to Clapham, *Haile-Selassie's Government*, xi.
21. Marcus, *A History of Ethiopia*, 182.
22. Ibid.
23. Ibid., 181.
24. Ibid.
25. Clapham, *Haile-Selassie's Government*, 54.

26. Tiruneh, *The Ethiopian Revolution*, 58.

27. Clapham, *Haile-Selassie's Government*, 57.

28. Ibid.

29. Johnson, *Managing the White House*, 236.

30. See Lijphart, *Patterns of Democracy*; Lijphart, *Parliamentary versus Presidential Government*.

31. Kowert, *Groupthink or Deadlock*, 155; see also the classic treatment of bureaucratic politics in Allison, "Conceptual Models and the Cuban Missile Crisis" or his *Essence of Decision*.

32. Garrison, *Games Advisors Play*, 17.

33. Allison, "Conceptual Models"; see also Allison, *Essence of Decision*, or Allison and Zelikow, *Essence of Decision*.

34. Allison, "Conceptual Models"; see also Allison, *Essence of Decision*, or Allison and Zelikow, *Essence of Decision*.

35. Hart et al., "Foreign Policy-making at the Top."

36. Hermann et al., "Resolve, Accept, or Avoid."

37. Kowert, *Groupthink or Deadlock*, 162.

38. Hart et al., "Foreign Policy-making at the Top," 13–14; see also Hermann et al., "Resolve, Accept, or Avoid."

39. Hart et al., "Foreign Policy-making at the Top," 13; see also Garrison, *Games Advisors Play*.

40. Hart et al., "Foreign Policy-making at the Top," 14–17; see also Herman et al., "Who Leads Matters."

41. Welch, "Culture and Emotion," 207.

42. Hart et al., "Foreign Policy-making at the Top," 21–22.

43. Ibid., 22.

44. Ibid., 17–19.

45. Ibid., 22–24.

46. Kowert, *Groupthink or Deadlock*, 160–1.

47. Herman et al., "Resolve, Accept, or Avoid," 137.

48. Allison and Halperin, "Bureaucratic Politics," 56.

49. Kaarbo, "Power and Influence."

50. Herman et al., "Resolve, Accept, or Avoid."

51. Simon, *The Sciences of the Artificial*.

52. Hart, Stern, and Sundelius, *Beyond Groupthink*; Hart, "Irving Janis' *Victims of Groupthink*"; Janis, *Groupthink*.

53. Perlmutter, "The Presidential Political Center and Foreign Policy"; Richards, "Coordination and Shared Mental Models," 261.

54. Hoyt, "The Political Manipulation of Group Composition"; Krasner, "Are Bureaucracies Important?"

55. Garrison, "Framing Foreign Policy Alternatives."

56. Garrison, *Games Advisors Play*, 17.

57. Bendor and Hammond, "Rethinking Allison's Models"; Rhodes, "Do Bureaucratic Politics Matter?"; Garrison, *Games Advisors Play*.

Chapter 5

Leaders in Context I: Domestic Constraints on Foreign Policy Making

Chapter Preview

- Explains how relations among government bureaucracies constrain foreign policy making.
- Explains the impact of domestic audiences on foreign policy decision making.
- Explains the role of the media in framing and focusing pubic attention on foreign policy.
- Explains the influence of national history and culture on foreign policy decision making.
- Explains the relevance of the democratic peace proposition for foreign policy making.

You Can't Always Get What You Want

Well before the United States was attacked at Pearl Harbor, President Roosevelt had become convinced that the Axis powers (Germany, Italy, and Japan) could not be stopped without U.S. involvement in World War II. He also knew that Congress would not permit the United States to enter the war at that point. In the period between the two World Wars, the United States had returned to **isolationism**, which meant that the country avoided an active role in world affairs. This policy was supported by the domestic public as well as the Congress, which made it difficult for President Roosevelt to get what he wanted.

This situation is not unusual. Leaders almost always face domestic constraints on foreign policy making. Policy options must not only respond appropriately to the situation, they must also be acceptable at home. In evaluating policy options, decision makers must therefore consider not only whether such options constitute effective and appropriate responses to the situation, they must also evaluate how such options will be received by the domestic audience. Depending on the country and the structural relationship between the executive and legislative branches, this may include the ability of the executive to convince the legislature, as well as a thorough understanding of domestic constituencies outside of government.

In chapter 3, we briefly alluded to the influence of domestic political considerations in decision making when we discussed the polihueristic theory. You may remember that this theory posits that the decision process is divided into two stages. During the first stage, options are excluded if they are not acceptable on one critically important dimension. Almost invariably, what is critically important to a leader is political survival.[1] In order to remain in office, leaders need the support, or at a minimum the acquiescence, of the domestic public. Hence, options that a leader judges to be unacceptable to (important segments of) the domestic audience will be eliminated during the first stage of the decision making process. To return to our example, President Roosevelt might have been convinced that the United States needed to come to the aid of the countries fighting the Axis powers, but he also knew that proposing direct American military involvement was not a politically feasible option. He knew he would not be able to convince either Congress or the domestic public. In other words, Roosevelt's options were constrained by the isolationist attitude that prevailed domestically.

Constraints narrow a leader's options, but can also lead to creative solutions. Before the attack on Pearl Harbor, the U.S. Congress passed the Lend-Lease Act, which provided for the shipment of large amounts of war materials, including not just ammunition and guns but also tanks and planes, to the Allied powers. It was a clever idea that stretched the boundaries of the domestic constraints to—and perhaps beyond—their limits. It placed the United States squarely on the side of the Allies at a time when the country was officially neutral with regard to the war that was raging in Europe. The lend-lease policy enabled Roosevelt to act on an international threat at a time when the domestic public and Congress were hesitant to involve the United States in wars between other countries. The policy provided support to the Allied war effort without directly involving the United States, making it a solution acceptable to Congress. The Lend-Lease Act shows that constraints may not just narrow the available policy options but may also lead to innovative policy responses.

How constraints are managed depends on leaders and their advisors. Their collective ability to evaluate the domestic environment and perceive not only the limitations but also the opportunities it presents affect the foreign policy decisions they make. In this chapter, the focus is on domestic constraints, and in chapter 6 we investigate how international constraints influence foreign policy decision making. Both are important, and foreign policy makers always navigate between domestic and international pressures.[2]

As you read both this and chapter 6, consider that decision makers are products as well as representatives of their society. Like all citizens of their society, they have been shaped by it through their upbringing and education, and they may have lesser or greater awareness of the extent to which their understanding of history and international affairs is culturally determined. To be sure, there are decision makers who have attained a great deal of comparative insight and who have achieved a deep appreciation for the different perceptual lenses with which the leaders of various countries view the world. But such insights cannot be assumed, as the Argentine decision making during the Malvinas/Falklands crisis demonstrates (see chapter 3).

More typically, decision makers have a sophisticated understanding of the political system of their own country. They also strive to achieve a thorough understanding of domestic constituencies. This is true irrespective of the system of government, albeit that the press freedom associated with democracies makes it easier for decision makers to acquire information about the reaction of the domestic public to their decisions and proposals.[3]

Hemmed in by the Political System?

At the end of chapter 4, we discussed bargaining among coalition partners. Whether or not a coalition cabinet is needed depends on the electoral system, or the rules that govern the elections of countries with parliamentary government. Countries that elect their representatives from single-member districts usually end up with two dominant political parties, although additional parties often do exist. Countries that elect multiple members of the legislature from one district are more likely to have a larger number of political parties, but each of those parties tends to control a smaller proportion of the seats in the parliament. When no single party obtains a majority in the legislature, a coalition of two or more political parties is needed to obtain the majority required to pass legislation and to form a government. In other words, how the members of parliament are elected has consequences for the type of government that results. Whether that government consists of a coalition cabinet or a cabinet dominated by a single party in turn influences the political decision making process. In chapter 4, we discussed the possibility that the junior coalition partner exercises influence beyond its numerical presence in the cabinet. This gives a junior coalition partner power beyond its numerical strength within the coalition.

A country's domestic political structure affects foreign policy in other ways as well. Unlike the advisory system or the governing coalition, leaders often have less direct influence over the structure and functioning of the agencies that make up the government bureaucracy. Yet much of their decision making is affected by government agencies: not only are agencies often responsible for implementing decisions, they are also an important source of information. Government agencies may facilitate the emergence of new ideas or make change difficult to achieve. In short, the government bureaucracy frequently functions as a constraint on leaders and their advisors.

To illustrate, we discuss the structural elements of the government bureaucracy and its constituent parts that influence both the flow of ideas and policy implementation. As you have probably discerned, the government's foreign policy bureaucracy consists of many organizations and agencies. The interrelationship between these agencies influences the capacity of any one agency to propagate its ideas beyond its own limited sphere.[4] Agencies can be classified as insulated or embedded. An **insulated agency** is an autonomous or independent entity within the government bureaucracy, which means that it has its own resources and organizational structure.[5] Agencies of this type have their own staff and develop their own criteria for advancement within the organization—they develop their own organizational culture, in other words. The U.S. Peace Corps is an example of such an insulated agency.

An **embedded agency**, on the other hand, may have a clear mandate, but is created as a subunit of a larger entity. As part of that larger entity, it will have a structure that is largely determined by the organization of which it is a part, and it will also depend on that larger organization for resources. Embedded agencies have less autonomy and are less able to develop their own organizational identity, criteria for advancement, or other unique structural features. The Bureau of Human Rights and Humanitarian Affairs, for example, was created as an embedded agency within the U.S. State Department.

Yet both the Peace Corps and the Bureau of Human Rights and Humanitarian Affairs are agencies that were established to serve a clear mission: both are **idea-based organizations**, rather than **interest-based organizations**. An idea-based organization is created to serve a specific goal: both its objective and its strategy for achieving that goal are usually widely shared by those who work for the organization.[6] Idea-based organizations often attempt to persuade those in other agencies within the government. If they can do so in ways that resonate with their counterparts in other agencies, an idea-based agency can over time influence other agencies within the government bureaucracy. In contrast, representatives of an interest-based organization can bargain with those in other organizations and, depending on its power and stature within the government bureaucracy, as well as the effectiveness of the bargaining strategies, may have greater or lesser success at doing so. In the end, the norms and values of idea-based organizations give such entities an advantage in their interactions with other agencies within the government. This is especially true for embedded idea-based organizations, although it is also more difficult for such agencies to successfully maintain their unique mission and identity over time. Maintaining a core identity is easier for insulated idea-based organizations, but it is also more difficult for such agencies to propagate their ideas successfully to other government agencies. The Peace Corps, which was founded in 1961, has been able to carve out a unique mission and autonomous identity, but has had little impact on other foreign policy agencies within the U.S. government. The founding ideas of the Peace Corps revolved around the promotion of development and, as a result, the creation of goodwill among allies in the developing world. In this, it was very much a creature of the Cold War, with its focus on allies and enemies. The direct action of the Peace Corps Volunteers was at the heart of the agency's strategy. Despite its survival and continued relevance, the Peace Corps has not had much impact beyond its own activities. It has influenced neither decision making regarding foreign aid and development nor U.S. foreign policy as a whole.[7]

The Bureau of Human Rights and Humanitarian Affairs, on the other hand, ultimately altered U.S. foreign policy to include human rights as an "important component of the American national interest."[8] This did not happen overnight: the bureau was established in 1977 during the Presidency of Jimmy Carter. It initially had highly conflictual relationships with other bureaus within the State Department.[9] In those early years, the political appointees of the bureau came from civil rights backgrounds and were unfamiliar with the diplomatic traditions of the State Department. During the subsequent Presidency of Ronald Reagan, the mission of the Bureau of Human Rights and Humanitarian Affairs was changed to no longer include economic rights. In this altered form, the bureau now focused on human rights violations and civil and political rights. By the end of the second Reagan administration, the bureau had begun to influence U.S. foreign policy, although the bureau had also moved away from its founding ideas.[10]

The examples of the Peace Corps and the Bureau of Human Rights and Humanitarian Affairs illustrate the potential power of idea-based organizations; they also illustrate that their placement within the larger government bureaucracy influences their capacity to propagate their ideas. An insulated agency, such as the Peace Corps, is more likely to stay true to its founding principles but less likely to infuse other agencies within the bureaucracy with its ideas. An embedded agency, such as the Bureau of Human Rights and Humanitarian Affairs, is less likely to stay true to its founding ideas, but more likely to infuse other agencies with its ideas, provided it remains in existence in some form. In sum, the structural relationships among the various agencies within the government bureaucracy influence whether new ideas remain isolated in small corners or provide the impetus for new directions in a state's foreign policy more broadly, including funneling innovative ideas up the chain of command for consideration by the leader and his or her immediate advisors.

Whether an agency is created as an insulated or embedded entity is a political decision and is subject to the same decision processes that characterize all political decision making. The example shows that the agency-creating process is not neutral. It has consequences for the functioning of the agency and especially for the likelihood that the agency's founding ideas will survive and influence policy. The structural relationships between agencies influence whether ideas thrive in isolation, have a more general influence on the state's foreign policy, or become muted and have little or no impact. The bottom line is that "ideas do not float freely";[11] they flourish or flounder depending on the institutional context within which they find themselves. In addition to the nature of government and the structure of the bureaucracy, the interrelation between a government and its people, as well as the "values and norms embedded in its political culture," matter in foreign policy decision making.[12] The subsequent sections of this chapter address these issues.

How Domestic Constituencies Influence Foreign Policy

Domestic pressures may take several different forms. There are explicit pressures exerted by interest groups, the media, and public opinion. The degree to which these domestic constituencies influence foreign policy is difficult to gauge. On the one hand, decision makers are constrained by the pressures exerted by domestic constituencies but, on the other hand, decision makers also try to set the agenda and shape the attitudes of these constituencies.[13] To what degree are domestic constituencies manipulable by decision makers? To what degree do they form a constraint on decision makers?

The relationship between decision makers and domestic constituencies is shaped in part by the political institutions of the society. Authoritarian governments provide very few, if any, avenues for citizens to explicitly influence foreign policy. This does not mean that the public has no impact, but it does mean that its impact is likely to be largely indirect or implied. Decision makers in authoritarian societies face few explicit domestic constraints. Citizens cannot join interest groups, it is difficult for polling firms to keep their pulse on the public's opinions and attitudes—if such polling is permitted at all—and the media are often not free. Despite this, leaders in such societies do seek to understand their public, if only because this helps them stay in power. They present foreign policy problems and decisions in terms of verbal imagery that they believe will resonate with their domestic audience and they, too, try to convince their domestic audience that their policies are in the national interest, as defined by the leader.

One problem faced by leaders of authoritarian societies, as well as **semi-authoritarian regimes**, is that, because such societies generally lack a free press, they are deprived of "credible information about public opinion."[14] Semi-authoritarian regimes are characterized by a "hollow" version of democracy. Such countries may hold elections and maintain a set of institutions that give the appearance of democracy without providing either citizens or the press with the freedoms necessary to foster political debate. In other words, semi-authoritarian regimes go through the motions but lack the substance of democracy.[15] Interestingly, leaders in such countries "are forced to listen to society, if only to be forewarned of potential opposition. These regimes may not be truly accountable to their publics . . . , but they are responsive—and perhaps vulnerable—to them."[16] In other words, the public may have few opportunities to make its opinions known, but this does not mean that public opinion is irrelevant to decision makers. It does mean that they must gauge it indirectly.

In addition to the indirect and implicit influence of domestic constraints in authoritarian societies that lack a free press, leaders in such countries are likely to pay far more attention to certain segments of the population than to others. Consider that the support of the military is often crucial to maintaining power—or perhaps more accurately: crucial to not losing it to the decision of military officers to stage a coup. This makes it important to understand the opinions among that segment of the population and among those civilian elites who could exercise influence on those in the military. Widespread dissatisfaction among a population, either with the leader or with the conditions within the country, could be (and has been) used by military officers as a justification for the overthrow of a leader. Why the military? In societies where people are not free to create (political) organizations, it may be difficult for citizens to build the organizational infrastructure necessary to plan effective action against a leader. The military differs from other groups in the society, because it is not only organized but also has ready access to weapons and the training to use them.

Semi-authoritarian societies differ from authoritarian societies in that there are wider possibilities for protest. The media are generally not fully free, although the press in such countries can be surprisingly bold in its criticism of government decision makers. Semi-authoritarian governments differ in terms of how much press freedom they are willing to tolerate. They may react to criticism by shutting down media outlets and jailing journalists. Despite such perils to freedom of expression, there is a "surprising array of collective action around the world in precisely those regimes that have ostensibly choked off avenues of protest," with much of that action aimed at changing policy rather than at overthrowing the government.[17]

The domestic audience in countries governed by nondemocratic regimes—whether authoritarian or semi-authoritarian—has fewer formal and readily available avenues for expressing dissent. As a result, leaders of such countries face fewer explicit domestic constraints than decision makers in democratic societies, but they ignore their domestic constituencies at their peril. Governing requires, at minimum, the acquiescence of the public.

In democratic societies, the public has more avenues formally available to express dissent. The degree to which such opinion is expressed, as well as the degree to which it constrains decision makers, depends on both institutional and societal factors.[18] The structure of the political institutions is more open to societal influence in some societies than in others. Open institutional structures provide greater access and more contact points for interest groups and other societal actors and hence more opportunity to influence decision making. For example, the American public has a greater impact on its country's foreign policy than the French public, which confronts a far more centralized set of political institutions.[19]

On the other hand, it has been argued that foreign policy is a "thin interest-group environment," meaning that, compared to domestic politics, interest groups are "smaller, less organized, less wealthy, and by extension less influential."[20] Not only are there relatively fewer interest groups, decision makers are also less clearly constrained by public opinion in foreign policy decision making than in domestic politics.[21] There are two reasons for this: One, citizens often perceive foreign policy as something that is quite distant. They are often poorly informed about international affairs.[22] Two, there is a distinct "asymmetry between what leaders know and what the public knows."[23] Indeed, it has been argued that the conduct of diplomacy requires secrecy.[24] As a result, the public has often been willing to defer to leaders on foreign policy, believing that leaders have more information and therefore deeper insight into the situation than they do.

Yet even if the public is largely willing to defer to leaders and is often inattentive to, as well as uninformed about, foreign policy, it is not altogether without relevance.[25] Policy makers try to anticipate the public's reactions to foreign policy decisions. At the same time, decision makers often also try to mold public opinion by presenting problems from a particular perspective. The public's impact on foreign policy is thus dependent on a delicate dance between decision makers' efforts to anticipate public opinion, their attempts to shape public reactions, and efforts by (segments of) the public to shape the set of options decision makers will perceive to be viable strategies. As we shall see in the next section, the public's impact on foreign policy can be more imagined than real because it "often arises from a circular process in which government officials respond to polling opinions, anticipated or perceived majorities, and priorities that many of them helped create."[26]

The limited impact of public opinion also tends to occur at specific phases of the decision making process, rather than occurring equally throughout. First, it is important to distinguish crisis and non-crisis foreign policy problems. The former usually focus the attention of the domestic audience for a short period of time, when the issue is highlighted in the media, while the latter can occupy decision makers for long periods of time without receiving much media attention during most of the decision process. Second, although it appears that the domestic audience plays a role at specific junctures of the decision making process, there is some debate as to when its impact is felt most clearly. One scholar argues that policy makers can usually define a problem's contours without much explicit attention to or input from the public,[27] while another argues that public opinion has a direct impact on getting issues on the agenda.[28] Both points of view make sense. Recent attention to the AIDS crisis and its impact on economic development and political stability in Africa owes much to celebrities like U2's Bono focusing the media's—and therefore the public's—attention on this continent.

On the other hand, the path that ultimately led to the war in Iraq first depended on the U.S. government's portrayal of Saddam Hussein's regime as tied to terrorism. Whether or not such a connection did indeed exist prior to the invasion is a matter of debate. Nevertheless, previous U.S. administrations had defined Iraq as a **rogue state**. What is a rogue state? There are no clear and transparent criteria for defining a state as such, but most countries that are classified as rogue states do not conduct their foreign relations according to the conventions of international diplomacy.[29] As a result, they are perceived as threats to international peace. The representation of Iraq as a rogue state—and later, more specifically, as tied to terrorism—was fostered largely by the U.S. government, rather than by public opinion. Hence, the problem representation phase in this case involved primarily the leader's circle of advisors. This suggests that crises and national security problems differ from other foreign policy issues in terms of how and when public opinion matters. In addition, it is often the leader and his or her immediate circle of advisors who define a situation as a crisis.

Although decision makers may have greater leeway in defining, or framing (see chapter 3), the problem during a crisis, the public's attention builds steadily and is usually greatest during the implementation phase.[30] This means that decision makers have less freedom in selecting a policy response. The decision may therefore "sacrifice strategic effectiveness to pacify a highly attentive domestic audience."[31] Close scrutiny also means that the public wants to see results. In other words, success (or failure) will not go unnoticed. Consider that the U.S. war in Iraq continues to make headlines well into 2007. Although there was quite a lot of public support at the beginning of the war in 2003, as time went on and a definitive conclusion to the war remained elusive, public support has waned. In other words, the public has been acutely aware of how the decision to invade Iraq has turned out.

In contrast, in non-crisis situations the public's attention usually starts to wane before the implementation of a decision. Instead, attention will be greatest during the decision phase, which means that decision makers are scrutinized as they weigh the various policy options but the public begins to lose interest before the implementation of the decision.[32] Failure of the policy may go unnoticed, and it will take effort to focus the public's attention on success. Most U.S. citizens know far less about the country's policy regarding the AIDS crisis in Africa than they do about its policy regarding Iraq.

These patterns of attention suggest that different types of policy problems present decision makers with different kinds of constraints. Leaders may choose to launch bold initiatives in response to non-crisis foreign policy problems even if they know such initiatives may not come to fruition, because the public will lose attention well before the fate of such an initiative is evident. In crises, however, public attention tends to crest at the implementation phase. Decision makers are likely to choose policies that are acceptable to the public, even if they consider such policies less optimal than alternative options. Remember that the poliheuristic theory suggests that during stage one of the decision process options are discarded if they do not meet one important criterion. For most leaders, the ability to maintain public support for their policies is a critical dimension that policy options must be able to meet.[33]

One caveat is probably in order: even if decision makers will consider only policy options they think will be acceptable to their domestic audience, this does not guarantee that the public will indeed support such options or continue to do so over time. Decision makers try to make educated guesses about whether they can persuade the public to support certain policies, but such assessments can be wrong. Similarly, decision makers make assessments about the likely success of policy options. Even when such assessments are done carefully and use the best information and intelligence available, the information is often incomplete. Remember that foreign policy problems are often best characterized as ill-structured problems (see chapter 3). So, while decision makers will discard any option they do not consider acceptable to the domestic public during the first stage of the decision process, this does not guarantee that the option they choose will continue to receive public support.

Framing the News

How do decision makers evaluate public attentiveness and public support? Quite often, they gauge this by the amount of media coverage a specific issue receives.[34] This gives the media enormous potential to focus not just the public's but also policy makers' attention. How this power of the press is used depends on the media tradition of a specific society. The press has greater freedom in some societies than in others. In democracies, the media usually face few, if any, restrictions. Differences exist nonetheless. In some countries, the media place their emphasis on balanced—or even objective—reporting, whereas in other countries the media are overtly partisan and freely mix commentary into their reporting.[35] In both cases, decision makers are likely to pay close attention to the media as one important way of keeping their finger on the pulse of their society and to gauge whether, and to what degree, the domestic audience presents a constraint with regard to a specific foreign policy problem. Indeed, the lack of press freedom deprives not only the public of information, it also makes it more difficult for decision makers to evaluate whether that public is likely to support their policy initiatives.[36]

Keep in mind, however, that the relationship between decision makers and public opinion is complex: decision makers need public support for their policies, but their assessments of public opinion follow their own attempts to shape that opinion. Moreover, the media do not merely reflect the views of decision makers. They choose what to report and how to report it. In doing so, they function as an intermediary that influences how the public frames or represents the issues.[37]

Consider how Canadian newspapers reported speeches by U.S. President Bush in the immediate aftermath of 9/11.[38] Although papers sometimes print transcripts of entire speeches, they often report on a presidential speech by highlighting specific quotes from it. When they do so, reporters select certain statements for quotation and not others. How do they choose which statements to incorporate into their story? A systematic analysis of reports on President Bush's post 9/11 statements shows that Canadian reporters tended to select those quotes that resonated with Canadian political values.[39] This means that a statement from a presidential speech is more likely to be quoted in a Canadian newspaper if it "reinforces a widely held value or set of values or reinforces one position in an ongoing debate about foreign policy values."[40] Conversely, statements that do not resonate with Canadian political values are much less likely to be cited.[41] This congruence is not the same as biased reporting. Although the Canadian reporters tended to privilege statements that fit with Canadian political values, they most often reported them in neutral language.[42] This suggests that there was not an overt attempt to portray the president's speeches in a certain light but that they selected quotes that they anticipated to be of interest to their audience. In other words, their definition of what was important in the President's speech was guided by the Canadian political values these reporters shared with their audience.

The example illustrates not only that the media function as an intermediary between the government and the public, it also suggests that the media's role is circumscribed by the **political culture** of a society.[43] Political culture is a rather amorphous concept that denotes the shared political values of a society's people. It is what led Canadian reporters to focus on certain quotes in President Bush's post 9/11 speeches that fit well with Canadian values. For instance, Bush advocated respect for Islam in these speeches, which resonated with Canadian multicultural values and was quoted extensively in Canadian newspapers.[44] In other words, the media tend to frame news in a way that is congruent with the political culture of its target audience.[45] Or rather, reporters frame their news stories according to their interpretation of that political culture as members of that society.

Political culture does not necessarily provide straightforward guidance.[46] In some situations it will. At those times, leaders can fairly easily frame the problem in such a way that they achieve broad agreement on the problem representation among their audience. At other times, the guidance from a country's political culture is ambiguous. This makes it possible for the media to present alternative points of view. The media thrive on controversy, but they also need informants to help them present an alternative point of view. Such informants are more readily available when they perceive public opinion to be undecided, or divided, on the issue than when they perceive the public to be solidly behind a leader. Ironically, this makes it more difficult for the media to perform its role as watchdog when it matters most. When leaders and their public have the greatest tendency to think alike, it is quite important for the media to encourage both to think critically so as to avoid policy failures.

The media do make an effort to do this, often by relying on criticisms from abroad. Whether such dissent receives attention has long depended on the perception of such sources as credible and authoritative.[47] As more and more people gain access to the Internet, and with it to sources world-wide, "the significance of foreign dissent on U.S. policy decisions may be greater in the twenty-first century than in the past."[48] This means that, more than in the past, the constraints on foreign policy making are inter-national as well as domestic.

Before turning to the international constraints on foreign policy mak-ing in greater detail, however, it is necessary to delve more fully into the constraints placed on foreign policy making by a society's political culture or, more specifically, the impact of national history and culture, as well as the well-supported notion that democracies do not go to war with one another.

A Window from Which to View the World

The concept of political culture and the notion that certain statements res-onate better with audiences in certain countries suggest that there are dif-ferences in the way the citizens of different countries view the world. This is true also for decision makers, who are products of their societies as well as representatives of their societies. Both citizens and decision makers have been shaped by their upbringing and education. Both may have lesser or greater awareness of the extent to which their understanding of history and international affairs is culturally determined.

Consider, for instance, the way that Americans and Europeans draw the world map: they place Europe and Africa in the center and split the globe across the Pacific Ocean. That image of the world map is used at all levels of education. It is so familiar that most citizens in the West never consider that this map might look very strange to people elsewhere. But it does. Students in China are taught global geography with a map that places their very large country near the center of the map and splits the globe across the Atlantic Ocean.[49] Whichever map you have been raised with, the first encounter with the other map will require a bit of an adjustment. There is nothing natural or inevitable about placing any specific country or continent at the center of the map, but the map to which you are accustomed will *seem* more natural. That sense of the customary as natural or inevitable is at the heart of enculturation. To the degree that foreign policy decision makers remain unaware that their way of understanding the world is not universally shared, they will also remain unaware that they are hemmed in to a certain perspective. This can have disastrous consequences, as it did for the leaders of Argentina during the Malvinas crisis (see chapter 3).

The discussion of the Europe-centered and China-centered world maps illustrates in a tangible manner that we are accustomed to viewing the world in a particular way. It also illustrates that it is often difficult, for citizens and decision makers alike, to understand that what is customary is not the only possible perspective. The failure to do so can lead to foreign policy failures, as was illustrated by the case of the Malvinas/Falklands crisis in chapter 3. Conversely, the ability to grasp the vantage point of the decision makers of other countries can substantially increase the likelihood of successful foreign policy making. Effective foreign policy making, in other words, requires the ability to see the world from multiple perspectives.

It is relatively easy to show how differently centered world maps can alter one's perspective. The role of national history and culture in the way we view the world is less easy to demonstrate. First, it is important to note that **national history** consists not merely, and not most importantly, of facts. National history is characterized in important ways by the meanings that are conveyed through tales that, although fact-based, are employed to communicate common values the society seeks to instill in the next generation. **Culture** is closely associated with national history: culture denotes the set of values that is transmitted through the teaching of national history. At the heart of a culture are generalized beliefs and attitudes about one's own state, about other states, and about the actual and desirable relationships between these.[50] These values and beliefs provide a "guiding constraint" on problem representation, as well as other aspects of thought and the use of information in foreign policy decision making.[51]

Just because it is difficult to demonstrate that policy makers are constrained by their enculturation into a specific society does not mean that national history and culture do not play a role.[52] It does mean that history and culture are often overlooked as factors that shape foreign policy decisions.[53] And when such influences are referenced, they tend to be used as a catchall explanation for any differences in perception and problem representation between the decision makers of two countries. Used in that way, references to culture tend to caricature the foreign policy responses of the leaders of other countries and are no better than stereotyping. Taking the impact of national history and culture seriously requires a deep understanding of the way in which national history reaches into the present to shape the sensibilities of leaders, in terms of both their own reflexive reactions and their perceptions of what their domestic public will accept. It additionally requires the recognition that decision makers, on the basis of personality and life experience, interpret their national history and culture in their own way. Hence, history and culture are not fixed guiding stars, although they do shape the boundaries of what is perceived as possible. They determine how decision makers think and judge, as well as their attitude toward information and intelligence.[54]

Untangling the impact of national history and culture of foreign policy can be difficult. It requires the ability to place oneself into the perspective of the leaders of another country. To illustrate the influence of history and culture on foreign policy decision making, we will make a comparison between two small states, Belgium and the Netherlands.[55] These two countries are both located in Western Europe. They are roughly equal in size, especially as compared to other surrounding states. The Netherlands is slightly larger and also more densely populated than Belgium. Both are heavily dependent on international trade, which makes it necessary to maintain positive relations with current and potential future trading partners. Both are democracies with **constitutional monarchies**. This means that the power of their monarchs has been circumscribed by a constitution that specifies the separation of powers between the various branches of their governments. In each, the monarch has a largely, but not entirely, symbolic function, and the country is effectively governed by a coalition cabinet with the support of the parliament. On the basis of these similarities, it would be reasonable to suspect that these two countries tend to pursue comparable foreign policies. However, the leaders of the Netherlands tend to be more eager to play a role in international affairs than are Belgian politicians. In particular, Dutch leaders have endeavored to position their state as a leader in development cooperation. What might explain the eagerness of the Dutch to play a role on the world stage when the Belgians are content to conduct diplomacy behind the scenes?

First, there are significant differences in the founding histories of the two countries. The Dutch achieved national independence in 1648, after having been at war with their Spanish rulers since 1568.[56] The war overlaps with the Dutch success as a commercial-maritime power during the seventeenth century, which accounts for their eventual ability to win their political independence.[57] The Dutch pride themselves in having won their freedom by means of their own resources. Both the history of the Eighty Years' War and the riches of the seventeenth century are featured prominently in Dutch history. In addition, the glory days of the seventeenth century are well preserved in architectural landmarks, art, and artifacts.

The Belgian independence, on the other hand, was brokered in the 1830s by the leaders of the great powers of the time at an international conference in London. Although the Belgians themselves initiated the revolt against the rule and policies of the Dutch King William I, their independence was not won on the battlefield. Rather, the leaders assembled at the London Conference decided that a neutral and independent Belgium was the most desirable solution to the Belgian Revolt.[58]

In sum, the Dutch look back on a heroic history that is associated with the founding of their state, whereas the Belgians were from the very inception of their country dependent on the larger, more powerful states around them. The leaders of those big powers thoroughly reinforced that dependency with their demand that Belgium remain neutral in conflicts between them, so that the new country could not upset the balance of power in Europe by siding with—and thus strengthening—the military capabilities of any of them. Although it is difficult to draw immediate causal links between contemporary foreign policy and the historical events associated with the founding of each country, these national histories are suggestive—especially since they continue to be transmitted from one generation to the next. These histories teach each country's citizens something about the state's capacity to assert itself in the international environment.

The relationship each country has had with the developing world is also different. Both Belgium and the Netherlands possessed colonies. This is relevant because former colonizers often began their development cooperation policies with aid to their former colonies. It is therefore not unreasonable to think that countries with similar histories in this regard might exhibit similar development cooperation policies. A simple way to characterize such policies is the proportion of gross national income they spend on development aid, which is a generally accepted indicator of a state's generosity. Belgium's development aid constitutes a considerably lower proportion of its gross national income than the Dutch aid.[59] What might explain this?

History provides some possible clues. The colonial experiences of the two countries were quite different, both in terms of the length of time and the way in which colonialism was tied into the society and economy of each country. The Belgian King Leopold II, whom we first encountered in chapter 2, acquired the Belgian Congo (now called the Democratic Republic of the Congo) in 1885 as a personal possession, which he used largely to enrich himself.[60] The Belgian state was not involved in its administration until the colony was transferred to it in 1908.[61] In the aftermath of World War I, the Belgian state furthermore acquired mandates over Rwanda and Burundi, which lie on the Congo's eastern border. The Belgian colonial era ended in the early 1960s when first Zaire and subsequently Rwanda and Burundi acquired independence.[62] Thus, Belgian colonialism was relatively short-lived and initially driven by the monarch's personal ambitions.

In contrast, Dutch colonialism has roots extending back to the 1600s, when merchant marine companies established trade connections in both Southeast Asia and the Americas.[63] The profits made through these early ventures helped finance the military success that secured Dutch statehood. Not surprisingly, colonialism was closely tied to the mythology regarding the founding of the Dutch state and the emergence of a merchant middle class at a time when wealth was still widely defined in terms of the possession of land and the landed estates of the nobility. The focus during the early period was on trade rather than the acquisition of territory, but during the nineteenth century the Dutch did establish territorial control over Indonesia, Surinam, and the Netherlands Antilles.[64] In 1949, the Dutch reluctantly gave up control over Indonesia. The end of the Dutch colonial era came slower in the western hemisphere: Surinam did not acquire independence until 1975 and the Netherlands Antilles remain an "overseas territory."

The intense debate over Indonesia's independence in the immediate aftermath of World War II demonstrates that Dutch policy makers saw the possession of colonies as essential to the economic well being of the state, a frame that harkens back to the trade profits that financed the wars that secured Dutch statehood several centuries earlier. As they had tightened their territorial control, however, the Dutch had added a sense of a "civilizing" mission to their desire for profit. This sense of mission entails a vision of the colony's future that reshapes its society in terms of the colonizer's value system, an idea that has been largely discredited today. This added a certain duality to Dutch policy, which has been characterized as driven by both profit and moral principles.[65] After Indonesia, its largest and most profitable colony, became independent, the Dutch policy makers had a rethink both the basis of their economic survival as a trade-dependent country and the role of principles in their foreign policy. Moral principles found a new voice by justifying the Dutch role as a beacon for the rich countries to follow as more and more countries initiated development cooperation policies.[66]

Belgian foreign policy has never aspired to such a role. Some scholars see its foreign policy, as well as its development cooperation, as driven at times by short-term commercial expediency, which is perhaps not unreasonable for a country that is highly dependent on international trade for its economic well being.[67] Most also agree that Belgium is a loyal alliance partner within NATO and works within the international political and economic structures, such as those of the European Union (EU), rather than seeking to serve as any other state's beacon or guide.[68] In sum, Belgian foreign policy makers tend to focus more narrowly than do the Dutch decision makers on satisfying their country's political and economic interests rather than on embarking on crusades to influence, for instance, the conduct of the development cooperation policies of other wealthy states. Perhaps this is not surprising in light of the history of the founding of the Belgian state.

This comparison provides only a small snapshot of the impact of history on the broad traditions of foreign policy making by these two small states. The Dutch have not always been as assertive, and the Belgians have at times had greater impact. Individual decision makers within each country have disagreed about the direction of their country's foreign policy. On the whole, however, the policy makers of the two countries have conducted their foreign policies in very different ways. It would be overstating the facts to claim that this difference is *caused* by the differences in the founding histories, but it does appear that the foreign policies of the two countries each share a logical consistency with their founding histories.

Despite the difficulties in pinning down the precise impact of national history and culture, the comparison between Belgium and the Netherlands makes clear that decision makers do not have absolute freedom in selecting their course of action in response to a foreign policy problem. This also helps us understand the approach to evaluating policy options during stage one of the decision making process posited by the poliheuristic theory (introduced in chapter 3). This first stage of the decision making process is characterized by a noncompensatory decision rule. You'll remember that during this stage, an option will be discarded if it is unacceptable on one single, but critical, dimension. What makes certain options unacceptable? One of the aspects that guides decision makers' evaluations is whether or not they can convince their domestic public of the merits of a proposed policy. If they are convinced that it is impossible to explain a policy in a manner that will resonate with the domestic public—in other words, in a way that will make sense within the context of national history and culture—it is extremely likely that such an option will be discarded during the first stage of the decision making process.[69]

Remember that President Roosevelt had concluded that the United States could not stay on the sidelines during World War II, but that he also knew that it would be enormously difficult to convince the domestic public and the Congress of this. National history and culture assert their influence on a state's foreign policy: they provide both the domestic audience and decision makers with a specific window on the world. Put another way, history and culture affect the role that decision makers can conceive for their country to play in international affairs.[70]

Peaceful Democracies?

Just as national history and culture influence foreign policy making, so does the domestic political system. Earlier in this chapter, we discussed how the domestic audience constrains decision makers. We distinguished between different institutional arrangements in democracies, as well as between democracies, semi-authoritarian, and authoritarian countries, and pointed out that the domestic audience's ability to influence foreign policy varies across these. The domestic audience has a greater impact in political systems where decision makers are accountable to that audience, as is the case in democracies. Do note, however, that democracies vary in their institutional arrangements and, as a consequence, in the degree to which they are open to domestic influence. On the basis of both these variations in political institutions and variations in national history and culture, we might expect that the nature of the constraints placed on foreign policy decision makers by that domestic audience is highly idiosyncratic. In other words, there should be little reason to expect that the foreign policies of democracies share much in common.

Before we conclude that this is so, we should take a look at the democratic peace theory. This theory suggests that countries that are governed democratically are less war-prone than non-democracies. Empirical studies have demonstrated that democracies rarely, if ever, go to war with one another.[71] They do, however, engage in violent conflict with non-democracies as often as non-democracies engage in conflict with one another. What restrains the leaders of democratic states in their actions vis-à-vis other democratic states? There are two types of explanations: normative and structural.[72]

Normative explanations for the democratic peace stress that decision makers in democratic states have become accustomed to resolving conflict by nonviolent means. Such societies value "tolerance, compromise, and sharing power."[73] Although democracies may be constituted differently and have different histories, they share basic norms. In disputes, leaders of democratic states expect that their counterparts in other democratic states will apply the same norms of behavior to which they each adhere domestically in their foreign policy behavior. However, the leaders of democratic states will not approach confrontations with leaders of nondemocratic states with that same set of expectations. In fact, they may adopt nondemocratic norms when confronting nondemocratic opponents. The reason for this is that democratic norms "can be more easily exploited to force concessions than nondemocratic ones."[74] Hence, in a conflict with a nondemocratic state, the leaders of a democracy may feel a heightened need to show strength despite their normative commitment to settling disputes through negotiation.

Structural or institutional explanations for the democratic peace empha-size that decision makers are hemmed in by institutions, which place con-straints on their behavior. Those constraints are a function of the separation of powers: not only do the various branches of government—the executive, legislative, and judiciary—each have their own mandates, they are also designed to restrain one another through oversight and the ability to, under certain circumstances, undo or override the decisions of one another. The institutional structure of democratic governments, in other words, deliberately limits the power of decision makers who function within that structure and makes the various parts of the government check one another. Moreover, leaders understand that their counterparts in other democratic states are subject to similar constraints. They will assume that there is "time for processes of international conflict resolution to operate, and they will not fear surprise attack" from another democratic state.[75]

In their relations with nondemocratic states, democratic leaders cannot make the same assumptions: they are aware that the leaders of nondemocra-tic states do not face the same institutional constraints. In fact, a nondemoc-ratic state may more easily engage in a surprise attack of another state, irrespective of whether this opponent is democratic or not. Furthermore, the leaders of nondemocratic states understand the constraints faced by demo-cratic leaders, and this can give them leverage in their dealings with democ-racies. The leaders of democracies, on the other hand, may choose war over giving in to the demands of a nondemocratic leader and appearing weak.

The normative and institutional explanations for the democratic peace are not mutually exclusive. The more well-established a democracy's insti-tutions are, the more deeply ingrained its norms will be and the more pow-erful will be their influence on the actions of its leaders.[76] Note, however, that such norms are more important in guiding foreign policy behavior vis-à-vis other democracies than they are in the interactions with non-democracies. This suggests that what guides decision makers is not just domestic norms and constraints but also their assessment of the norms and constraints that guide the behavior of their opponents.[77] Since the fre-quency of interaction is higher with states in the immediate neighborhood, this means that whether or not domestic values and constraints influence foreign policy depends on whether a democratic state is located in a dem-ocratic neighborhood or is surrounded by nondemocratic countries. In other words, foreign policy behavior may not only be constrained by a state's domestic norms and institutions, but also by its geographic location: whether or not it is located in a neighborhood (or region) with many dem-ocratic states.[78]

This suggests that geographic location may influence foreign policy decisions and behaviors. Whether this and other international factors serve as constraints and, if so, how they influence foreign policy decisions and behaviors is the subject matter of chapter 6.

Chapter Summary

- The agencies that collectively make up the government bureaucracy influence foreign policy making. Agencies can be idea- or interest-based, and they can be insulated or embedded.
- Domestic audiences influence foreign policy making in both democracies and non-democracies, but the extent of, and the mechanisms through which, that influence is exercised differ in different political systems. Public attentiveness varies across the life span of foreign policy problems, and does so differently in crisis and non-crisis situations.
- The media frame foreign policy and focus public attention within the context of the society's political culture.
- National history and culture predispose leaders to give greater credence to certain problem representations and pursue foreign policies congruent with them.
- The democratic peace theory holds that democracies are less likely to go to war (with one another) than non-democracies. Leader expectations are shaped by their knowledge of the political system of countries with which they interact.

Terms

Isolationism
Insulated agency
Embedded agency
Idea-based organization
Interest-based organization
Semi-authoritarian regimes
Rogue state
Political culture
National history
Culture
Constitutional monarchy
Democratic peace

Study Questions

1. Do all relevant bureaucratic agencies influence foreign policy making equally?
2. Do domestic audiences influence foreign policy making in non-democracies? If so, how?
3. How do domestic audiences in democratic societies affect foreign policy making?
4. What is the role of the media in foreign policy?
5. In what way do national history and culture constrain foreign policy making?
6. What is the democratic peace? How does it affect foreign policy decision making by leaders in democratic states?

Suggestions for Further Reading

The impact of the domestic political structures on foreign policy decision making is elaborated in Lyall, "Pocket Protests: Rhetorical Coercion and the Micropolitics of Collective Action in Semiauthoritarian Regimes"; Drezner, "Ideas, Bureaucratic Politics, and the Crafting of Foreign Policy"; and Risse-Kappen, "Ideas Do Not Float Freely: Transnational coalitions, domestic structures, and the end of the cold war."

A well-respected work on public opinion is Holsti, Public Opinion and American Foreign Policy, rev ed. The role of the media is detailed in Entman, *Projections of Power: Framing News, Public Opinion, and U.S. Foreign Policy.*

Political culture has not received much attention. One good source is: Hudson, ed., *Culture and Foreign Policy.* The democratic peace is the subject of numerous books and scholarly articles. A recent contribution to this literature is Goldsmith, "A Universal Proposition? Region, Conflict, War and the Robustness of the Kantian Peace."

Notes

1. Mintz, "Integrating Cognitive and Rational Theories"; James and Zhang, "Chinese Choices."
2. Farnham, "Impact of the Political Context," 459; Putnam, "Diplomacy and Domestic Politics."
3. Van Belle et al., *Media, Bureaucracies, and Foreign Aid*, 21.
4. This discussion is derived from Drezner, "Ideas, Bureaucratic Politics, and the Crafting of Foreign Policy."

5. Drezner, "Ideas, Bureaucratic Politics, and the Crafting of Foreign Policy," 736.
6. Ibid., 735.
7. Ibid., 743.
8. Ibid., 746.
9. Ibid., 744.
10. Ibid., 746.
11. Risse-Kappen, "Ideas Do Not Float Freely," 187.
12. Ibid. 187.
13. Holsti, *Public Opinion*, see also Van Belle, *Press Freedom*.
14. Lyall, "Pocket Protests," 387.
15. Ibid.
16. Ibid., 388.
17. Ibid., 381.
18. Müller and Risse-Kappen, "From the Outside In and from the Inside Out"; Risse-Kappen, "Public Opinion."
19. Risse-Kappen, "Public Opinion"; Risse-Kappen, "Ideas Do Not Float Freely"; see also Chan and Safran, "Public Opinion as a Constraint against War" for a discussion of the influence of electoral systems on the impact of public opinion on foreign policy.
20. Drezner, "Ideas, Bureaucratic Politics, and the Crafting of Foreign Policy," 735.
21. Knecht and Weatherford, "Public Opinion and Foreign Policy," 705; see also Entman, *Projections of Power*, 163.
22. Holsti, *Public Opinion*, 23; see also Entman, *Projections of Power*, 163.
23. Knecht and Weatherford, "Public Opinion and Foreign Policy," 719.
24. See the discussion in Holsti, *Public Opinion*, 290–93.
25. Powlick and Katz, "Defining the American Public Opinion/Foreign Policy Nexus"; Knecht and Weatherford, "Public Opinion and Foreign Policy"; Entman, *Projections of Power*.
26. Entman, *Projections of Power*, 142; see also Gaubatz, "Intervention and Intransitivity."
27. Foyle, *Counting the Public In*.
28. Graham, "Public Opinion and U.S. Foreign Policy Decision Making."
29. Caprioli and Trumbore, "Identifying 'Rogue' States"; Hoyt, "The 'Rogue State' Image."
30. Knecht and Weatherford, "Public Opinion and Foreign Policy," 712, 717.
31. Ibid., 712.
32. Ibid., 712, 717.
33. James and Zhang, "Chinese Choices."
34. Knecht and Weatherford, "Public Opinion and Foreign Policy," 709; Holsti, *Public Opinion and American Foreign Policy*, 302; Van Belle et al., *Media, Bureaucracies, and Foreign Aid*.
35. Hallin and Mancini, *Comparing Media Systems*.
36. Lyall, "Pocket Protests," 387
37. Entman, *Projections of Power*, 142.

38. This example is drawn from Frensley and Michaud, "Public Diplomacy and Motivated Reasoning."
39. Ibid.
40. Ibid., 211–12.
41. Ibid., 212.
42. Ibid., 215.
43. Entman, *Projections of Power*, 147–49.
44. Frensley and Michaud, "Public Diplomacy and Motivated Reasoning," 217.
45. Entman, *Projections of Power*, 147.
46. This paragraph relies heavily on Entman, *Projections of Power*, Chapter 7.
47. Entman, *Projections of Power*, 150; see also Van Belle, *Press Freedom*.
48. Entman, *Projections of Power*, 153.
49. Personal communication, Zheng Wang, July 30, 2006.
50. Vertzberger, *The World in their Minds*, 268.
51. Ibid., 261, see also Hudson, *Culture and Foreign Policy*.
52. Vertzberger, *The World in their Minds*, 261.
53. Hudson, *Culture and Foreign Policy*; Goldstein and Keohane, *Ideas and Foreign Policy*; Farnham, "Political Cognition and Decision Making."
54. Vertzberger, *The World in their Minds*, 270.
55. This comparison draws heavily upon Breuning, "Culture, History, Role."
56. Voorhoeve, *Peace, Profits and Principles*.
57. Kennedy, *The Rise and Fall of the Great Powers*.
58. Witte et al., *Politieke Geschiedenis van België*; Fishman, *Diplomacy and Revolution*; Vermeersch, *Vereniging en Revolutie*.
59. The data on which this comparison is based are from OECD, various years.
60. Hochschild, *King Leopold's Ghost*.
61. Pakenham, *The Scramble for Africa*; Van Bellinghen, "Belgium and Africa"; Witte et al., *Politieke Geschiedenis van België*.
62. Bouveroux, *België uit Afrika?* Luykx and Platel, *Politieke Geschiedenis van België*.
63. Kennedy, *The Rise and Fall of the Great Powers*; Voorhoeve, *Peace, Profits and Principles*; Wels, *Aloofness and Neutrality*.
64. Voorhoeve, *Peace, Profits and Principles*; Wels, *Aloofness and Neutrality*.
65. Voorhoeve, *Peace, Profits and Principles*; Wels, *Aloofness and Neutrality*.
66. Voorhoeve, *Peace, Profits and Principles*; see also Breuning, "Words and Deeds."
67. Coolsaet, *Buitenlandse Zaken*.
68. Dewachter, *Besluitvorming in Politiek België*; see also Dewachter and Verminck, "De Machtsbases van België."
69. Farnham, "Impact of the Political Context," 443.
70. Breuning, "Culture, History, Role"; see also Holsti, "National Role Conceptions"; Walker, *Role Theory and Foreign Policy Analysis*.
71. Chan, "Mirror, Mirror on the Wall"; Chan, "In Search of Democratic Peace"; Gat, "The Democratic Peace Theory Reframed"; Maoz and Abdolali, "Regime Type and International Conflict"; Maoz and Russett, "Normative

and Structural Causes of Democratic Peace"; Russett *Grasping the Democratic Peace*; Russett and Oneal, *Triangulating Peace*.

72. Russett, *Grasping the Democratic Peace*, chapter 2.
73. Chan, "In Search of Democratic Peace," 66.
74. Russett, *Grasping the Democratic Peace*, 35.
75. Ibid., 40.
76. Cederman, "Back to Kant."
77. Schafer and Walker, "Democratic Leaders and the Democratic Peace," 579.
78. Russett, "Bushwhacking the Democratic Peace," 406; see also Goldsmith, "A Universal Proposition?"

Chapter 6

Leaders in Context II: International Constraints on Foreign Policy Making

Chapter Preview

- Explains how a state's capabilities shape its role on the world stage.
- Explains the usefulness and limitations of classifying states into small, middle, and great powers.
- Explains the patterns in the foreign policy behavior of dependent states.
- Explains the value of soft power and the role of norm entrepreneurs in international politics.

All the World's a Stage

The international environment is the stage on which foreign policy decision makers find themselves. Their foreign policies are designed to navigate that stage. As they seek their way across the global stage, decision makers must take into account how the international environment constrains the policy options that are realistically available to them. They must also recognize opportunities that may present themselves, especially if these help secure their state's interests. It is not easy to recognize such opportunities, as the leaders of Argentina discovered after they occupied the Malvinas, and as Iraq's Saddam Hussein discovered after his military occupied Kuwait (see chapters 3 and 1). Perceiving opportunities accurately is a challenge that demands great insight into the decision makers of other countries. It requires the ability to view the world, and specific situations in it, from the vantage point of other countries' leaders. It also requires the ability to understand the domestic and international constraints such leaders perceive.

The importance of the ability to put oneself into the shoes of another country's leadership is evident from the previous chapters. Here, the primary focus is on the more enduring constraints the international environment places on decision makers. Consider the following questions: Does it make a difference for policy makers what sort of states lie across the border? Or even with how many states their country shares borders? Whether those borders are sea or land, whether they are across flat and open terrain, mountainous, or demarcated by rivers? Does it make a difference whether the state is large or small in terms of its geographic size, either objectively or in the context of its neighbors? Does it matter whether a state possesses resources or wealth?

In thinking about these questions, consider the foreign policies of the states that were mentioned in earlier chapters. Do the decision makers of the Argentina, Belgium, Britain, China, Ethiopia, Iraq, the Netherlands, or the U.S. view the international environment in similar or different ways? The states they represent have very different **capabilities**, which can be used as an indicator of their potential power. Capabilities are measurable assets, such as a country's geographic size, its population, its natural resources, and the size of its economy and military. Although such measures may seem straightforward, they also leave many questions yet unanswered. The significance of specific natural resources will depend on technological advances. For instance, oil has been quite important to Iraq's economy, but the importance of it rose only after the invention of the internal combustion engine. In addition, resources—or the lack thereof—are not always reliable indicators of a state's role in the international environment. Belgium has few natural resources but a highly developed economy. Indeed, the average Belgian is much wealthier than the average Iraqi.[1] The Gulf War in the early 1990s and the current conflict have increased, but not caused, this gap. Of course, Belgium's economy has in the past benefited from the rather unequal trade relationship with its colonies, whereas Iraq was first part of the Ottoman Empire and then a British colonial possession prior to acquiring independence in 1932.[2]

Belgium is economically wealthy but also resource poor. Its very open economy depends heavily on international trade. This means that natural resources can be helpful but also that a lack of natural resources does not make it impossible for a country to create a thriving economy. It also means that information about a country's resource base is of only limited usefulness in understanding its potential power. It is not wholly irrelevant, however. It tells us something about the constraints under which decision makers function. Belgian decision makers have traditionally shied away from a high profile foreign policy. Their focus has been on the country's economic external relations, including also efforts to further develop European economic integration.[3] Not all countries with very open economies are equally cautious. The Netherlands is also highly dependent on international trade, but its decision makers have not focused equally strongly on their state's economic external relations (see chapter 5). Hence, a state's smallness and economic openness may make it logical for its decision makers to focus primarily on economic external relations, but it does not guarantee it.

Both Belgium and the Netherlands are democratic countries and are located in a neighborhood of democracies. As was noted in the discussion of the democratic peace in the chapter 5, there is evidence that democracies are much less likely to go to war with one another. In addition, it appears that this result is not equally strong in all regions of the world.[4] This suggests that perhaps it is not only the sort of government a country has domestically that matters, but also its membership and participation in regional organizations. Belgium and the Netherlands are both founding members of the European Union (EU) and its predecessors. Both also belong to the North Atlantic Treaty Organization (NATO). These and other regional organizations create rules that guide the interactions of the states that belong to them. The leaders of such states are therefore constrained not only by domestic factors, but their decision making also takes place within the confines of the norms, rules, and expectations of these regional organizations. This may not affect all of their external relations, but it does influence relations with the states in the neighborhood that also belong to the same regional organization. In the European landscape, democracies and regional organizations are both important. It is unclear which contributes more to the relative peacefulness of this region. What *is* clear is that the states in this region do have their disputes, but that their leaders manage these disputes through negotiation, often within the confines of organizations like the EU or NATO.

Measuring Up: Size and Power

The relationship between a state's foreign policy behavior and its capabilities is not always straightforward. Most of the time, decision makers play an important role as intermediary: their perceptions of the relative power of their own and other states, as well as their perceptions of opportunities and constraints, determine the actions taken. After all, it is the decisions made by leaders that the determine the foreign policy behavior of states, and those leaders do not always accurately evaluate the relative capabilities of their own and other states. Does it make a difference whether a decision maker represents a small or large state? If so, how? What other aspects of a state's capabilities might affect decision making?

Let's first examine some basic measures of state capabilities that form the parameters of the stage on which leaders act. Subsequently, we will examine to what degree such objective indicators guide foreign policy decision making and behavior.

Geographic size and population size may suggest a state's power potential. The United States is slightly larger geographically than China, but its population is somewhat less than a quarter the size of China's, as is shown in table 6.1. There are few countries in the world that control such enormous territories. In fact, China is the fourth largest country in the world. The largest is Russia, followed by Canada, and the United States is in third place. A state's size alone does not make it powerful, but size helps: before the Soviet Union broke apart and left Russia with a smaller (but still enormous) territory, it was known as a **superpower**. This term became popular during the Cold War and denotes a state that can project power globally. The United States was the other superpower. Other labels, such as *hyperpower*, have been used to describe the United States since the end of the Cold War, when the United States was widely perceived as the single most powerful country in the world. It makes little sense to use increasingly superlative terms for the few countries that have the capabilities to project power around the globe. What matters is that we understand that some states are endowed with greater capabilities than others. In addition, it is also important to recognize that strong capabilities do not always translate into the motivation or the ability to define the state's interests as global in scale, just as lesser capabilities can under favorable circumstances be translated into a substantial ability to project power.

Currently, China is seen as an **emerging power**, which means that it is rapidly becoming more powerful and likely to rival the prowess of the United States in the near future. Hence, of the four countries that are the largest geographically, three either have played important roles in world politics or are likely to do so in the future.

When capability is measured in terms of population, the United States comes in third, also. China and India have larger populations.[5] Indeed, in addition to China, India is now also often mentioned as an emerging power. Both countries have higher population densities than the United States. Russia and Canada, on the other hand, have vast territories but much smaller populations. Russia's population is just under half that of the United States, whereas Canada's population is somewhat smaller than Argentina's.

Table 6.1 Measures of capabilities

	Geographic size (total square km)	Population (estimated number)	Size of economy (gdp/ppp in billions of dollars)	Per capita size of economy (gdp/per capita)	Military expenditure (percent of gdp)
Argentina	2,766,890	39,921,833	599.1	15,000	1.3
Belgium	30,528	10,379,067	330.4	31,800	1.3
Britain	244,820	60,609,153	1,903.0	31,400	2.4
China	9,596,960	1,313,973,713	10,000.0	7,600	4.3
Ethiopia	1,127,127	74,777,981	71.6	1,000	3.4
Iraq	437,072	26,783,383	94.1	1,900	-
Netherlands	41,526	16,491,461	512.0	31,700	1.6
U.S.	9,826,630	298,444,215	12,980.0	43,500	4.1

Source: Data from CIA World Factbook

Whether population density is an advantage or not depends on other factors. Consider that Ethiopia is smaller but much more populous than Argentina, but the latter has a much larger and more diversified economy. Argentina is sometimes still classified as a **developing country**, a designation that is imprecise but generally denotes countries that are not as technologically advanced or industrialized as countries like the United States or others with wealthy and advanced economies. Many developing countries are postcolonial states, and most achieved their independence in the years after World War II. Neither Argentina nor Ethiopia fit that mold: the former declared its independence from Spain in 1816 (albeit not with its current borders), and Ethiopia was never colonized, although it was occupied by Italy in the period between the two world wars. Currently, Argentina is at the upper income end of the developing countries, whereas Ethiopia is among the poorest and has an economy that is highly dependent on agriculture. An important distinction between the two countries' populations is that Argentina's is well educated, whereas less than half of Ethiopia's adult population is literate.[6] Not only is the economy of Argentina bigger in absolute terms, it is also larger than Ethiopia's when adjusted for each country's population size—as is shown by the vastly different figures for the per capita size of each country's economy in table 6.1. Interestingly, the same measure shows that the economic performances of Belgium, Britain, and the Netherlands are very similar. Of course, Britain has a much larger economy than either Belgium or the Netherlands and, as a result, has greater capabilities.

In addition to geographic, population, and economic size, a country's military prowess determines its relative power capabilities. There are many ways to measure military might, such as the number of people employed in the military or the guns, missiles, tanks, ships, planes, and so on at its disposal. A problem with many such comparisons is that countries vary in their defense needs, depending in part on their geographic circumstances. For instance, a country with predominantly land borders may want to include more tanks in its military, whereas a state with mostly sea borders might want to have a stronger navy. Here, we employ a simpler and more easily comparable measure: military expenditure as a proportion of the size of a country's economy. This implies that a state's military capability depends on its economic wealth. Although leaders may choose to devote a smaller or larger proportion of the state's wealth to their militaries, a state with a poorly developed economy usually has a lesser capability to project military strength—and is usually limited to less technologically sophisticated weaponry. Remember that the focus here is on the capacity to project military strength, not on the actual use of the military instrument in settling disputes or the propensity to go to war.

As table 6.1 shows, the United States and China allocate a larger proportion to their militaries than the other countries, as dictated by a desire to be able to project power globally. Interestingly, Ethiopia also devotes a rather substantial share of its economy to its military. Given the relatively small size of its economy, this does not constitute the ability to project power in the same way as it does for the United States or China, but it indicates a desire to play a significant role in the politics of the Horn of Africa, the region in which the country is located. Interestingly, it spends slightly more than its larger neighbor, the Sudan.

In comparison, Argentina, Belgium, and the Netherlands spend anemic amounts on their militaries. These countries do not seek to project military power beyond an ability to defend their borders. All three have also participated in UN peacekeeping missions. As described previously, Belgium and the Netherlands are located in a corner of the world that is populated by states that are democratic, and they are closely connected with the states with which they share borders through participation in organizations like the EU and NATO. In addition, the Netherlands has traditionally played an important role in the transshipment of goods to Germany, and Belgium has gained recognition as the crossroads of Western Europe and the home to the headquarters of both the EU and NATO.

Traditionally, sea borders were regarded as more easily defended than land borders, unless those land borders were mountainous and difficult to penetrate, as is the case with Switzerland and Afghanistan. Consider that Britain has primarily sea borders and has proved difficult to invade. Belgium, on the other hand, has primarily land borders and also borders on two much larger countries. It was invaded and occupied by Germany during both World War I and World War II. Modern military technology has perhaps made such geographic features less valuable than they were in the past. Nevertheless, table 6.2 provides the proportion of the total borders that are constituted by each country's coastline. Notice that the United States has a rather substantial proportion of coastline borders, whereas Iraq and Ethiopia have little to none. Ethiopia is located on a high plateau and has a mountain range in its center but also borders on the largest country in Africa, the Sudan. Iraq finds itself wedged between three countries larger than itself—Iran, Saudi Arabia, and Turkey—and sharing a strategic location along the Persian Gulf with Iran, Kuwait, and Saudi Arabia, which is significant with regard to the shipment of oil. Both Iraq and Ethiopia are located in regions that have seen substantial instability dating back many decades. There are no current figures available for Iraq's military expenditure due to the U.S. occupation, but Ethiopia's geographic location in an unstable neighborhood suggests a partial explanation for its military spending.

These descriptive features—coastline borders, neighboring countries, and relative size, as well as the measures of capabilities previously discussed—provide only a small glimpse at the positions of states in the larger international environment. These measures cannot tell us what foreign policies the decision makers of various states will pursue, but they help us understand the set of constraints they face. The leaders of superpowers may be able to project power globally. Although leaders of the United States long perceived their state to have favorable geographic circumstances by being wedged between two oceans, geographic location may matter less when a state commands vast power capabilities. The leaders of smaller states vary greatly in their ability to project power, since the "small state" label encompasses states of dramatically different capabilities. The leaders of states with limited capabilities must find ways to secure their states' interests that rely less on the ability to project power. For such states, the context of their geographic location may be quite significant in helping us understand the sort of foreign policies they pursue and how they choose to employ their (limited) capabilities.

In sum, the discussion of capabilities and geographic circumstances has given us an initial understanding of the variety of circumstances faced by the decision makers of various countries. Large countries, by virtue of their larger territory, have a better likelihood of also being well endowed with natural resources. All other things being equal, the leaders of states with smaller territories, populations, and economies should perceive greater constraints as they navigate the international environment than the leaders of larger states, with more resources, more population and larger economies.

Table 6.2 Geographic circumstances

Country	Coastline percentage of total border	Border countries	Size, relative to neighbors
Argentina	33.6%	5: Bolivia, Brazil, Chille, Paraguay, Uruguay	Second-largest country in South-America, after Brazil.
Belgium	4.6%	4: France, Germany, Luxembourg,	Smaller than three of its neighbors. France is Western Europe's largest country and Germany is large and strategically located. The Netherlands is only slightly larger. Belgium is the "crossroads" of Western Europe.
Britain	97.2%	1: Ireland	More than 3 times as large as the only country with which it shares a land border. Smaller than France or Germany.
China	39,6%	14: Afghanistan, Bhutan, Burma,India, Kazakhstan, North Korea, Kyrgystan, Laos, Mongolia, Nepal, Pakistan, Russia Tajikistan, Vietnam	Borders on the largest country in the world Russia, and is itself the fourth largest country in the world, and the largest in Asia.
Ethiopia	0 (land-locked)	5: Djibouti, Eritrea, Kenya, Somalia, Sudan	Borders on the largest country in Africa (Sudan), is substantially larger than its remaining neighbors. Its smaller neighbors to the east have strategic locations.
Iraq	1.6%	6: Iran, Jordan, Kuwait, Saudi Arabia, Syria, Turkey	Smaller than half of its neighbors (Iran, Saudi Arabia, and Turkey) and larger than the remaining three. Shares a strategic location with several of its neighbors.
Netherlands	30.5%	2: Belgium, Germany	Borders on large and strategically located Germany, for which it provides transshipment. Slightly larger than Belgium.
U.S.	62.3%	2: Canada, Mexico	World's third largest country, after Russia and Canada.

Source: Based on data from CIA World Factbook

Beyond Measurement: Classifying States

Thus far, this chapter's discussion has focused on using objective measures to describe the positions of states in the international environment. Now, we will turn to a more comprehensive classification of states that is built upon the notion that size matters in more than just its geographic sense. Size is related to power as well as to a state's **interdependence** with other states. Interdependence denotes the structure of a state's interactions with other states and will be discussed in greater detail in the next section, where we will delve further into the interrelations between unequal states.

As you read this and the next section, remember that a state's size is a very rough guide to estimating its foreign policy behavior. Size may set the parameters for action, but it does not predetermine how decision makers navigate constraints and perceive or create opportunities for their country.

The concept of size is not limited to the geographic dimensions of a state. A frequently used classification is a division of states into small, middle, and great powers. Others have used terms like **weak state**,[7] which is sometimes synonymous with small state but has also been used to define countries with ineffective institutions of government. In that last definition, a weak state is similar to a **failed state**, which is defined by the failure of the institutions of government to control the state's territory, and also the absence of effective institutions of government.[8] States like Somalia, the Democratic Republic of the Congo, and Afghanistan fit this description.

The classification of states as great, middle, or small powers is rather imprecise, because the concept of size lacks specificity. This is less problematic at the extremes than in delineating the boundaries between the categories. Few will challenge the notion that the United States qualifies as a **great** (or also **super-**) **power**. It has the political, economic, and military strength to exert influence on a global scale. What other states also fit this category of states? Above, China and India were described as emerging powers. Both are large and populous states with fast-growing economies.

Another way to evaluate great power status is to look to those states that have been recognized as significant players on the world stage by their status as permanent members of the UN Security Council. Alongside the United States, we find Britain, China, France, and Russia. Permanent membership in the UN Security Council is not the only way to define great power status, however. Another group that is generally recognized as consisting of powerful countries is the Group of Eight (G8). Its eight members together represent well over half of the world economy. The group meets to discuss global economic governance. It started out with six members but soon became seven. The initial six were Britain, France, Germany, Italy, Japan, and the United States, but Canada was added very soon after the group's inception in 1975. Representatives of Russia started attending the

meetings shortly after the end of the Cold War and became a full partici-
pant in 1997, when the group officially became the G8.

The membership of the UN's Security Council and the G8 each reflects
their missions as well as the history behind these organizations. The UN
was created in the waning days of World War II to maintain international
peace and security, promote social and economic progress, and safeguard
human rights. The G8 emerged in the aftermath of the 1973 oil crisis and
in response to the economic recession and changes in the world economic
system that followed on its heels. Its main focus is the functioning of the
global economy. The histories of these two bodies provide a partial explanation for their membership.

Interestingly, Canada, which is a member of the G8, is a self-described
middle power. Its decision makers began to use this concept to describe
their role in the international environment.[9] Middle powers are states that
can wield a measure of influence, albeit not through the projection of military might. Consider, for instance, the role Norway played in the negotiations between representatives of Israel and the Palestinians that culminated
in the Oslo Accords of 1993. Middle powers are usually affluent states that
employ their resources to foster peace and to lessen global economic
inequality. In addition to Canada and Norway, the Netherlands and
Sweden have employed this label. The leaders of these states have at times
characterized their countries as "like minded" and have acted as **norm
entrepreneurs** in the international environment.[10] Norm entrepreneurs
advocate for the adoption of certain international standards and work
diplomatically to persuade the representatives of other states to also adopt
these norms. The countries listed here, which have at times also labeled
themselves as middle powers, have played such a role in the area of international development cooperation. The decision makers of these countries
advocated not only for more aid for development for especially the poorest
countries, but also for sustainable development.[11]

Defined in this way, the concept of middle power is not synonymous
with the notion of a **regional power**, which is defined as a state that has the
resources to exert influence in its own region of the world. Countries like
Brazil, India, Indonesia, Iran, Nigeria, South Africa, and Turkey are often
named in this category. This list is not exhaustive. Other states either are, or
have the capacity to be, regional power brokers. Whether or not states do in
fact play such a role often depends on whether its leaders decide to position
their state in such a way.

Furthermore, middle powers like the Netherlands and Norway are sometimes also listed among the **small states**.[12] Small states are less easily
defined.[13] The category includes a large and varied group of states. Consider
that the UN currently counts 192 member states and that only a fraction of

these can be considered either great, middle or regional powers. This is true even if we expand the category of regional powers to include additional states and thereby reduce the pool of states eligible for the small state label. Here, small states are defined as those that have a rather limited capacity to exert influence on other states. In general, the leaders of small states have a smaller range of instruments they can effectively employ in their relations with other states. Diplomacy is always an option, but force rarely. In addition, the decision makers of small states can be quite adept at working through international organizations such as the UN or regional organizations like the European Union (EU) to exert influence beyond their own, independent capacity.[14]

Size is a relative concept: a state that is small in the global context may be able to exert influence over a neighboring state that is smaller, has fewer resources, or has weak and ineffective institutions of governance. Conversely, a small state that is strategically placed may be less in the shadow of a larger neighbor than it would otherwise be. Consider that tiny but strategically placed Djibouti is an important transshipment point for goods into and out of its much larger but landlocked neighbor, Ethiopia. This strategic position does not give Djibouti power over Ethiopia, but it provides an incentive for the latter to maintain a stable relationship with the former.

The classification of states into small, middle, and great powers leaves much to be desired. It may be easy to identify the few great powers and to name some of the very smallest states, but beyond the extremes of the spectrum of state capabilities it becomes more difficult to differentiate between small and middle, or middle and great, powers. Despite the difficulties in pinning down these concepts, the differences among states have consequences for foreign policies. Ultimately, size and power are about the degree to which states are constrained in the range of foreign policy options available to their decision makers. Very few states have the capabilities to project power across the globe. Only a small number can exert influence over other states within their own region of the world. Most states lack the political, economic, and military strength to project power or exert influence over other states. The foreign policies of such states are circumscribed by the limitations imposed not only by their size but also by their geographic location and the structure of their relations with other states. That brings us to the subject of interdependence.

Interdependence and the Inequality of States

There is much more to be said about interdependence than the simple definition previously provided. *Inter*dependence suggests that the relations between states are characterized by mutuality and equality. But we have already seen that states are not equal. They differ in terms of size as well as resources. These differences have consequences for the interactions between states. The effects of smallness are felt most acutely by the smaller developing states in the global South. Their foreign policy is constrained by their **dependence**, which is best defined as an asymmetric pattern of inter-actions between a more and a less powerful state. The general condition of inequality does not mean that the foreign policies of small, dependent states are easily compared. Indeed, four distinct foreign policy orientations have been identified that characterize the foreign policies of small states.[15]

One, the leaders of some small states pursue a **consensus-oriented foreign policy**. This means that the leaders of a small state voluntarily align their external policy with that of a larger more powerful state that has the capacity to exert influence over them. If a small state does not do so, the more powerful state has the capacity to pressure the smaller state's leaders to align their foreign policy with it, resulting in a **compliant foreign policy**, the second foreign policy orientation. In both cases, the observed foreign policy behavior of the small state consists of actions that are in alignment with the desires of the more powerful country. What distinguishes the two types of foreign policy behavior is the motivations behind these actions: the first is the result of voluntary choices by leaders who recognize that their state lacks the resources to act independently, whereas the second reflects foreign pol-icy actions undertaken only after the decision makers of a more powerful state exerted their influence. In practice, it will be difficult to determine from a small state's foreign policy behavior alone whether consensus or compliance best explains it. The only thing that distinguishes the two is the *motivation* behind the behavior, not the behavior itself. In other words, it would be necessary to have insight into the decision making process to understand why the small state's policy makers decided as they did.

Three, **counterdependent foreign policy** represents a defiant reaction to dependence. The leaders of such states are frustrated with the dependent situation of their state and try to find ways to reduce the consequences of that dependence, usually inviting the displeasure of the leaders of more powerful states in the process.

Lastly, there is **compensation**, which is a foreign policy that antagonizes the leaders of powerful states in an effort to appease domestic audiences. Like the difference between consensus-oriented and compliant foreign policy behavior, the difference between counterdependent and compensa-tion-oriented foreign policies will be difficult to discern from a state's behavior alone. Here, too, the difference is primarily in the motivations that drive the policy choices. Would you characterize the Argentine occu-pation of the Malvinas, as described in chapter 3, as counterdependence or compensation? Was the Argentine government frustrated with the progress of its negotiations with Britain, leading them to make a decision to take a stand and invade the islands? Or was the decision motivated more by a desire to please a domestic audience? There is some evidence to support both explanations in this instance. More information than that presented in chapter 3 would be necessary to determine whether this decision is more accurately characterized as counterdependence or compensation.

Insight into the decision making process can help untangle the motivations behind the foreign policy actions. The first two types of small state foreign policies, consensus and compliance, recognize the existence of power differentials. The resulting foreign policy behaviors demonstrate a willingness to work within the constraints of smallness and dependence. The latter two types, counterdependence and compensation, reflect a desire to work around or even defy the existing power differences. Such strategies may work on occasion. At other times, such strategies may invite diplomatic, or more forceful, retribution from more powerful states. What these four types of foreign policy behavior illustrate is that leaders have choices in the face of the limitations that size and dependence place upon the policy options available to them. They can seek to stretch the limits of the possible (as leaders pursuing counterdependent foreign policies do), they can accept the constraints and pursue a consensus-oriented foreign policy, or they can comply with the wishes of the policy makers of larger powers even if they would have preferred to make a different decision.

Lastly, compensation-oriented foreign policy reminds us that the leaders of small and dependent states, like those of any other type of state, face dual pressures: the international environment is one source of constraints—and sometimes opportunities—but the imperatives of the domestic environment cannot be ignored. Foreign policy decision makers, in other words, are always engaged in a two-level game, needing to satisfy simultaneously both their domestic audience and their counterparts in other countries.[16]

Power and Decision Making

The discussion of size, capabilities, power, as well as the classification of states based on those distinctions, has largely focused on observable and measurable differences between states. These differences form the backdrop against which foreign policy making takes place. Decision makers are well aware of their own state's capabilities relative to those of the states surrounding them and of those more distant states with which they have active relationships. Yet it frequently is not the measurable differences in capabilities or the classification of those states that matter most in their interactions with the leaders of other states.

That is not to say that the capabilities of states are unimportant. We have already noted that a state's capabilities delineate at best a range of possibilities for foreign policy action. A great power does not always bring all its weight to bear on its interactions with other states. Furthermore, capabilities measure power resources and the possibility for a state to be powerful, but not whether a state and its leaders are willing and able to make effective use of those power resources. Conversely, the leaders of small states are sometimes very effective in using an advantageous attribute of their state to play a role beyond what might be expected given its capabilities. In short, information about the capabilities of states or the classification of one's own and other states in the world is at best a very rough guide to the roles they play in international politics. This means that in addition to knowledge about the capabilities of other states, decision makers are often interested in the historical patterns of interactions between states.[17] It is a combination of such historical patterns and measurable indicators that shapes the expectations decision makers hold of the behavior of other states. Leaders make foreign policy in the long shadow cast by the history of the foreign relations between their own and other states. Hence, the distribution of capabilities in the international environment only partially describes the international constraints perceived by decision makers. Those constraints are also, and importantly, determined by the expectations decision makers have on the basis of past interactions between their own and other states.[18]

Such patterns of interactions tend to take on a life of their own, and it becomes difficult for decision makers to perceive the international environment other than through the lens of the history of their state's relations with other states.[19] Such perceptions may be grounded in both the distribution of capabilities and in actual historical events, but they make it difficult for decision makers to perceive novel situations clearly[20] or to recognize the implications of changes in the international environment. Indeed, as the Cold War ended, one scholar argued we would soon miss the predictability that it had given to international politics.[21] Another argued that "without the cold war's mutual attributions of threat and hostility to define their identities, [the United States and the Soviet Union] seem unsure of what their 'interests' should be."[22] It was not just the decision makers of the superpowers who were less certain of the principles that should guide their foreign policies. The momentous changes in the international environment that resulted from the end of the Cold War and the fragmentation of the Soviet Union into Russia and the various former Soviet republics created a radical change that left many decision makers initially unsure as to how best to confront this altered international stage. Their established understandings of the world around them no longer fit this new reality. This time period nicely illustrates that foreign policy making is guided by the expectations decision makers bring to the task—and that these expectations are as forceful as the measurable capabilities of their own and other states.[23]

The predictability that stems from the usually relatively stable and slowly changing nature of the pattern of interactions among states has led to the notion that leaders perceive their states as playing certain roles in the international environment. The accompanying **national role conception** is delineated by the decision makers' definition of the types of foreign policy decisions and behaviors that are appropriate for their state to undertake.[24] This national role conception guides decision makers both in unique situations and also in ongoing relationships, such as their state's role in the region in which the state is located, the state's role in relation to a specific other type of state, or even the state's global role.

For instance, Nigerian leaders increasingly position their state to play the role of peacekeeper in West Africa, the region in which their state is located. The decision makers of Sweden and several other states have used the middle power label and have positioned their states in a leadership role as norm entrepreneurs in the effort to lessen global inequality. This has resulted in relatively larger development cooperation budgets for these countries. It has also prompted among these states' decision makers a commitment to fostering the development of norms and standards within international organizations that favor an increased transfer of resources to especially the poorest countries.[25] American policy makers have long conceived their country as playing a global role, although the strategies employed in doing so have changed dramatically over time.

The middle power label used by Sweden and others is less about power status than about a specific set of foreign policy interests. Used in this way, the label obscures that decision makers often perceive their state to play several roles simultaneously. The middle power label is used to communicate a specific set of values with respect to relations with developing countries. The states that employed this label play very different roles in other areas of their foreign policy. Whereas Canada's decision makers have tried to fashion a relatively independent role for their state and Sweden has long taken a strong position in favor of neutrality, the decision makers of the Netherlands long have perceived their state as playing the role of a faithful ally with respect to the United States and the other NATO partners. But leaders of all three states also saw their states as having a special obligation with respect to developing countries.[26] The decision makers of the Netherlands especially sought to position their state in a leadership role with regard to development cooperation.[27] Hence, national role conceptions often function in issue-specific domains and the decision makers of one state may perceive multiple roles that each pertain to different sets of foreign policy relationships.

In addition, national role conceptions, like more general notions of capabilities or power status, suggest only the broad outlines of foreign policy objectives. As indicated, American policy makers have long perceived a global role for their country, but its foreign policy has clearly changed. In the aftermath of World War II, the United States was instrumental in the creation of international organizations—such as the UN, the World Bank, and NATO—that played an important role in structuring and regulating political and economic relations between countries in the international environment, and that provided security for West European countries during the Cold War period. In the past decade, however, the United States has increasingly acted unilaterally. Although some see this as a temporary shift resulting from the preferences and perceptions of specific decision makers,[28] another interpretation suggests that the incentives presented by the post–Cold War international environment encourage American decision makers to act in this manner.[29] If so, this would mean that American unilateralism does not merely reflect the preferences of a specific set of decision makers within the United States but rather is the result of a changed set of circumstances that makes cooperation with other states in international organizations less attractive than it used to be. After all, America's allies have become increasingly insistent that the United States act in accordance with the rules of international organizations, while at the same time being less willing to follow the American lead.[30] This means that the costs of cooperation are now higher and the benefits more difficult to achieve. As the most powerful actor on the global stage, the United States cannot be compelled to cooperate, and it may see little benefit from trying to persuade the reluctant leaders of smaller countries.

Although it may be tempting for American decision makers to go it alone because their country has the capacity, doing so may have negative consequences in the long run. In chapter 3, we introduced the concept of **soft power**, which we defined as the ability to shape the preferences of others.[31] The concept is mainly associated with American foreign policy but merits further investigation. Does it apply to other states as well?

Soft Power and the Instruments of Foreign Policy

Soft power is a concept that has emerged relatively recently.[32] Traditionally, power has been defined primarily in military terms. In a world in which the economies of states have become ever more intertwined, economic power has gained in popularity as well. Economic power can be effective, but it is a less precise instrument. It has long been clear that the leaders of countries that receive aid from the United States do not always return the favor by voting as U.S. leaders might like them to in the UN.[33] Economic sanctions have a problematic record as well. There have been a few instances where sanctions have been successful, such as the oil embargo instituted by the countries of the Organization for Petroleum Exporting Countries (OPEC) in the early 1970s. Most of the time, sanctions can be circumvented. Nevertheless, both military and economic power can be expressed through tangible foreign policy action.

Soft power is different. It relies not so much on specific actions as on what a country represents. Soft power is the "values a government champions in its behavior at home (for example, democracy), in international institutions (working with others), and in foreign policy (promoting peace and human rights)."[34] Soft power is less tangible than other forms of power. It has a strong psychological dimension because it involves making others *want* to do what you would like them to do—rather than *making* them do it. It uses "an attraction to shared values and the justness and duty of contributing to the achievement of those values."[35] This requires skill and subtlety rather than the weight of raw power. It is also likely to require patience because it means figuring out how to motivate the leaders of another country to want to pursue a course of action that you want them to pursue.

The concept of soft power has been closely associated with American foreign policy, largely because it was first coined in that context. It has served as a critique of the country's recent unilateralism.[36] This critique recognizes that, as we note in the previous section, the incentives presented by the post Cold War international environment encourage American decision makers to act in this manner.[37] However, it takes the position that this unilateralism is shortsighted and that "America's success will depend upon our developing a deeper understanding of the role of soft power . . . in our foreign policy."[38]

Perhaps it is difficult for a great power with the ability to project military power across the globe to understand and utilize the benefits of soft power. Yet for smaller states, it may be the only way in which their leaders can hope to exercise influence on the world stage. Think back to the description of the self-described middle powers that function as norm entrepreneurs earlier in this chapter. Whereas the United States has received its share of "hate mail" in the form of distrust and negative statements by the leaders of other countries, Sweden and the other like-minded countries are generally perceived quite positively. As a result, the leaders of Sweden carry weight in international diplomacy beyond what one might expect on the basis of the power capabilities of their state. The United States, on the other hand, can impose its will on the leaders and populations of other states, which resent its actions. Consider how soft power might complement America's power capabilities to achieve a more positive reaction to its foreign policy actions.

The ideas of soft power run counter much of the thinking about international politics, which has been heavily influenced by Realist theory (see chapter 3). Realists perceive a world of sovereign, independent states. **Sovereignty** is the doctrine that the government of a state is the legitimate and ultimate authority over that state. The government of a sovereign state recognizes no other authority over itself. This is in first instance a legal concept. The meaning of sovereignty in practice depends on a state's power and capabilities: the leaders of powerful states can impose their will on those of smaller states. Whether such smaller states pursue compliant or counterdependent foreign policies, their leaders are acutely aware that their size limits their capacity to make their legal sovereignty a practical reality.

In addition to the variation in the abilities of states to realize their sovereignty in practice, the leaders of states have accepted limitations on their sovereign rights through membership in international organizations and by signing treaties, conventions, and declarations. Through such mechanisms they express a willingness to abide by common rules and norms. However, sovereignty also means that international organizations and agreements largely depend on the voluntary cooperation of the member states. After all, as Realists are quick to point out, the international environment is anarchic. **Anarchy** means that there is no central power, that each sovereign entity is left to its own devices. In the final analysis, whether anarchy or voluntary cooperation best describe the nature of the international environment is an empirical question. Or perhaps it depends on how leaders interpret the international environment. After all, leaders make foreign policy decisions on the basis of their—and their advisors'—expectations and understandings of the international environment. Those expectations are grounded in the actions of the leaders of other states in the international arena, but are also shaped in important ways by interpretation of the meanings of, and motivations for, those actions. And that brings us back to the role of decision makers in foreign policy.

Chapter Summary

- The capabilities of states are their measurable assets, such as their size, population, economy, and military. These are at best a rough guide to the role of a state in international politics. A state's capabilities shape its role on the world stage.
- Classifications of states into small, middle, and great powers are often as much about the roles states play in international politics as about objective power differences.
- Small and dependent states may engage in four different patterns of foreign policy behavior: consensus, compliance, counterdependence, and compensation.
- Soft power is increasingly important in international politics. Some small countries function as norm entrepreneurs and influence international politics beyond what their size or capabilities should lead one to expect.

Terms

Capabilities
Superpower
Emerging power
Developing country
Interdependence
Weak state
Failed state
Great power
Middle power
Norm entrepreneur
Regional power
Small state
Dependence
Consensus-oriented foreign policy
Compliant foreign policy
Counterdependent foreign policy
Compensation-driven foreign policy
National role conception
Sovereignty
Anarchy

Study Questions

1. Do a state's capabilities predict what sort of foreign policy its leaders will pursue? Why or why not?
2. Do the concepts of small, middle, and great (or even super) power help decision makers understand the constraints placed on them by the international environment?
3. What small-state foreign policy behavior patterns have been identified? Do these help in understanding the connection between size, power, and foreign policy behavior?
4. What patterns in dependent state foreign policy behavior have been identified? What do these patterns explain about power differences in international politics?
5. What is soft power? What are norm entrepreneurs? What do these concepts share in common?

Suggestions for Further Reading

Not much attention has been devoted to size and capability. An early work is East, "Size and Foreign Policy Behavior: A Test of Two Models." A more recent theoretical essay is: Neack, "Linking State Type with Foreign Policy Behavior."

Small states have recently attracted renewed attention; see Hey, ed., *Small States in World Politics: Explaining Foreign Policy Behavior.* Another recent book that reprints (excerpts from) many classics and offers new contributions is Ingebritsen, Neumann, Gstöhl, and Beyer, *Small States in International Relations.*

Dependent foreign policy has received less attention than it deserves. A good overview is Hey, "Foreign Policy in Dependent States."

There is a small literature on national role conceptions, dating back to Holsti, "National Role Conceptions in the Study of Foreign Policy." More recent work is represented by Walker, ed., *Role Theory and Foreign Policy Analysis,* and Breuning, "Words and Deeds: Foreign Assistance Rhetoric and Policy Behavior in the Netherlands, Belgium, and the United Kingdom."

Notes

1. As measured in terms of Gross Domestic Product per capita (GDP/cap), see the UNDP's HDI (Human Development Reports) or CIA World Fact Book.

2. See Hochschild, *King Leopold's Ghost*, for a gripping account of Belgian predatory colonialism. Interestingly, Belgium is a comparatively young state in the West European context, dating its independence to 1830.
3. Coolsaet, *België en zijn Buitenlandse Politiek*; see especially the conclusion.
4. Goldsmith, "A Universal Proposition?"
5. Based on data from the Central Intelligence Agency, *The CIA World Fact Book*.
6. See the UNDP's *Human Development Reports*, various years.
7. Handel, *Weak States in the International System*.
8. See, e.g., Rotberg, *When States Fail*; Milliken, *State Failure*; Zartman, *Collapsed States*.
9. Neack, "Linking State Type with Foreign Policy Behavior," 224.
10. Ingebritsen, "Norm Entrepreneurs."
11. Ibid.; see also Breuning, "Why Give Aid?"; Breuning, "Words and Deeds"; Stokke, *Western Middle Powers and Global Poverty*.
12. See Katzenstein, *Small States in World Markets*; East, "Size and Foreign Policy Behavior."
13. For examples of definitions and discussions of the concept of a small state, see Baehr, "Small States"; East, "National Attributes and Foreign Policy"; East, "Size and Foreign Policy Behavior"; Hey, *Small States in World Politics*; Ingebritsen et al., *Small States in International Relations*; Keohane, "Lilliputians' Dilemmas"; Rothstein, *Alliances and Small Powers*; Vital, *The Survival of Small States*.
14. Hey, *Small States in World Politics*; East, "Size and Foreign Policy Behavior."
15. Hey, "Foreign Policy in Dependent States"; see also Biddle and Stephens, "Dependent Development and Foreign Policy"; Moon, "Consensus or Compliance?"; Moon, "The Foreign Policy of the Dependent State"; Singer, *Weak States in a World of Powers*.
16. Putnam, "Diplomacy and Domestic Politics."
17. Wendt, "Anarchy," 397.
18. Ibid.
19. Ibid., 423; also relevant in this regard is Kwitny's argument in *Endless Enemies*.
20. Houghton, "The Role of Analogical Reasoning"; Peterson, "The Use of Analogies."
21. Mearsheimer, "Why We Will Soon Miss the Cold War."
22. Wendt, "Anarchy," 399.
23. Ibid.
24. See Holsti, "National Role Conceptions," 12; see also Walker, *Role Theory*.
25. Ingebritsen, "Norm Entrepreneurs," 283.
26. Holsti, "National Role Conceptions," 16–25.
27. Breuning, "Words and Deeds."
28. Nye, *The Paradox of American Power*; Prestowitz, *Rogue Nation*.
29. Skidmore, "Understanding the Unilateralist Turn."
30. Ibid.

31. Nye, *Soft Power*, 5.
32. Nye (*Soft Power*, xi) dates the concept to his own earlier book, *Bound to Lead*.
33. Lai and Morey, "Impact of Regime Type"; Hagan, "Domestic Political Regime Changes."
34. Nye, *Soft Power*, 14.
35. Ibid., 7.
36. Nye, *Soft Power*.
37. Skidmore, "Understanding the Unilateralist Turn."
38. Nye, *Soft Power*, 147.

Chapter 7

Who or What Determines Foreign Policy?

Chapter Preview

- Explains why foreign policy analysis puts the human decision maker at the center of its endeavor.
- Explains the importance and appropriateness of multicausal explanations of foreign policy decision making.
- Outlines prospects and challenges for the field of foreign policy analysis.

Looking for Explanations

Where are the best explanations of foreign policy to be found? Over the course of the chapters in this book, we investigated numerous factors at various levels of analysis that each have the potential to affect foreign policy: leader personality and worldview; perceptions, problem representations, the use of analogies, and reasoning; the role of advisors, group decision making, and the impact of institutional arrangements; domestic audiences, national history, culture, and the state's political institutions; capabilities, size, and geographic location. At this point, it is tempting to argue that they all matter. This is not wrong, because multicausal explanations are often the most appropriate ones. However, it is also important to recognize that different causes sometimes explain slightly different things—such as decisions, behaviors, and outcomes—and require that we investigate phenomena at different levels of analysis—the individual, state, and international system.

Looking back, you will readily notice that the emphasis in the previous chapters has been on decisions, decision making, and decision makers. The book started with the observation that world history is rife with the sometimes puzzling and frequently disastrous decisions that leaders have made. We argued that foreign policy analysis is first and foremost interested in explaining how and why such decisions came about. This is where foreign policy analysis differs most clearly from the broader study of international relations. Foreign policy analysts proceed from the conviction that "human decision makers acting singly or in groups" are at the heart of international relations.[1] It is ultimately *leaders* who make foreign policy decisions. They are the ones committing their country and its resources to certain foreign policy behaviors. The resulting outcomes may not be what they intended, but that does not altogether absolve leaders from responsibility for the consequences of their decisions. Granted, outcomes depend on the complex interplay between decisions made by the leaders of several countries and are often not what any one of those leaders intended to happen.[2] Perhaps there are times when outcomes are beyond the capacities of leaders to control. Frequently, however, leaders get caught up in tangled webs of their own making: sometimes they wear the blinders of historical memory, sometimes the bureaucratic agencies on which they rely distort information, and sometimes they suffer the consequences of relying on faulty intelligence or bad advice. Despite these mitigating factors, it is in the end the decisions of leaders that shape the course of world history.

Hence, leaders—human decision makers—are at the heart of world politics. Would World War II have happened if Hitler had not made his fateful decisions to annex and conquer? Would it have made a difference if Chamberlain had drawn a line in the sand, as President George H. W. Bush did decades later when confronting Saddam Hussein's invasion of Kuwait? (And would President Bush have done so if he had not known of the failure of Chamberlain's appeasement?) Could a better grasp of Prime Minister Thatcher's personality have prevented the Malvinas/Falklands debacle for the Argentine leaders?

It is impossible to answer these questions definitively. Yet gaining insight into the personalities and perceptions of leaders, the advisors and the agencies on which they rely, and even the domestic and international constraints they face helps us understand not just how and why they arrived at their decisions, but also that much of world history could have been different. Better advice, more information, greater effort to see the world from the perspective of one's opponent, each of these could have influenced the course of history. Hence, if we want to understand international politics, we must understand leaders and their advisors. Decision makers and decision making are, so to speak, the ground (or the core) of international politics.[3]

The Stage and the Actors, or, Structure and Agency

Understanding decision makers and decision making is the key to understanding foreign policy behavior and the eventual outcomes of events. This does not mean that international and domestic constraints are unimportant. After all, leaders and their advisors do not function in a vacuum but are embedded in a domestic and international environment that they defy at their peril. It is important to understand the contours of those environments and also to obtain a grasp of the manner in which decision makers understood those environments at the time of the decision we seek to explain. Both the domestic and international environment are best categorized as **institutions**, in the sense that both are human creations rather than natural phenomena.[4] As used here, institutions are defined as "any collectively accepted system of rules (procedures, practices) that enable us to create institutional facts."[5] Institutions are therefore inherently social phenomena.

Institutional facts, in turn, are those things that can exist only in the context of human institutions.[6] Institutional facts are accepted as fact only within the context of human society and can therefore also be called **social facts**.[7] The borders between countries are a social (or institutional) fact, as is anything that flows from the existence of these borders, such as the need to carry a passport when you travel. Government is an institution, both as a concept and in terms of the specifics of its design, e.g., whether it is democratic or not. If government is an institution, you might guess that foreign policy and international relations are conducted within the boundaries of institutions and proceed very largely on the basis of social facts.

This is not to say that institutions and social facts are not real. For example, although there are many places in the world where the borders between countries are not demarcated in the landscape, we generally accept that borders exist and we behave accordingly—we bring along our passport when we travel. In other words, social facts influence our behavior. In fact, we frequently behave as if social facts are immutable forces of nature. This is most obvious when social facts change. At such times, our long-held assumptions are less useful in navigating the world around us. As discussed in chapter 6, after the end of the Cold War, decision makers were initially less sure of how to define their country's national interest.[8] The balance of power between the two superpowers, the United States and the Soviet Union, had dominated their framing of the international environment. Without it, decision makers suddenly faced an international environment that no longer fit their representation of it. The end of the Cold War provides a tangible moment when decision makers had to confront the socially constructed nature of international relations and had to arrive at a new understanding of the international environment.

Most of the time, decision makers are more likely to experience the international environment as a constraint or a given, rather than a human creation (and therefore alterable). Decision makers may perceive themselves as having the capacity to influence the domestic environment but simultaneously experience much of it as a constraint or a given as well. Hence, even if foreign policy decision making takes place in the context of human institutions and social facts, rather than in the context of natural phenomena, the individuals engaged in policy making often—but not always—experience the international environment as dominated by unchangeable facts. This is especially evident for the leaders of small states. Even the decision makers of those countries that have played the role of norm entrepreneur (see chapter 6), understand that outside of the specific issue area in which their country seeks to influence international politics, that same country exists in an international environment that is largely a constraint on their state's foreign policy behavior.

From this point of view, the domestic and international environment, as institutions and their accompanying social facts, are the stage on which foreign policy making takes place. The contours of that stage delimit the possibility for action. On occasion, foreign policy decisions and behaviors have the power to significantly alter those institutions and social facts that delimit the world stage—but more frequently, change in these environments requires cumulative effort across time. For example, decolonization can be dated back to the eighteenth century.[9] This is not only much earlier than the conventionally referenced period of decolonization in the post–World War II period (and primarily the 1960s) that had its roots in the early twentieth century ideas of national self-determination, but it also suggests that the beginning of decolonization pre-dates the end of the second phase of European expansionism by at least a century. Colonialism continued and expanded even as the idea of self-determination was beginning to take root. The rapid decolonization of the 1960s was, in effect, the culmination of a trend that had long been developing. Social facts may be human constructions, but once they are in place, they are often quite resistant to change. Hence, the domestic and international environment are often perceived as constraints—the boundaries within which policy making takes place.

As a result, foreign policy analysis privileges the individual level of analysis—and with it the consideration of options and the making of decisions. Foreign policy analysis does not deny that the state and system levels of analysis have their roles to play. It has been argued that especially the constraints presented by the international environment are "under-theorized," meaning that there has not been much attention for—or good ideas about—how exactly the international environment affects foreign policy decision making.[10] The discussion of the international constraints in chapter 6 supports this contention: capabilities make a difference, but we cannot say exactly how. Geographic location makes a difference, but we cannot say exactly how. Size matters, but we lack both a precise conceptualization of size and propositions about the expected behaviors of states of various sizes.[11] In comparison, there are many more plentiful and well-developed ideas about domestic constraints (chapter 5), and even more so about the influence of advisors, advisory systems, and bureaucratic agencies on foreign policy making (chapter 4). The largest proportion of foreign policy analysis, however, has placed the emphasis on leaders and psychological dynamics that impact decision making at the individual level (chapters 2 and 3).[12]

Foreign policy analysis, as an approach to the study of world politics, shares this notion that human decision makers are its ground with the social sciences more generally,[13] yet this same focus has been oddly absent from some of the classic works in the study of world politics, which privileged the system level of analysis.[14] Additionally, classical Realism, first introduced in chapter 3, proceeded from a rather narrow perception of what motivated decision makers. This perspective on the study of world politics encouraged analysts to think "in terms of interest defined as power."[15] The national interest was defined largely in terms of hard power or military might. In contrast, foreign policy analysis does not assume interests; rather, it seeks to empirically determine how decision makers actually define their state's interests.

As discussed in chapter 6, the leaders of some small states define their interest in terms of their role as norm entrepreneurs. In doing so, they are not interested in expanding their military prowess. Instead, they seek to influence international norms to popularize certain values and encourage behaviors consistent with those values.[16] In other words, they seek to alter the institutions of international politics.

Foreign policy analysis shares with classical Realism the emphasis on decision makers but differs in its assumptions about human behavior. The difference is similar to that between normative and empirical theories of rationality—with Realism generally more akin to normative and foreign policy analysis more akin to empirical approaches to rationality.

Making Sense of Multiple Simultaneous Explanations

Explaining foreign policy decisions is rarely simple. Usually, multiple causes help to generate a rich and complex explanation of the foreign policy behaviors of states. Early efforts in the field of foreign policy analysis presented comprehensive conceptual frameworks of the decision making process and the various constraints on that process.[17] These efforts were too unwieldy to serve as ready-made frameworks for research projects, but they did serve to define foreign policy analysis as a field of study. In essence, these efforts included all the elements an author might wish to include in a text introducing the field of study (such as this one). Since the introduction of these global frameworks, foreign policy analysis has grown to be an eclectic field that brings together a variety of ideas and types of studies. Rarely does one scholar investigate the entire, comprehensive scope of factors that might impinge on foreign policy making. Most often, investigations are limited to narrowly specified problems, and individual researchers often limit their work to specific slices of the study of foreign policy as a whole. Some spend much of their professional life analyzing leader personality, whereas others choose to focus on problem representations or the use of analogies in reasoning. Specialists may focus on the advisory system and sometimes on specific aspects of it, such as the impact of institutional arrangements of the advisory system on decision making processes. Other foreign policy analysts seek to understand when, how, and why public opinion or the media matter. There has been relatively little work on the impact of culture and national history or the influence of size, capabilities, and geographic location.

The fact that some aspects of foreign policy decision making have received less attention than others does not make those aspects irrelevant, but it does mean the field lacks well-developed theories about them.[18] It would also be inaccurate to assume that analysts who focus on one aspect of decision making perceive other aspects as unimportant and therefore not worthy of their attention. They simply focus on those areas that most hold their interest or those where they think they can make a contribution to our collective understanding of foreign policy making—and thereby international relations.

As scientists, foreign policy analysts carve out small problems to study, not because they think these are the only ones that matter, but because it is much easier to make sense of a small aspect than the entire foreign policy process at once. Foreign policy analysts readily agree that the decisions, behaviors, and outcomes they study are multicausal, but single research projects usually seek to isolate the impact of one or a small set of variables. It's a matter of how best to increase our knowledge and understanding of our subject. We are interested, first and foremost, in knowing which variables contribute *most* to the decision, behavior, or outcome in the cases we study. The next step is to investigate whether those same variables matter most in other cases as well. If they do, we can say that our findings are more generalizable than if they do not. Either way, it is through a sequence of small studies that we begin to understand how widely or narrowly our explanations apply. Some explanations will obtain only under a narrow set of circumstances, others will be more generally valid, some will apply under certain circumstances, and other will explain other sets of circumstances. The task is to develop further insight into which explanations apply to what type of cases and under what circumstances.

Prospects and Challenges for Foreign Policy Analysis

The field of foreign policy analysis is comparatively young. It is an approach to the study of international relations that dates back to the 1950s.[19] As already mentioned, the early efforts presented comprehensive conceptual frameworks of the decision making process and included also all the various constraints on that process. These efforts were too unwieldy to serve as ready-made frameworks for research projects, but they did serve to define the field of study.

What defines foreign policy analysis? One, and as previously pointed out, foreign policy analysis privileges the human decision maker. Although the individual level of analysis predominates in foreign policy analysis today, the field also includes state level analyses. This is especially true for large-scale event data sets focusing on foreign policy behavior. The development of these data sets dominated the field in the 1970s. This was well before machine coding became a possibility. As a result, the creation of these large data sets was extremely labor intensive. Although these efforts were largely abandoned by the end of the 1980s, there is now a new generation of efforts at event data collection that employs machine coding.[20] These event data sets focus in the foreign policy actions or behaviors of states but do not deny that human decision makers are ultimately responsible for those behaviors.

Two, the focus of foreign policy analysis is most often on decision makers and decision making processes, treating foreign policy behavior as the result of decision making rather than something that can be understood on its own terms. Efforts to understand decision makers and the decision making process are most often motivated by a desire to generate useful knowledge.[21] Foreign policy analysis is often motivated by the desire to have scholarship serve to improve the practice of foreign policy decision making.

Three, foreign policy analysis is methodologically eclectic, but various approaches share an emphasis on carefully explicated empirical analysis. Research may be quantitative or qualitative in nature, but it always strives for transparency in research design—making it possible for other scholars to understand precisely how evidence was employed and evaluated and to replicate the findings if they wish. Quantitative studies have the advantage of being the most easily replicable, but some questions are not easily answered through quantitative analysis. In addition, whether or not a specific concept can be quantified depends the state of the field: for example, the operational code (introduced in chapter 2) started out as a set of questions that researchers evaluated on the basis of case study analysis, but it has more recently been refashioned to into a quantitative method of analysis that employs machine coding of text.

Four, foreign policy analysis seeks to develop and test generalizable propositions about foreign policy decision making and foreign policy behavior. This last point deserves elaboration. As noted earlier, initial efforts in the study of foreign policy often presented grand, comprehensive, and integrated theories that encompassed the entire scope of subjects from individual and advisory system via bureaucracies and domestic constraints to questions of size and power, as well as the other states in the international environment.[22] Such schemes served their purpose. However, most contemporary theory is much more modest in scale. It tends to be **mid-range**, conditional, and bounded.[23] This means that such theories endeavor to provide explanations for only some aspect of foreign policy (rather than its totality) and do not claim universal applicability. Instead, such theories specify the conditions under which it applies or the range of cases to which the findings are expected to be generalizable. Such more modest theorizing helps the field to develop cumulative knowledge of certain aspects of foreign policy. It also demonstrates that the seminal early works have become a paradigmatic umbrella that unifies a diverse set of efforts.

Under that large umbrella, foreign policy analysts often focus on a specific element or dynamic of the decision making process. They formulate expectations and test these on the basis of empirical analyses that are relatively small in scale, such as a set of case studies, either historical or contemporary, that is chosen to specifically because they are similar in some ways but differ in other respects. What is held constant and what is permitted to vary will depend on the specific research question, but each carefully designed small-scale study can help expand our knowledge. In this way, foreign policy analysis provides better prospects for the cumulation of knowledge than other research efforts in international relations, because it seeks to "expand the debate across as many independent sources of empirical information as possible."[24]

Despite this advantage, foreign policy analysis has maintained a rather strong focus on U.S. foreign policy and on crisis decision making. Several scholars in foreign policy analysis have remarked that "foreign policy decision making in the *absence* of crisis-related factors has gone largely unexplored."[25] Indeed, analysis of economic foreign policy making, decision making regarding foreign aid and development cooperation, the negotiation of international environmental treaties, and a range of other subjects remain a small proportion of the total volume of studies in foreign policy analysis. As the world becomes more interconnected, it will be important to begin to explore foreign policy making on subjects beyond crises more earnestly.

In addition, there has been a distinct bias in favor of U.S. foreign policy making as the subject of investigation. This evidences the American origins of the field of study but has other roots as well. Data availability has been an important element. Foreign policy analysts based in the United States have frequently delved into archival records at presidential libraries and interviewed former and current decision makers. When the foreign policies of other countries are the subject of investigation, the emphasis is frequently on great and emerging powers or states that are in other ways relevant to U.S. foreign policy at the time. On the one hand, this is to be expected of a field of study that seeks to provide useful knowledge. On the other hand, there are also missed opportunities both for theory development and for a deeper understanding of the dynamics of international system change over time.

The application of propositions regarding the organization of the American executive to the court of Emperor Haile Selassie of Ethiopia in chapter 4 represents an effort in this book to apply theoretical propositions developed in the context of U.S. foreign policy to other another country. In this case, the example helps us understand the problems that emerged at the center of power as the Emperor aged. Interestingly, the strong centralization of foreign policy making power in the American executive suggests the possibility that theories developed in the context of U.S. foreign policy may be more helpful in the study of authoritarian (and perhaps also semi-authoritarian) regimes than in studying the foreign policies of parliamentary democracies. This may explain the observation that: "Rarely have students of international relations systematically analyzed the foreign policy decision making processes of non-U.S., nonauthoritarian regimes such as democratic, parliamentary systems."[26]

Analysts of the foreign policies of parliamentary democracies with coalition governments require theories that deal specifically with the diffuse authority structure that is common in such political systems. Theories created for the study of presidential systems, which have a single leader at the pinnacle of government, are a poor fit for understanding the foreign policy making of countries with coalition governments. In such governments, as described in chapter 4, the junior coalition partner can under certain circumstances exercise control well beyond its numerical representation within the coalition. In other words, in coalition governments the buck does not automatically stop at the prime minister's desk.

Lastly, irrespective of government structure, small states are also understudied in foreign policy analysis. There has been a general perception that small states are less important than large states because of their lesser power capabilities. Such a perception may be inaccurate on two grounds: One, size and capabilities are, as explained in chapter 6, at best a rough guide to a state's foreign policy behavior. Two, small states have occasionally positioned themselves as norm entrepreneurs in specific foreign policy issue areas. They may not have the resources to engage in extensive foreign policy making efforts on a wide range of issues, but by targeting their efforts in a narrow, well-defined set of interconnected issues, the decision makers of such states may be able to affect the behavior of other states in that specific domain. The connection of the efforts of norm entrepreneurs with the American concept of soft power demonstrates that small states, and especially norm entrepreneurs, may be useful subjects for investigation as we seek to understand foreign policy influence apart from concept of raw, hard power.

In sum, foreign policy analysis is a dynamic approach to the study of international relations. It is characterized by a strong emphasis on human decision makers and a focus on the cumulation of knowledge through the shared enterprise of many scholars engaged in small-scale, systematic, and empirical efforts. There are aspects of the field that are as yet underdeveloped, as well as areas in which we have gained important insights. Among the latter is the realization that foreign policy disasters almost always have at their root the inability of foreign policy decision makers to perceive the world from the vantage point of the decision makers of one or more other countries. Although there are no guarantees that carefully crafted foreign policy decisions will always yield the intended outcomes, the odds are much better when human decision makers have the ability to perceive the world from multiple perspectives. Foreign policy analysis, at its core, is about understanding the multiple perspectives of the world that either collide or connect when the foreign policy decision makers of different countries meet—and it holds out the hope that there might be less collision and more cooperation.

Chapter Summary

- Foreign policy analysis puts the human decision maker at the center of its endeavor. The subject matter of foreign policy analysis concerns institutions created by human beings. These institutions often function as constraints but are nonetheless the products of accepted norms, rules, and practices.
- Multicausal explanations are most appropriate in explanations of foreign policy decision, behaviors, and outcomes. Foreign policy analysts are interested in generalizable theories. Repeated tests, using different case studies or different data, help to evaluate the generalizability of any specific theory.
- Foreign policy analysis has often privileged the study of U.S. foreign policy and crisis decision making and paid relatively less attention to non-crisis decision making and small-state foreign policy.

Terms

Institutions
Institutional facts
Social facts
Mid-range theory

Study Questions

1. What level of analysis is most appropriate for efforts to understand foreign policy decision making? Foreign policy behavior? Outcomes?
2. How do foreign policy analysts approach the study of the complex and multicausal phenomena that interest them?
3. What four elements define foreign policy analysis as a field of study?

Suggestions for Further Reading

Two excellent essays on the current state of the field of foreign policy analysis are: Hudson, "Foreign Policy Analysis: Actor-Specific Theory and the

Ground of International Relations," and Houghton, "Reinvigorating the Study of Foreign Policy Decision-making: Toward a Constructivist Approach."

Most of the early efforts in foreign policy analysis that presented comprehensive conceptual frameworks are now out of print. An exception is Snyder, Bruck, and Sapin, *Foreign Policy Decision-making: An Approach to the Study of International Politics.*

In addition, the journal *Foreign Policy Analysis* is a good source for current research in foreign policy analysis.

Notes

1. Hudson, "Foreign Policy Analysis," 1, 21.
2. A point made long ago by Allison, "Conceptual Models and the Cuban Missile Crisis."
3. Hudson, "Foreign Policy Analysis," 1.
4. Searle, "What is an Institution?"; see also Houghton, "Reinvigorating the Study of Foreign Policy Decision-Making."
5. Searle, "What is an Institution?" 21.
6. Ibid., 3.
7. Adler, "Constructivism and International Relations," 95; Houghton, "Reinvigorating the Study of Foreign Policy Decision-Making," 28.
8. Wendt, "Anarchy," 399.
9. Szirmai, *The Dynamics of Socio-Economic Development*, 50.
10. Houghton, "Reinvigorating the Study of Foreign Policy Decision-Making," 34.
11. It is significant that much of the work dealing with size and capabilities is rather dated, although there is some renewed interest in small states, as exemplified by Ingebritsen et al., *Small States in International Relations.*
12. Houghton, "Reinvigorating the Study of Foreign Policy Decision-Making," makes precisely this point.
13. Hudson, "Foreign Policy Analysis," 1.
14. Notably classics such as: Singer, "The Level-of-Analysis Problem in International Relations"; Waltz, *Man, the State, and War: A Theoretical Analysis*; Waltz, *Theory of International Politics.*
15. E.g., Morgenthau, *Politics Among Nations*, 13.
16. Ingebritsen, "Norm Entrepreneurs"; see also Finnemore, *National Interests in International Society.*
17. Rosenau, "Pre-Theories and Theories of Foreign Policy"; Snyder et al., *Foreign Policy Decision-Making*; Sprout and Sprout, *The Ecological Perspective on Human Affairs.*
18. Houghton, "Reinvigorating the Study of Foreign Policy Decision-Making," 34.

19. Rosenau, "Pre-Theories and Theories of Foreign Policy"; Snyder et al., *Foreign Policy Decision-Making*; Sprout and Sprout, *The Ecological Perspective on Human Affairs*. Several essays have recounted the field's history and development. See Gerner, "The Evolution of the Study of Foreign Policy"; Hudson, "Foreign Policy Analysis"; Hudson, "Foreign Policy Decision-Making"; Hudson with Vore, "Foreign Policy Analysis."

20. Hudson, "Foreign Policy Analysis," 9–10 and 20; For information on the KEDS system and its uses, see Gerner et al., "Machine Coding of Event Data Using Regional and International Sources"; Schrodt and Gerner, "Validity Assessment of a Machine-Coded Event Data Set for the Middle East, 1982–92"; The Kansas Event Data System (KEDS) Project, http://web.ku.edu/keds/.

21. See, e.g., George, *Bridging the Gap*; Nincic and Lepgold, *Being Useful*.

22. See, for instance, Snyder, Bruck, and Sapin, *Foreign Policy Decision-Making*.

23. Gerner, "The Evolution of the Study of Foreign Policy," 30; Hermann, "Epilogue: Reflections on Foreign Policy Theory Building," 252.

24. Van Belle, "Dinosaurs and the Democratic Peace," 294.

25. Astorino-Courtois and Trusty, "Degrees of Difficulty," 29, italics in original. See also Drezner, "Ideas, Bureaucratic Politics, and the Crafting of Foreign Policy"; Kowert, *Groupthink or Deadlock*.

26. Kaarbo, "Power and Influence in Foreign Policy Decision Making," 503; see also Hagan, *Political Opposition and Foreign Policy*.

Glossary

Accountability—The idea that decision makers cannot do as they please but must take responsibility for their decisions and actions and must explain themselves to the people they govern. The concept is often associated with democracy but is not exclusive to it. (Chapter 2)

Active-negative—A category used in the study of presidential character. These are individuals who invest a lot of energy in their leadership role but also perceive the job as a chore. (Chapter 2)

Active-positive—A category used in the study of presidential character. These are leaders who invest a lot of energy and derive a lot of satisfaction from the job. (Chapter 2)

Analogical reasoning—A process of comparing a poorly understood problem to a historical problem that is deemed similar and about which more is known. (Chapter 3)

Anarchy— Characterizes the international system. Means that there is no central power. Each state is sovereign and must secure its own interests. (Chapter 6)

Balance of power—Refers to a situation in which there is a rough parity among the large powers in the international system. In addition, the effort to arrive at, or to maintain, a balance of power leads analysts to prescribe certain policies. (Chapter 2)

Bargaining—Implies that the decision making process involves give-and-take and that the preferences of any one policy maker never fully shape the decision but often partially do so. (Chapter 4)

Behavior—See **Foreign policy behavior**. (Chapter 1)

Bounded rationality—Holds that actors are rational are rational within the scope of what they know. Recognizes that human decision makers are not omniscient. (Chapter 3)

Bureaucratic politics model—One of three models of decision making outlined in this book. It describes policy making as the outcome of multiple bargaining processes between individual decision makers at multiple levels within the government. (Chapter 4)

Cabinet government—An executive branch of government in which collective responsibility for decision making rests with a cabinet. (Chapter 4)

Capabilities—Measurable assets, such as a country's geographic size, its population, its natural resources, the size of its economy and its military, which can be used as an indicator of the potential power of a state. (Chapter 6)

Citizen diplomacy—The efforts and effects abroad of actions by actors who are not official representatives of the state or its government. (Chapter 1)

Coalition—Associated with parliamentary systems and electoral systems that employ proportional representation. Two or more political parties jointly form the government, because no single party has a majority of the seats in parliament. (Chapter 4)

Coalition agreement—The negotiated agreement that provides the basis for cooperation between the coalition partners. (Chapter 4)

Coalition cabinet—A government in a parliamentary system that consists of ministers who represent two or more political parties. (Chapter 4)

Coalition partners—The parties that join together to form a coalition government. (Chapter 4)

Cognitive biases—Identifiable and systematic errors in human reasoning. (Chapter 3)

Collective responsibility—An approach to cabinet government in which each minister is expected to publicly support all cabinet (or government) decisions. (Chapter 4)

Collegial approach—An approach to organizing the executive that emphasizes teamwork and debate rather than competition. The leader seeks out multiple sources of information and encourages multiple viewpoints. (Chapter 4)

Command center—Relates to small-group decision making. The group develops options, evaluates them, selects the most viable ones, and ultimately makes a decision. (Chapter 4)

Compensation foreign policy—A dependent state's foreign policy that antagonizes the leaders of powerful states in an effort to appease domestic audiences. (Chapter 6)

Competitive approach—An approach to organizing the executive that actively and systematically employs multiple channels of information. Results in a competitive relationship between advisors but provides the leader with multiple viewpoints on issues. (Chapter 4)

Complexifiers—Describes theorists who perceive good judgment to be connected to the ability to think critically. (Chapter 3)

Compliant foreign policy—A dependent state's foreign policy alignment with that of a larger, more powerful state on the basis of influence exerted by the latter to achieve such an alignment. (Chapter 6)

Conceptual complexity—A concept used in leadership trait analysis. It measures whether a decision maker perceives the world in complex and nuanced ways or in simpler back-and-white terms. (Chapter 2)

Concurrence—A decision process marked by little discussion of options. The decision makers quickly settle on an option they jointly perceive as a reasonable solution. (Chapter 4)

Consensus-oriented foreign policy—A dependent state's voluntarily alignment of their external policy with that of a larger, more powerful state that has the capacity to exert influence over the dependent state. (Chapter 6)

Constitutional monarchy—Describes a specific type of democratic political system in which monarchy has been circumscribed by a constitution that specifies the separation of powers between the various branches of government and limits the political role of the monarch. (Chapter 5)

Content analysis—A term used for various ways of analyzing text. It can vary from interpretive schemes guided by a set of questions to counting the frequency of specific words in text. (Chapter 2)

Counterdependent foreign policy—A dependent state's defiant foreign policy that usually invites the displeasure of the large, more powerful state on which it is dependent. (Chapter 6)

Counterfactuals—Decisions, behaviors, or outcomes that differ from the actual facts of history. Careful exploration of counterfactuals can enhance our understanding of causality in international politics. (Chapter 1)

Crisis—Situation defined by three elements: a high threat to something that is highly valued, a short amount of time to make a decision, and its occurrence surprises the decision makers. (Chapter 1)

Culture—A set of values held in common by the people of a state. (Chapter 5)

Deadlock—The result of a decision making process in which the decision makers fail to achieve agreement. (Chapter 4)

Decision—See **Foreign policy decision**.

Decision frame—The manner in which a decision maker has framed, or represented, a specific decision making situation. (Chapter 3)

Decision units—The individual or group of individuals who are in a position not only to make a foreign policy decision but also to prevent any other entity within the government from explicitly reversing that decision. (Chapter 4)

Democratic peace theory—A set of propositions that suggests that countries that are governed democratically are less likely to initiate wars (with one another) than non-democracies. There is substantial empirical evidence that supports these propositions. (Chapter 5)

Dependence—An asymmetric pattern of interactions between a more and a less powerful state. (Chapter 6)

Dependent variable—The effect in a cause-and-effect relationship. Its value depends on the effect of the independent variables. In scientific investigation, the occurrence or value(s) of dependent variable is what we seek to understand. (Chapter 1)

Developing country—A designation that is imprecise and encompasses a wide variety of countries. Generally denotes countries that are not as technologically advanced or industrialized as states with advanced economies. (Chapter 6)

Diversionary theory of war—Holds that leaders may take their country to war to focus the public's attention on foreign policy rather than on the domestic problems to enhance support for the government. (Chapter 3)

Dominant solution—The only credible option for dealing with a foreign policy situation; the obvious choice of all decision makers. (Chapter 4)

Electoral system—The rules that govern the elections of countries with elected legislatures or other elected governmental offices. These rules determine how votes are translated into seats in that legislature or how it is determined which candidate gets to hold the office. (Chapter 4)

Embedded agency—An entity that is created as a subunit of a larger government agency. (Chapter 5)

Emerging power—A state that is rapidly becoming more powerful; one developing its capabilities into usable assets. (Chapter 6)

Emotions—Consist of both psychological and physical components. The first are described as feelings and the second as physical changes. Emotions are often also described as spontaneous reactions. (Chapter 2)

Empirical theory of rationality—A theory about rationality that favors empirical investigation into human reasoning and decision making. (Chapter 3)

Failed state—A state in which the government effectively does not control the state's territory. The phrase describes the absence of (effective) institutions of government. (Chapter 6)

Foreign policy—The totality of a country's policies toward and interactions with the environment beyond its borders. (Chapter 1)

Foreign policy behavior—The enactment of a **foreign policy decision**. (Chapter 1)

Foreign policy decision—The foreign policy option that was chosen. (Chapter 1)

Foreign policy options—The range of possible choices for responding to a specific problem or situation. (Chapter 1)

Foreign policy outcomes—The end result of a state's foreign policy behavior in interaction with the foreign policy behaviors of other states. (Chapter 1)

Formalistic approach—An approach to organizing the executive that emphasizes hierarchy and has a clear chain of command. (Chapter 4)

Formative event—A major event that strongly influences a decision maker's thinking about the nature of world politics and foreign policy. (Chapter 3)

Framing—Describes the systematic effects of a person's perspective on the interpretation of situations and events, e.g., a tendency to judge risk in terms of how a problem is presented. (Chapter 1)

Good decision—A decision (1) in which a sound decision making process was followed or (2) from which a good outcome resulted. Neither is an entirely satisfactory definition. (Chapter 1)

Great power—A term for classifying a state that has the political, economic, and military strength to exert influence on a global scale. (Chapter 6)

Groupthink—The premature closure of the search for options. Decision makers quickly concur but may have overlooked or ignored options. (Chapter 4)

Groups—Refers to small groups of advisors at the pinnacle of government. Policy makers meet face-to-face in small groups where decisions are fashioned on the basis of the information and analysis provided by the various agencies and departments. (Chapter 4)

Heuristic—A shortcut in decision making; also called a *rule of thumb*. (Chapter 3)

Idea-based organization—A government entity that is created to serve a specific policy goal. Its objective and its strategy for achieving it are shared by those who work for the organization. This type of organization is mission driven. (Chapter 5)

Ill-structured problem—A problem that is not well defined, usually because of incomplete information. (Chapter 3)

Independent variable—The causes in a cause-and-effect relationship. Factors that determine the value of the dependent variable. Independent variables explain the value or the occurrence of the dependent variable. (Chapter 1)

Individual level of analysis—The most specific of the three levels of analysis. It focuses on individuals, such as leaders and their advisors, to explain foreign policy. (Chapter 1)

Insulated agency—An autonomous or independent entity within the government bureaucracy. (Chapter 5)

Institutional facts—Facts that owe their existence to human society, such as borders between countries or citizenship. Also called **social facts**. (Chapter 7)

Institutions—Systems of rules, procedures, and practices that are shared by collectivities of individuals, states, or even the international community as a whole. (Chapter 7)

Integrative solution—A result that represents the preferences of all members of the group, albeit modified to some degree. (Chapter 4)

Interdependence—The structure of a state's interactions with other states. Usually refers to states that have active trading relationships with one another. (Chapter 6)

Interest-based organization—A government entity that is characterized by bargaining with other organizations within the government bureaucracy. It is driven less by organizational mission than by a desire to maintain or improve the organization's standing within the larger government bureaucracy. (Chapter 5)

Irredentism—The quest to include an ethnic kinship group that lives across the border into the territory of the state, usually by incorporating the territory in which that group lives into the state. (Chapter 3)

Isolationism—Describes the basic foreign policy attitude of the United States prior to World War I, when the country avoided an active role in world affairs. (Chapter 5)

Issue area—A set of interrelated concerns in policy making that can be distinguished from other sets of interrelated concerns. (Chapter 1)

Large-N comparison—A research strategy in which a large number of cases is systematically compared, usually with the aid of statistical methodologies. This research strategy enables researchers to evaluate general cause-and-effect patterns (or relationships). (Chapter 1)

Leadership trait analysis—An approach to the study of leader personality. (Chapter 2)

Levels of analysis—The specificity or abstraction of the entities studied. Most often, three levels of analysis are employed in the study of international relations: individual, state, and system. (Chapter 1)

Machiavellian—Used to connote duplicity and unscrupulous behavior. Named after Niccolo Machiavelli, a fifteenth century political thinker, who counseled policy makers that it is more important to appear good than to be good. (Chapter 2)

Middle power—A state that can wield a measure of influence, albeit not through the projection of military might. (Chapter 6)

Mid-range theory—Provides explanations for only (a) specific aspect(s) of foreign policy. Such a theory specifies the conditions under which it applies or the range of cases to which the findings are expected to be generalizable. Not a universally applicable theory. (Chapter 7)

National history—Conveys and communicates common values that a society seeks to instill in the next generation. Uses tales that are (usually) factually accurate but chosen because they convey values and meanings that are deemed significant. Does not necessarily present a comprehensive record of events. (Chapter 5)

National interest—Traditionally defined in terms of security issues, such as the ability to maintain the integrity of the state's borders through military defense. Foreign policy analysis does not impose such a definition but instead asks how decision makers define the national interest. (Chapter 3)

National role conception—The scope and type of foreign policy decisions and behaviors that decision makers perceive as appropriate for their state to undertake. (Chapter 6)

National self-determination—The desire of a group of people sharing a common national or ethnic identity to govern itself in its own state. (Chapter 3)

Noncompensatory principle—Suggests that policy options are excluded if they are unacceptable on one critical dimension, irrespective of other attractive features such options may have. A decision rule associated with stage one of the poliheuristic theory. (Chapter 3)

Normative theory of rationality—A theory of rationality that specifies a specific model of rational decision making. (Chapter 3)

Norm entrepreneur—Actors, such as states or individuals, who advocate for the adoption of certain international standards and work diplomatically to persuade the representatives of other states to also adopt these norms. (Chapter 6)

Operational code—An approach to the study of leader personality. (Chapter 2)

Options—See **Foreign policy options**.

Organizational process model—One of three models of decision making outlined in this book. It describes government as a collection of organizations and decision making as the product of organizational processes. (Chapter 4)

Outcomes—See **Foreign policy outcomes**.

Parliamentary system—A system of government in which the executive and legislative branches of government are linked. Parliamentary elections determine the composition of both the parliament and the executive. (Chapter 4)

Passive-negative—A category used in the study of presidential character. These are leaders who perceive the presidency as a chore but are motivated by a sense of duty to country. (Chapter 2)

Passive-positive—A category used in the study of presidential character. These are leaders who are less energetic but find the job satisfying. (Chapter 2)

Personality—The enduring qualities, or character, of a person. (Chapter 2)

Persuasion—Describes the process by which one or more decision makers are successful at convincing others in a decision making group to adopt their point of view. Persuasion generates agreement on a solution in a decision making group. (Chapter 4)

Poliheuristic theory—A theory of foreign policy decision making that specifies a two-stage decision process, with different decision rules characterizing decision making at each stage. (Chapter 3)

Political culture—Encompasses the shared political values of a society's people. This includes generalized beliefs about one's own state and about other states, as well as the actual and desired relations between these. See also **culture**. (Chapter 5)

Presidential character—An approach to the study of leader personality. (Chapter 2)

Presidential system—A system of government in which the executive branch of government is separate from the legislative branch. The president and legislature are elected independently of one another and have their own independent mandate. (Chapter 4)

Problem representation—A mental representation of a problem or situation that has an impact on the decision making process. (Chapter 3)

Prospect theory—A set of propositions about the impact of framing or problem representation on the evaluation of options in decision making. (Chapter 3)

Public diplomacy—A government's diplomatic efforts that target citizens, the press, and constituencies in other countries rather than the governments of those countries. (Chapter 1)

Public opinion—The attitudes and opinions of the population of a society. Often measured through the use of surveys. (Chapter 2)

Public persona—The public image of a decision maker. It may or may not reflect her or his private personality. (Chapter 2)

Rationality—Suggests a thought process that starts with a purpose and revolves around weighing options and making choices in a manner that best achieves that predetermined end. This rather thin definition of rationality is expanded upon in Chapter 3. (Chapter 1)

Rational policy model—One of three models of decision making outlined in this book. It describes policy *as if* made by a single, rational decision maker. (Chapter 4)

Realist theory—An influential perspective in the study of world politics characterized by a concern with maintaining and possibly enhancing a state's power and, thereby, the integrity and autonomy of the state. (Chapter 3)

Regional power—A state that has the resources to exert influence in the region of the world in which it is located. (Chapter 6)

Rogue state—A state whose decision makers do not conduct their foreign policy according to the conventions of international diplomacy. Their violation of these conventions and of international law makes them threats to other states in the international environment. (Chapter 5)

Satisficing—Choosing the first acceptable solution; "good enough" decision making. (Chapters 3 and 4)

Schema—A generalized mental representation of a concept. (Chapter 3)

Semi-authoritarian regimes—Governments that hold elections and have the institutional framework of democracy (or representative government) without the substantive commitment to democratic values. (Chapter 5)

Simplifiers—Describes theorists who hold that good judgment is the ability to discern simple patterns that define even the most complex of events. (Chapter 3)

Skeptics of good judgment—Describes theorists who judge that the complex nature of international politics makes it near impossible to fully grasp the myriad consequences of any decision; they attribute good outcomes largely to luck. (Chapter 3)

Small-N comparison—A research strategy in which a small number of cases is systematically compared. Such comparisons permit a rich and nuanced understanding of similarities and differences between cases, but findings are not as easily generalized. (Chapter 1)

Small state—A state with a comparatively limited capacity to exert influence on other states. Generally has a smaller range of foreign policy instruments they can effectively employ in their relations with other states. (Chapters 2 and 6)

Social facts—See **Institutional facts**. (Chapter 7)

Soft power—The ability to shape the preferences of others through compelling ideas and values. It may involve both the modeling of desirable behaviors and persuasion. Contrasted with hard power. (Chapter 3)

Sovereignty—The doctrine that the government of a state is the legitimate and ultimate authority over that state; i.e., it recognizes no other authority above itself. (Chapter 6)

Standard operating procedures—The customary, or standardized, processes that describe most of the decision making in organizations. Associated with the organizational process model. (Chapter 4)

State level of analysis—The middle of the three levels of analysis. It focuses on factors internal to the state as the ones that compel states to engage in specific foreign policy behaviors. (Chapter 1)

Subset solution—A result in which one faction's ideas dominate over the preferences of other members or factions within the group. (Chapter 4)

Superpower—A state that can project power globally. (Chapter 6)

System level of analysis—The most abstract of the three levels of analysis. It focuses on the interactions between states. Foreign policy analysis rarely employs this level of analysis, although it uses system level attributes descriptively to understand the context of foreign policy making. (Chapter 1)

Think tank—A group of advisors who work jointly to create a problem representation, generate options, or evaluate options. Groups (or teams) are considered superior to single decision makers especially when problems are ill-structured. Relates to small-group decision making. (Chapter 4)

Two-level game—Describes the delicate balancing act that is required when foreign policy decision makers try to satisfy domestic constituencies and international imperatives simultaneously. (Chapter 1)

Unitary actor—The assumption that the state acts as if it were a homogeneous entity (rather than a collectivity of individual decision makers). (Chapter 3)

Weak state—Describes a country with ineffective institutions of government, sometimes used synonymously with small state. (Chapter 6)

Bibliography

Adler, Emanuel. "Constructivism and International Relations." In *Handbook of International Relations*, ed. Walter Carlsnaes, Thomas Risse, and Beth A. Simmons. London, UK: Sage, 2002.

Allison, Graham T. *Essence of Decision: Explaining the Cuban Missile Crisis*. Boston: Little, Brown, and Company, 1971.

———. "Conceptual Models and the Cuban Missile Crisis." *American Political Science Review* 63 (1969): 689–718.

Allison, Graham T., and Morton H. Halperin. "Bureaucratic Politics: A Paradigm and Some Implications." *World Politics* 24/supplement (1972), 40–79.

Allison, Graham T., and Philip Zelikow. *Essence of Decision: Explaining the Cuban Missile Crisis, 2nd ed.* New York: Addison Wesley Longman, 1999.

Andargachew Tiruneh. *The Ethiopian Revolution, 1974-1987: A Transformation from an Aristocratic to a Totalitarian Autocracy*. New York: Cambridge University Press, 1993.

Astorino-Courtois, Allison, and Brittani Trusty. "Degrees of Difficulty: The Effect of Israeli Policy Shifts on Syrian Peace Decisions." In *Integrating Cognitive and Rational Theories of Foreign Policy Decision Making*, ed. Alex Mintz. New York: Palgrave, 2003.

Barber, James D. *The Presidential Character: Predicting Performance in the White House*. Englewood Cliffs, NJ: Prentice Hall, 1992.

Baehr, Peter R. "Small States: A Tool for Analysis?" *World Politics* 27/3 (1975): 456–66.

Bendor, Jonathan, and Thomas H. Hammond. "Rethinking Allison's Models" *American Political Science Review* 86 (1992): 301–22.

Biddle, William J., and John D. Stephens. "Dependent Development and Foreign Policy: The Case of Jamaica." *International Studies Quarterly* 33 (1989): 411–34.

Bless, Herbert. "The Interplay of Affect and Cognition: The Mediating Role of General Knowledge Structures." In *Feeling and Thinking; The Role of Affect in Social Cognition*, ed. Joseph P. Forgas. Cambridge, UK: Cambridge University Press, 2000.

Bouveroux, Jos. *België uit Afrika? Rwanda, Boeroendi, en Zaire [Belgium out of Africa? Rwanda, Burundi, and Zaire]*. Antwerp, Belgium: Standaard, 1994.

Braveboy-Wagner, Jacqueline Anne, ed. *The Foreign Policies of the Global South: Rethinking Conceptual Frameworks*. Boulder, CO: Lynne Rienner, 2003.

Breuning, Marijke. "The Role of Analogies and Abstract Reasoning in Decision-making: Evidence from the Debate over Truman's Proposal for Development Assistance." *International Studies Quarterly* 47 (2003): 229–45.

———. "Culture, History, Role: Belgian and Dutch Axioms and Foreign Assistance Policy." In *Culture and Foreign Policy*, ed. Valerie M. Hudson. Boulder, CO: Lynne Rienner, 1997.

———. "Words and Deeds: Foreign Assistance Rhetoric and Policy Behavior in the Netherlands, Belgium, and the United Kingdom." *International Studies Quarterly* 39/2 (1995): 235–54.

———. "Why Give Foreign Aid? Decision Maker Perceptions of the Benefits to the Donor State." *Acta Politica* 29 (1994): 121–45.

Brzezinski, Zbigniew. *The Grand Chessboard: American Primacy and Its Geostrategic Imperatives*. New York: Basic Books, 1998.

Caprioli, Mary, and Peter Trumbore. "Identifying 'Rogue' States and Testing their Interstate Conflict Behavior." *European Journal of International Relations* 9/3 (2003): 377–406.

Cederman, Lars-Erik. "Back to Kant: Reinterpreting the Democratic Peace as a Macrohistorical Learning Process." *American Political Science Review* 95/1 (2001): 15–31.

Central Intelligence Agency (CIA), *The World Factbook*. http://www.cia.gov/cia/publications/factbook/index.html.

Chan, Steve. "In Search of Democratic Peace: Problems and Promise." *Mershon International Studies Review* 41/Supplement 1 (1997): 59–91.

———. "Mirror, Mirror on the Wall: Are the Free Countries More Pacific?" *Journal of Conflict Resolution* 28 (December 1984).

Chan, Steve, and William Safran. "Public Opinion as a Constraint against War: Democracies' Responses to Operation Iraqi Freedom." *Foreign Policy Analysis* 2/2 (2006): 137–56.

Clapham, Christopher. *Haile-Selassie's Government*. New York: Frederick A. Praeger, 1969.

Coolsaet, Rik. *België en zijn Buitenlandse Politiek, 1830–1990* [*Belgium and its Foreign Policy, 1830–1990*]. Leuven, Belgium: Van Halewyck, 1998.

———. *Buitenlandse Zaken* [*(Belgian) Foreign Affairs*]. Leuven, Belgium: Kritak, 1987.

Crawford, Neta C. "The Passion of World Politics: Propositions on Emotion and Emotional Relationships." *International Security* 24/4 (2000): 116–56.

Crichlow, Scott. "Idealism or Pragmatism? An Operational Code Analysis of Yitzhak Rabin and Shimon Peres." *Political Psychology* 19/4 (1998): 683–706.

Dahl, Robert A. "The Behavioral Approach in Political Science: Epitaph for a Monument to a Successful Protest." *American Political Science Review* 55 (1961): 763–72.

Danilovic, Vesna. "The Rational-Cognitive Debate and Poliheuristic Theory." In *Integrating Cognitive and Rational Theories of Foreign Policy Decision Making*, ed. Alex Mintz. New York: Palgrave, 2003.

DeRouen, Karl, Jr. "The Decision Not to Use Force at Dien Bien Phu: A Poliheuristic Perspective." In *Integrating Cognitive and Rational Theories of Foreign Policy Decision Making*, ed. Alex Mintz. New York: Palgrave, 2003.

Dewachter, Wilfried. *Besluitvorming in Politiek België* [*Decision Making in Belgian Politics*]. Leuven, Belgium: Acco, 1992.

Dewachter, Wilfried, and Mieke Verminck. "De Machtsbases van België in de Internationale Politiek [The Powerbases of Belgium in International Politics]." *Res Publica* 29 (1987): 21-27.

Drezner, Daniel W. "Ideas, Bureaucratic Politics, and the Crafting of Foreign Policy." *American Journal of Political Science* 44/4 (October 2000), pp. 733–49.

Dyson, Stephen B. "Personality and Foreign Policy: Tony Blair's Iraq Decision." *Foreign Policy Analysis* 2/3 (2006): 289–306

———. "Drawing Policy Implications from the 'Operational Code' of a 'New' Political Actor: Russian President Vladimir Putin," *Policy Sciences* 34/3 (2001): 329–46.

Dyson, Stephen B., and Thomas Preston. "Individual Characteristics of Political Leaders and the Use of Analogies in Foreign Policy Decision Making." *Political Psychology* 27/2 (2006): 265–88.

East, Maurice A. "National Attributes and Foreign Policy." In *Why Nations Act*, ed. Maurice A East, Stephen A Salmore, and Charles F. Hermann. Beverly Hills, CA: Sage, 1978.

———. "Size and Foreign Policy Behavior: A Test of Two Models." *World Politics* 25/4 (1973): 556–57.

Entman, Robert M. *Projections of Power: Framing News, Public Opinion, and U.S. Foreign Policy*. Chicago: University of Chicago Press, 2004.

Elster, Jon. "Sadder but Wiser? Rationality and the Emotions." *Social Science Information* 24 (1985): 375–406.

Etheredge, Lloyd S. "Wisdom and Good Judgment in Politics." *Political Psychology* 13/3 (1992): 497–516.

Evans, Peter B., Harold K. Jacobson, and Robert D. Putnam, eds. *Double-Edged Diplomacy: International Bargaining and Domestic Politics*. Berkeley: University of California Press, 1993.

Farnham, Barbara. "Impact of the Political Context on Foreign Policy Decision-Making." *Political Psychology* 25/3 (2004): 441–63.

———. "Perceiving the End of Threat: Ronald Reagan and the Gorbachev Revolution." In *Good Judgment in Foreign Policy: Theory and Application*, ed. Stanley A. Renshon and Deborah Welch Larson. Lanham, MD: Rowman and Littlefield, 2003.

———. "Political Cognition and Decision Making." *Political Psychology* 11/1 (1990): 83–111.

Fearon, James D. "Counterfactuals and Hypothesis Testing in Political Science." *World Politics* 43 (1991), 169–95.

Fishman, J. S. *Diplomacy and Revolution: The London Conference of 1830 and the Belgian Revolt.* Amsterdam: CHEV, 1988.

Fiske, Susan T., and Shelley E. Taylor. *Social Cognition*. New York: Random House, 1984.

Foyle, Douglas C. *Counting the Public In: Presidents, Public Opinion and Foreign Policy*. New York: Columbia University Press.

Frensley, Nathalie, and Nelson Michaud. "Public Diplomacy and Motivated Reasoning: Framing Effects on Canadian Media Coverage of U.S. Foreign Policy Statements." *Foreign Policy Analysis* 2/3 (2006), 201–21.

Garrison, Jean A. "Framing Foreign Policy Alternatives in the Inner Circle: The President, His Advisors, and the Struggle for the Arms Control Agenda." *Political Psychology* 22/4 (2001), 775–807.

———. *Games Advisors Play: Foreign Policy in the Nixon and Carter Administrations*. College Station, TX: Texas A&M University Press, 1999.

Gat, Azar. "The Democratic Peace Theory Reframed: The Impact of Modernity." *World Politics* 58 (2005), 73–100.

Gaubatz, Kurt T. "Intervention and Intransivity: Public Opinion, Social Choice, and the Use of Military Force Abroad." *World Politics* 47 (1995), 534–54.

Gentner, Dedre. "The Mechanics of Analogical Learning." In *Similarity and Analogical Reasoning*, ed. Stella Vosniadou and Andrew Ortony. Cambridge: Cambridge University Press, 1989.

George, Alexander L. *Bridging the Gap: Theory and Practice in Foreign Policy*. Washington, DC: United States Institute of Peace Press, 1993.

———. *Presidential Decisionmaking in Foreign Policy: The Effective Use of Information and Advice*. Boulder, CO: Westview, 1980.

———. "Case Studies and Theory Development: The Method of Structured, Focused Comparison." In *Diplomacy: New Approaches in History, Theory, and Policy*, ed. Paul Gordon Lauren. New York: Free Press, 1979.

———. "The Causal Nexus Between Cognitive Beliefs and Decision-Making Behavior: The 'Operational Code' Belief System." In *Psychological Models in International Relations*, ed. Lawrence S. Falkowski. Boulder, CO: Westview, 1979.

———. "The 'Operational Code': A Neglected Approach to the Study of Political Leaders and Decision-Making." *International Studies Quarterly* 13 (1969), 190–222.

George, Alexander L. and Juliette L. George. *Presidential Personality and Performance*. Boulder, CO: Westview Press, 1998.

———. *Woodrow Wilson and Colonel House: A Personality Study*. New York: Dover, 1964.

George, Alexander L., and Timothy J. McKeown. "Case Studies and Theories of Organizational Decision Making." *Advances in Information Processing in Organizations* 2 (1985): 21–58.

Gerner, Deborah J. "The Evolution of the Study of Foreign Policy." In *Foreign Policy Analysis: Continuity and Change in its Second Generation*, ed. Laura Neack, Jeanne A. K. Hey, and Patrick J. Haney. Englewood Cliffs, NJ: Prentice Hall, 1995.

Gerner, Deborah J., Philip A. Schrodt, Ronald A. Francisco, and Judith L. Weddle. "Machine Coding of Event Data Using Regional and International Sources." *International Studies Quarterly* 38/1 (1994): 91–119.

Goldgeier, James M. "Psychology and Security." *Security Studies* 6 (1997): 137–66.

Goldsmith, Benjamin E. "A Universal Proposition? Region, Conflict, War and the Robustness of the Kantian Peace." *European Journal of International Relations* 12/4 (2006): 533–63.

———. *Imitation in International Relations: Observational Learning, Analogies and Foreign Policy in Russia and Ukraine.* New York: Palgrave, 2005.

Goldstein, Judith, and Robert O. Keohane, eds. *Ideas and Foreign Policy: Beliefs, Institutions, and Political Change.* Ithaca, NY: Cornell University Press, 1993.

Graham, Thomas W. "Public Opinion and U.S. Foreign Policy Decision Making." In *The New Politics of American Foreign Policy*, ed. David A. Deese. New York: St. Martin's Press, 1994.

Greenstein, Fred. *Personality and Politics: Problems of Evidence, Inference, and Conceptualization.* Chicago: Markham, 1969.

Hagan, Joe D. *Political Opposition and Foreign Policy in Comparative Perspective.* Boulder, CO: Lynne Rienner, 1993.

———. "Domestic Political Regime Changes and Third World Voting Realignments in the United Nations, 1946–84." *International Organization* 43/3 (1989): 505–41.

Handel, Michael. *Weak States in the International System.* London: Frank Cass, 1981.

Hallin, Daniel C., and Paolo Mancini. *Comparing Media Systems: Three Models of Media and Politics.* Cambridge: Cambridge University Press, 2004.

Hart, Paul 't. "From Analysis to Reform in Policy-making Groups." In *Beyond Groupthink: Political Group Dynamics and Foreign Policy-making*, ed. Paul 't Hart, Eric K. Stern, and Bengt Sundelius. Ann Arbor: University of Michigan Press, 1997.

———. "Irving Janis' *Victims of Groupthink*." *Political Psychology* 12 (1991): 247–78.

Hart, Paul 't, Eric K. Stern, and Bengt Sundelius. *Beyond Groupthink: Political Group Dynamics and Foreign Policy-making.* Ann Arbor: University of Michigan Press, 1997.

———. "Foreign Policy-making at the Top: Political Group Dynamics." In *Beyond Groupthink: Political Group Dynamics and Foreign Policy-making*, ed. Paul 't Hart, Eric K. Stern, and Bengt Sundelius. Ann Arbor: University of Michigan Press, 1997.

Hemmer, Christopher. *Which Lessons Matter? American Foreign Policy Decision Making in the Middle East, 1979–1987.* Albany, NY: SUNY Press, 2000.

Hermann, Charles F. "Epilogue: Reflections on Foreign Policy Theory Building." In *Foreign Policy Analysis: Continuity and Change in Its Second Generation*, ed. Laura Neack, Jeanne A. K. Hey, and Patrick J. Haney. Englewood Cliffs, NJ: Prentice Hall, 1995.

———. *Crises in Foreign Policy: A Simulation Analysis.* Indianapolis, IN: Bobbs-Merrill, 1969.

Hermann, Charles F., Janice Gross Stein, Bengt Sundelius, and Stephen G. Walker. "Resolve, Accept, or Avoid: Effects of Group Conflict on Foreign Policy Decisions." *International Studies Review* 3/2 (2001): 133–68.

Hermann, Margaret G. "Assessing Leadership Style: A Trait Analysis." Hilliard, OH: Social Science Automation, 1999. http://www.socialscienceautomation.com.

———. "Presidential Leadership Style, Advisory Systems, and Policy Making: Bill Clinton's Administration after Seven Months." *Political Psychology* 15/2 (1994): 363–74.

———. "Assessing the Foreign Policy Role Orientations of Sub-Saharan African Leaders." In *Role Theory and Foreign Policy Analysis*, ed. Stephen G. Walker. Durham, NC: Duke University Press, 1987.

———. "Personality and Foreign Policy Decision Making: A Study of 53 Heads of Government." In *Foreign Policy Decision Making: Perception, Cognition, and Artificial Intelligence*, ed. Donald A. Sylvan and Steve Chan. New York: Praeger, 1984.

———. "Explaining Foreign Policy Behavior Using the Personal Characteristics of Political Leaders." *International Studies Quarterly* 24 (1980): 7–46.

———. "Leader Personality and Foreign Policy Behavior." In *Comparing Foreign Policies: Theories, Findings, and Methods*, ed. James N. Rosenau. New York: Sage/Wiley, 1974.

Hermann, Margaret G. and Charles F. Hermann. "Who Makes Foreign Policy Decisions and How: An Empirical Inquiry." *International Studies Quarterly* 33/4 (1989): 361–87.

Hermann, Margaret G., Charles F. Hermann, and Joe D. Hagan. "How Decision Units Shape Foreign Policy Behavior." In *New Directions in the Study of Foreign Policy*, ed. Charles F. Hermann, Charles W. Kegley Jr., and James N. Rosenau. Boston: Allen and Unwin, 1987.

Hermann, Margaret G., and Thomas Preston. "Presidents, Advisers, and Foreign Policy: The Effects of Leadership Style on Executive Arrangements." *Political Psychology* 15/1 (1994): 75–96.

Hermann, Margaret G., Thomas Preston, Baghat Korany, and Timothy M. Shaw. "Who Leads Matters: The Effect of Powerful Individuals." *International Studies Review* 3/2, Special Issue (2001): 83–131.

Hey, Jeanne A. K., ed. *Small States in World Politics: Explaining Foreign Policy Behavior*. Boulder, CO: Lynne Rienner, 2003.

———. "Foreign Policy in Dependent States." In *Foreign Policy Analysis: Continuity and Change in Its Second Generation*, eds. Laura Neack, Jeanne A. K. Hey, and Patrick J. Haney. Englewood Cliffs, NJ: Prentice Hall, 1995.

Hill, Christopher. *The Changing Politics of Foreign Policy*. New York: Palgrave, 2003.

Hirsh, Michael. *At War with Ourselves: Why America Is Squandering Its Chance to Build a Better World*. New York: Oxford University Press, 2003.

Hochschild, Adam. *King Leopold's Ghost: A Story of Greed, Terror, and Heroism in Colonial Africa*. New York: Mariner Books, 1999.

Holsti, Kal J. "National Role Conceptions in the Study of Foreign Policy." In *Role Theory and Foreign Policy Analysis*, ed. Stephen G. Walker. Durham, NC: Duke University Press, 1987.

———. "National Role Conceptions in the Study of Foreign Policy." *International Studies Quarterly* 14 (1970): 233–309.

Holsti, Ole R. *Public Opinion and American Foreign Policy, rev. ed.* Ann Arbor: University of Michigan Press, 2004.

———. "The Operational Code as an Approach to the Analysis of Belief Systems," *Final Report to the National Science Foundation*, Grant No. SOC75–15368. Durham, NC: Duke University, 1977.

———. "The 'Operational Code' Approach to the Study of Political Leaders: John Foster Dulles' Philosophical and Instrumental Beliefs." *Canadian Journal of Political Science* 3 (1970): 123–57.

Houghton, David Patrick. "Reinvigorating the Study of Foreign Policy Decision Making: Toward a Constructivist Approach." *Foreign Policy Analysis* 3/1 (2007): 24–45.

———. "The Role of Analogical Reasoning in Novel Foreign Policy Situations." *British Journal of Political Science.* 26 (1996): 523–52.

Hoyt, Paul. "The 'Rogue State' Image in American Foreign Policy." *Global Society* 14/ 2 (2000): 297–310.

Hoyt, Paul. "The Political Manipulation of Group Composition: Engineering the Decision Context." *Political Psychology* 18 (1997): 771–90.

Hoyt, Paul, and Jean Garrison. "Political Manipulation within the Small Group: Foreign Policy Advisers in the Carter Administration." In *Beyond Groupthink: Political Group Dynamics and Foreign Policy-making*, ed. Paul 't Hart, Eric K. Stern, and Bengt Sundelius. Ann Arbor: University of Michigan Press, 1997.

Hudson, Valerie M. "Foreign Policy Analysis: Actor-Specific Theory and the Ground of International Relations." *Foreign Policy Analysis* 1/1 (2005): 1–30.

———. "Foreign Policy Decision-Making: A Touchstone for International Relations Theory in the Twenty-first Century." In *Foreign Policy Decision-Making (Revisited)*, Richard C. Snyder, H. W. Bruck, and Burton Sapin. New York: Palgrave, 2002.

———, ed. *Culture and Foreign Policy.* Boulder, CO: Lynne Rienner Publishers, 1997.

Hudson, Valerie M., with Christopher S. Vore. "Foreign Policy Analysis Yesterday, Today, and Tomorrow." *Mershon International Studies Review* 39/2 (1995): 209–38.

Hughes, Barry B., *Continuity and Change in World Politics: Competing Perspectives, 4th ed.* Upper Saddle River, NJ: Prentice Hall, 2000.

Ingebritsen, Christine. "Norm Entrepreneurs: Scandinavia's Role in World Politics." In *Small States in International Relations.* Ed. Christine Ingebritsen, Iver Neumann, Sieglinde Gstöhl, and Jessica Beyer. Seattle: University of Washington Press, 2006.

Ingebritsen, Christine, Iver Neumann, Sieglinde Gstöhl, and Jessica Beyer, eds. *Small States in International Relations.* Seattle: University of Washington Press, 2006.

James, Patrick, and Enyu Zhang. "Chinese Choices: A Poliheuristic Analysis of Foreign Policy Crises, 1950–1996." *Foreign Policy Analysis* 1/1 (2005): 31–54.

Janis, Irving. *Groupthink: Psychological Studies of Policy Decisions and Fiascoes, 2nd ed.* Boston, Houghton Mifflin, 1983.

Jervis, Robert. *Perception and Misperception in International Politics*. Princeton, NJ: Princeton University Press, 1976.

Johnson, Loch. "The Operational Code of Senator Frank Church." In *A Psychological Examination of Political Leaders*, ed. Margaret G. Hermann. New York: Free Press, 1977.

Johnson, Richard Tanner. *Managing the White House: An Intimate Study of the Presidency*. New York: Harper and Row, 1974.

Kaarbo, Juliet. "Power and Influence in Foreign Policy Decision Making: The Role of Junior Coalition Partners in German and Israeli Foreign Policy." *International Studies Quarterly* 40/4 (1996): 501–30.

Kaarbo, Juliet, and Margaret G. Hermann. "Leadership Styles of Prime Ministers: How Individual Differences Affect the Foreign Policy Making Process." *Leadership Quarterly* 9 (1998): 243–63.

Kansas Event Data System (KEDS) Project, http://web.ku.edu/keds/.

Katzenstein, Peter. *Small States in World Markets*. Ithaca, NY: Cornell University Press, 1985.

Keane, Mark T., Tim Ledgeway, and Stuart Duff. "Constraints on Analogical Mapping: A Comparison of Three Models." *Cognitive Science* 18 (1994): 387–438.

Kegley, Charles W., Jr., and Eugene R. Wittkopf, *World Politics: Trend and Transformation, 7th ed.* New York: St. Martin's/Worth, 1999.

Kennedy, Paul. *The Rise and Fall of the Great Powers: Economic Change and Military Conflict from 1500 to 2000*. New York: Random House, 1987.

Keohane, Robert O. *Neorealism and its Critics*. New York: Columbia University Press, 1986.

———. "Lilliputians' Dilemmas: Small States in International Politics." *International Organization* 23/2 (1969): 291–310.

Khong, Yuen Foong. *Analogies at War: Korea, Munich, Dien Bien Phu, and the Vietnam Decisions of 1965*. Princeton, NJ: Princeton University Press, 1992.

King, Gary, Robert O. Keohane, and Sidney Verba. *Designing Social Inquiry: Scientific Inference in Qualitative Research*. Princeton: Princeton University Press, 1994.

Knecht, Thomas, and M. Stephen Weatherford. "Public Opinion and Foreign Policy: The Stages of Presidential Decision Making." *International Studies Quarterly* 50/3 (2006): 705–27.

Knill, Christopher, and Andrea Lenschow. "'Seek and Ye Shall Find!' Linking Different Perspectives on Institutional Change," *Comparative Political Studies* 34/2 (March 2001): 187–215.

Korany, Bahgat, with contributors. *How Foreign Policy Decisions Are Made in the Third World: A Comparative Analysis*. Boulder and London: Westview, 1986.

Kowert, Paul A. *Groupthink or Deadlock: When Do Leaders Learn from Their Advisors?* Albany, NY: State University of New York Press, 2002.

Krasner, Stephen D. "Are Bureaucracies Important? (Or Allison in Wonderland)." *Foreign Policy* 7:159–79.

Kwitny, Jonathan. *Endless Enemies: The Making of an Unfriendly World*. New York: Congdon and Weed, 1984.

Lai, Brian, and Daniel S. Morey. "Impact of Regime Type on the Influence of U.S. Foreign Aid." *Foreign Policy Analysis* 2/4 (2006): 385–404.

Larson, Deborah W. "Politics, Uncertainty, and Values." In *Good Judgment in Foreign Policy: Theory and Application,* ed. Stanley A. Renshon and Deborah Welch Larson. Lanham, MD: Rowman and Littlefield, 2003.

Lebow, Richard Ned. "What's So Different About a Counterfactual?" *World Politics* 52 (July 2000): 550–85.

———. *Between Peace and War: The Nature of International Crisis.* Baltimore, MD: Johns Hopkins University Press, 1981.

Leites, Nathan. *A Study of Bolshevism.* Glencoe, IL: Free Press, 1953.

———. *The Operational Code of the Politburo.* New York: McGraw-Hill, 1951.

Levy, Jack S. "Loss Aversion, Framing, and Bargaining: The Implications of Prospect Theory for International Conflict." *International Political Science Review* 17 (1996): 179–95.

———. "An Introduction to Prospect Theory." *Political Psychology* 13 (1992): 171–86.

Levy, Jack S. "The Diversionary Theory of War." In: Handbook of War Studies, ed. Manus I. Midlarsky. Boston: Unwin Hyman, 1989.

Levy, Jack S. and Lily I. Vakili. "Diversionary Action by Authoritarian Regimes: Argentina in the Falkslands/Malvinas Case." In: *The Internationalization of Communal Strife,* ed. Manus I. Midlarsky. New York: Routledge, 1992.

Lijphart, Arend, ed. *Parliamentary versus Presidential Government.* Oxford: Oxford University Press, 1992.

———. "The Comparable-Cases Strategy in Comparative Research." *Comparative Political Studies* 8/2 (1975): 158–77.

———. "Comparative Politics and the Comparative Method." *American Political Science Review* 55 (1971): 682–93.

Lijphart, Arend. *Patterns of Democracy: Government Forms and Performance in Thirty-six Countries.* New Haven, CT: Yale University Press, 1999.

Luykx, Theo, and Marc Platel. *Politieke Geschiedenis van België* [*Political History of Belgium*]. Vol. 2. Antwerp, Belgium: Kluwer Rechtswetenschappen, 1985.

Lyall, Jason M. K. "Pocket Protests: Rhetorical Coercion and the Micropolitics of Collective Action in Semiauthoritarian Regimes." *World Politics* 58 (April 2006): 378–412.

Machiavelli, Niccolo. "The Prince." In *The Portable Machiavelli,* ed. and trans. Peter Bondanella and Mark Musa. New York: Penguin, 1979.

Malici, Akan, and Johnna Malici. "The Operational Codes of Fidel Castro and Kim Il Sung: The Last Cold Warriors?" *Political Psychology* 26/3 (2005): 387–412.

Marcus, Harold G. *A History of Ethiopia, Updated Edition.* Berkeley: University of California Press, 2002.

Maoz, Zeev. "Framing the National Interest: The Manipulations of Foreign Policy Decisions in Groups Settings," *World Politics,* 43 (1990), 77–110.

Maoz, Zeev, and Nasrin Abdolali. "Regime Type and International Conflict, 1816–1976." *Journal of Conflict Resolution* 33/1 (1989): 3-35.

Maoz, Zeev, and Bruce Russett. "Normative and Structural Causes of Democratic Peace." *American Political Science Review* 87/3 (1993): 624–38.

Marfleet, Gregory. "The Operational Code of John F. Kennedy during the Cuban Missile Crisis: A Comparison of Public and Private Rhetoric." *Political Psychology* 21/3 (2000): 545–58.

Marfleet, B. Gregory, and Colleen Miller. "Failure after 1441: Bush and Chirac in the UN Security Council." *Foreign Policy Analysis* 1/3 (2005): 333–60.

Mearsheimer, John J. "Why We Will Soon Miss the Cold War." *The Atlantic* 266 (August 1990): 35–50.

Milliken, Jennifer. *State Failure, Collapse, and Reconstruction.* Malden, MA: Blackwell, 2003.

Mintz, Alex, ed. *Integrating Cognitive and Rational Theories of Foreign Policy Decision Making.* New York: Palgrave, 2003.

———. "Integrating Cognitive and Rational Theories of Foreign Policy Decision Making: A Poliheuristic Perspective." In *Integrating Cognitive and Rational Theories of Foreign Policy Decision Making*, ed. Alex Mintz. New York: Palgrave, 2003.

———. "Foreign Policy Decision Making: Bridging the Gap Between the Cognitive Psychology and Rational Actor 'Schools.'" In: *Decision Making on War and Peace: The Cognitive-Rational Debate*, ed. Nehemia Geva and Alex Mintz. Boulder, CO: Lynne Rienner, 1997.

———. "The Decision to Attack Iraq: A Non-Compensatory Theory of Decision Making." *Journal of Conflict Resolution* 37 (1993): 595–618.

Mintz, Alex, and Nehemia Geva. "The Poliheuristic Theory of Foreign Policy Decision Making." In *Decision Making on War and Peace: The Cognitive-Rational Debate*, ed. Nehemia Geva and Alex Mintz. Boulder, CO: Lynne Rienner, 1997.

Mintz, Alex, Nehemia Geva, Steven Redd, and Amy Carnes. "The Effect of Dynamic versus Static Choice Sets on Strategy and Outcome in Political Decision Making." *American Political Science Review* 91 (1997): 553–66.

Mitchell, David. "Centralizing Advisory Systems: Presidential Influence and the U.S. Foreign Policy Decision-Making Process." *Foreign Policy Analysis* 1/2 (2005): 181–206.

Moon, Bruce E. "Consensus or Compliance? Foreign Policy Change and External Dependence." *International Organization* 39 (1985): 297–329.

———. "The Foreign Policy of the Dependent State." *International Studies Quarterly* 27 (1983): 315–40.

Morgenthau, Hans J., and Kenneth W. Thompson. *Politics among Nations: The Struggle for Power and Peace, 6th ed.* New York: Knopf, 1985.

Morrow, James D. *Game Theory for Political Scientists.* Princeton, NJ: Princeton University Press, 1994.

Müller, Harald, and Thomas Risse-Kappen. "From the Outside In and from the Inside Out: International Relations, Domestic Politics, and Foreign Policy." In *The Limits of State Autonomy: Societal Groups and Foreign Policy Formation*, ed. David Skidmore and Valerie Hudson. Boulder, CO: Westview Press. 1993.

Neack, Laura. "Linking State Type with Foreign Policy Behavior." In *Foreign Policy Analysis: Continuity and Change in Its Second Generation*, eds. Laura Neack, Jeanne A. K. Hey, and Patrick J. Haney. Englewood Cliffs, NJ: Prentice Hall, 1995.

Neustadt, Richard E., and Ernest R. May. *Thinking in Time: The Uses of History for Decision Makers*. New York: Free Press, 1986.

Nincic, Miroslav, and Joseph Lepgold, eds. *Being Useful: Policy Relevance and International Relations Theory*. Ann Arbor, MI: University of Michigan Press, 2000.

Novick, Laura R. "Analogical Transfer, Problem Similarity, and Expertise." *Journal of Experimental Psychology: Learning, Memory, and Cognition* 14 (1988): 510–20.

Nye, Joseph S., Jr. *Soft Power: The Means to Success in World Politics*. New York: Public Affairs, 2004.

———. *The Paradox of American Power: Why the World's Only Superpower Can't Go It Alone*. New York: Oxford University Press, 2002.

———. *Understanding International Conflicts: An Introduction to Theory and History*, 3rd ed. New York: Longman, 2000.

———. *Bound to Lead: The Changing Nature of American Power*. New York: Basic Books, 1990.

Organisation for Economic Co-operation and Development (OECD). Development Co-operation Report. Paris: OECD, Various Years.

Pakenham, Thomas. *The Scramble for Africa*. New York: Random House, 1991.

Perham, Margery. Foreword to *Haile-Selassie's Government*, by Christopher Clapham. New York: Frederick A. Praeger, 1969.

Perlmutter, Amos. 1974. "The Presidential Political Center and Foreign Policy: A Critique of the Revisionist and Bureaucratic-Political Orientations." *World Politics* 27:87–106.

Peterson, M. J. "The Use of Analogies in Developing Outer Space Law." *International Organization* 51 (1997): 245–74.

Preston, Thomas. "Following the Leader: The Impact of U.S. Presidential Style upon Advisory Group Dynamics, Structure, and Decision." In *Beyond Groupthink: Political Group Dynamics and Foreign Policy-making*, ed. Paul 't Hart, Eric K. Stern, and Bengt Sundelius. Ann Arbor: University of Michigan Press, 1997.

Prestowitz, Clyde. *Rogue Nation: American Unilateralism and the Failure of Good Intentions*. New York: Basic Books, 2003.

Powlick, Philip J., and Andrew Z. Katz. "Defining the American Public Opinion/Foreign Policy Nexus." *Mershon International Studies Review* 42/1 (May 1998): 29–61.

Putnam, Robert. "Diplomacy and Domestic Politics: The Logic of Two-level Games." *International Organization* 42 (Summer 1988): 427–260.

Reiter, Dan. *Crucible of Beliefs: Learning, Alliances, and World Wars*. Ithaca, NY: Cornell University Press, 1996.

Renshon, Stanley A. "Psychological Sources of Good Judgment in Political Leaders: A Framework for Analysis." In *Good Judgment in Foreign Policy: Theory and*

Application, ed. Stanley A. Renshon and Deborah Welch Larson. Lanham, MD: Rowman and Littlefield, 2003.

Renshon, Stanley A., and Deborah Welch Larson, eds. *Good Judgment in Foreign Policy: Theory and Application*. Lanham, MD: Rowman and Littlefield, 2003.

Rhodes, Edward. 1994. "Do Bureaucratic Politics Matter? Some Disconfirming Findings from the Case of the U.S. Navy." *World Politics* 47:1–41.

Richards, Diana. "Coordination and Shared Mental Models." *American Journal of Political Science* 45/2 (2001): 259-76.

Ripley, Brian. "Cognition, Culture, and Bureaucratic Politics." In *Foreign Policy Analysis: Continuity and Change in the Second Generation*, ed. Laura Neack, Jeanne A. K. Hey, and Patrick J. Haney. Englewood Cliffs, NJ: Prentice Hall, 1995.

Risse-Kappen, Thomas. "Ideas Do Not Float Freely: Transnational Coalitions, Domestic Structures, and the End of the Cold War." *International Organization* 48 (Spring 1994): 185–214.

———. "Public Opinion, Domestic Structure, and Foreign Policy in Liberal Democracies." *World Politics* 43 (1991): 479–511.

Rosati, Jerel A. "The Power of Human Cognition in the Study of World Politics." *International Studies Review* 43 (2000): 45–75.

Rosenau, James N. *The Scientific Study of Foreign Policy*. London: Frances Pinter, 1980.

———. "Pre-Theories and Theories of Foreign Policy." In *Approaches in Comparative and International Politics*, ed. R. Barry Farrell. Evanston, IL: Northwestern University Press, 1966.

Rotberg, Robert I., ed. *When States Fail: Causes and Consequences*. Princeton, NJ: Princeton University Press, 2004.

Rothstein, Robert. *Alliances and Small Powers*. New York: Columbia University Press, 1968.

Rourke, John T. *International Politics on the World Stage, 8th ed.* Guilford, CT: McGraw-Hill/Dushkin, 2001.

Russett, Bruce. "Bushwhacking the Democratic Peace." *International Studies Perspectives* 6 (2005): 395–408.

———. *Grasping the Democratic Peace*. Princeton, NJ: Princeton University Press, 1993.

Russett, Bruce, and John Oneal. *Triangulating Peace: Democracy, Independence and International Organizations*. New York: W. W. Norton, 2001.

Schafer, Mark. "Bill Clinton's Operational Code: Assessing Source Material Bias." *Political Psychology* 21/3 (2000): 559–71.

———. "Issues in Assessing Psychological Characteristics at a Distance: An Introduction to the Symposium," *Political Psychology* 21/3 (2000): 511–27.

———. "Explaining Groupthink: Do the Psychological Characteristics of the Leader Matter?" *International Interactions* 25 (1999): 1–31.

Schafer, Mark, Sam Robison, and Bradley Aldrich. "Operational Codes and the 1916 Easter Rising in Ireland: A Test of the Frustration-Aggression Hypothesis." *Foreign Policy Analysis* 2/1 (2006): 63–82.

Schafer, Mark, and Stephen G. Walker. "Democratic Leaders and the Democratic Peace: The Operational Codes of Tony Blair and Bill Clinton." *International Studies Quarterly* 50/3 (2006): 561–83.

Schrodt, Philip A., and Deborah J. Gerner. "Validity Assessment of a Machine-Coded Event Data Set for the Middle East, 1982–92." *American Journal of Political Science* 38/3 (1994): 825–54.

Schwarz, Norbert, and Herbert Bless. "Happy and Mindless, but Sad and Smart? The Impact of Affective States on Analytic Reasoning." In *Emotion and Social Judgments*, ed. Joseph P. Forgas. Oxford: Pergamon Press, 1991.

Shannon, Vaughn, and Jonathan W. Keller. "Leadership Style and International Norm Violation." *Foreign Policy Analysis* 3/1 (2007): 79–104.

Shirer, William L. *The Rise and Fall of the Third Reich*. New York: Simon and Schuster, 1960.

Simon, Herbert A. "Human Nature in Politics: The Dialogue of Psychology with Political Science." *American Political Science Review* 79 (1985): 293–304.

———. *The Sciences of the Artificial, 2nd ed.* Cambridge, MA: MIT Press, 1981.

Singer, J. David. "The Level-of-Analysis Problem in International Relations." In *International Politics and Foreign Policy, rev. ed.*, ed. James N. Rosenau. New York: Free Press, 1969.

———. "The Level-of-Analysis Problem in International Relations." *World Politics* 14 (1961): 77–92.

Singer, Marshall R. *Weak States in a World of Powers: The Dynamics of International Relationships*. New York, Free Press, 1972.

Skidmore, David. "Understanding the Unilateralist Turn in U.S. Foreign Policy." *Foreign Policy Analysis* 1/2 (2005): 207–28.

Snyder, Richard C., H. W. Bruck, and Burton Sapin. *Foreign Policy Decision-making (Revisited)*. New York: Palgrave, 2002.

———. *Foreign Policy Decision Making: An Approach to the Study of International Politics*. New York: Free Press, 1962.

Stanford, Karin L. *Beyond the Boundaries: Reverend Jesse Jackson in International Affairs*. Albany: State University of New York Press, 1997.

Spellman, Barbara, and Keith Holyoak. "If Saddam Hussein is Hitler Then Who is George Bush? Analogical Mapping Between Systems of Social Roles." *Journal of Personality and Social Psychology* 62 (1992): 913–33.

Sprout, Harold, and Margaret Sprout. *The Ecological Perspective on Human Affairs, with Special Reference to International Politics*. Princeton, NJ: Princeton University Press, 1965.

Stokke, Olav, ed. *Western Middle Powers and Global Poverty: The Determinants of the Aid Policies of Canada, Denmark, the Netherlands, Norway, and Sweden*. Uppsala, Sweden: The Scandinavian Institute of African Studies.

Sylvan, Donald A. Introduction to *Problem Representation and Foreign Policy Decision Making*, ed. Donald A. Sylvan and James F. Voss. New York: Cambridge University Press, 1998.

Sylvan, Donald A., and Deborah Haddad. "Reasoning and Problem Representation in Foreign Policy: Groups, Individuals, and Stories." In *Problem Representation and Foreign Policy Decision Making,* ed. Donald A. Sylvan and James F. Voss. New York: Cambridge University Press, 1998.

Sylvan, Donald A., and James F. Voss. *Problem Representation in Foreign Policy Decision Making.* New York: Cambridge University Press, 1998.

Sylvan, Donald A., Ashol Goel, and B. Chandrasekaran. "Analyzing Political Decision Making from an Information Processing Perspective: JESSE." *American Journal of Political Science* 34/1 (1990): 74–123.

Sylvan, Donald A., Thomas M. Ostrom, and Katherine Gannon, "Case-Based, Model-Based, and Explanation-Based Styles of Reasoning in Foreign Policy." *International Studies Quarterly* 38 (1994): 61–90.

Szirmai, Adam. *The Dynamics of Socio-Economic Development: An Introduction.* Cambridge, UK: Cambridge University Press, 2005.

Tetlock, Philip E. "Good Judgment in International Politics: Three Psychological Perspectives." *Political Psychology* 13/3 (1992): 517–39.

Tetlock, Philip E., and Aaron Belkin. *Counterfactual Thought Experiments in World Politics: Logical, Methodological, and Psychological Perspectives.* Princeton, NJ: Princeton University Press, 1996.

Truman, Harry. "The President's Farewell Address to the American People." *Truman Presidential Museum & Library.* http://trumanlibrary.org/calendar/viewpapers.php?pid=2059.

Truman Presidential Museum & Library. "'The Buck Stops Here' Desk Sign." http://www.trumanlibrary.org/buckstop.htm.

Tversky, Amos, and Daniel Kahneman. 1981. "The Framing of Decisions and the Psychology of Choice." *Science* 211/4481 (1981): 453–58.

Tweraser, Kurt K. *Changing Patterns of Political Beliefs: The Foreign Policy Operational Codes of J. William Fulbright, 1943–1967.* Beverly Hills: Sage, 1974.

UNDP. *Human Development Report.* New York: UNDP, various years. Also online at http://hdr.undp.org/

Van Belle, Douglas A. "Dinosaurs and the Democratic Peace: Paleontological Lessons for Avoiding the Extinction of Theory in Political Science." *International Studies Perspectives* 7/3 (2006): 287–306.

———. *Press Freedom and Global Politics.* Westport, CT: Praeger, 2000.

Van Belle, Douglas A., Jean-Sébastien Rioux, and David M. Potter. *Media, Bureaucracies and Foreign Aid: A Comparative Analysis of the United States, the United Kingdom, Canada, France, and Japan.* New York: Palgrave, 2004.

Van Bellinghen, Jean-Paul. "Belgium and Africa." In *Modern Belgium*, ed. Marina Boudart, Michel Boudart, and René Bryssinck. Palo Alto, CA: Society for the Promotion of Science and Scholarship, 1990.

Vermeersch, A. J. *Vereniging en Revolutie: De Nederlanden 1814–1830* [*Union and Revolution: The Netherlands 1814–1830*]. Bussum: Fibula-Van Dishoeck, 1970.

Vertzberger, Yaacov Y. I. *The World in Their Minds: Information Processing, Cognition, and Perception in Foreign Policy Decision Making.* Stanford, CA: Stanford University Press, 1990.

———. *Risk Taking and Decisionmaking: Foreign Military Intervention Decisions.* Stanford, CA: Stanford University Press, 1998.

Vital, David. *The Survival of Small States: Studies in Small Power/Great Power Conflict.* London: Oxford University Press, 1971.

Voorhoeve, Joris J. C. *Peace, Profits and Principles: A Study of Dutch Foreign Policy.* Leiden, the Netherlands: Martinus Nijhoff, 1985.

Voss, James F. "On the Representation of Problems: An Information-processing Approach to Foreign Policy Decision Making." In *Problem Representation and Foreign Policy Decision Making,* ed. Donald A. Sylvan and James F. Voss. New York: Cambridge University Press, 1998.

Walker, Stephen G. "Assessing Psychological Characteristics at a Distance: Symposium Lessons and Future Research Directions." *Political Psychology* 21/3 (2000): 597–602.

———. "Psychodynamic Processes and Framing Effects in Foreign Policy Decision-Making: Woodrow Wilson's Operational Code," *Political Psychology* 16/4 (1995): 697.

———. "The Evolution of Operational Code Analysis." *Political Psychology* 11/2 (1990): 403–18.

———, ed. *Role Theory and Foreign Policy Analysis.* Durham, NC: Duke University Press, 1987.

———. "The Motivational Foundations of Political Belief Systems: A Re-Analysis of the Operational Code Construct." *International Studies Quarterly* 27 (1983): 179–201.

———. "The Interface Between between Beliefs and Behavior: Henry Kissinger's Operational Code and the Vietnam War." *Journal of Conflict Resolution* 21/1 (1977): 129–68.

Walker, Stephen G., and Mark Schafer. "The Political Universe of Lyndon B. Johnson and His Advisors: Diagnostic and Strategic Propensities in Their Operational Codes." *Political Psychology* 21/3 (2000): 529–43.

Walker, Stephen G., Mark Schafer, and Michael D. Young. "Systematic Procedures for Operational Code Analysis: Measuring and Modeling Jimmy Carter's Operational Code." *International Studies Quarterly* 42/1 (1998): 175–90.

Waltz, Kenneth N. *Theory of International Politics.* Reading, MA: Addison-Wesley, 1979.

———. *Man, the State, and War: A Theoretical Analysis.* New York: Columbia University Press, 1959.

Welch, David. "Culture and Emotion as Obstacles to Good Judgment." In: *Good Judgment in Foreign Policy: Theory and Application,* ed. Stanley A. Renshon and Deborah Welch Larson. Lanham, MD: Rowman and Littlefield, 2003.

———. "Remember the Falklands? Missed Lessons of a Misunderstood War." *International Journal* 53/3 (1997): 483–507.

Wels, Cornelis B. *Aloofness and Neutrality: Studies in Dutch Foreign Relations and Policy-Making Institutions.* Utrecht, the Netherlands: HES, 1982.

Wendt, Alexander. "Anarchy is What States Make of It: The Social Construction of Power Politics." *International Organization* 46/2 (1992): 391–425.

Williams, Victoria C. Internal Woes, External Foes? Exploring the Theory of Diversionary War (Egypt, Israel, Argentina, Grenada). Ph.D. Diss., University of Kentucky, 2000.

Wish, Naomi Bailin. "Foreign Policy Makers and Their National Role Conceptions." *International Studies Quarterly* 24/4 (1980): 532–54.

Witte, Els, Jan Craeybeckx, and Alain Meynen. *Politieke Geschiedenis van België van 1830 tot Heden* [*Political History of Belgium from 1830 to Present*], 5th ed. Antwerpen, Belgium: Standaard, 1990.

Woodward, Bob. *The Commanders*. New York: Simon and Schuster, 1991.

Zartman, I. William. *Collapsed States: The Disintegration and Restoration of Legitimate Authority*. Boulder, CO: Lynne Rienner, 1995.

Index